JOHN MORGAN

A Pers

JOHN MORGAN'S WALES

WALES

A Personal Anthology

CHRISTOPHER DAVIES

For Jen and Euryn

Gwelir gwir gyfeillgarwch
Yn y drain a'r niwl yn drwch

Anon. 20th Century

Contents

Publisher's Note and Acknowledgement

Before John Morgan died he drafted a rough acknowledgement page for inclusion in this volume. There had been difficulty in collecting and selecting pieces for inclusion, as by his own admission, he had neglected to keep a file of his work.

However he did wish to thank a number of people for their kind assistance and the following paragraphs are from the original draft.

C.D.

Anthony Howard of *The Observer* found material for me. So did John Lloyd at *The New Statesman* and Gareth Jenkins, Features Editor of *the Western Mail*. My radio producers, Alastair Osborne and Julian Coles at Broadcasting House, London, found many talks; as did Teleri Bevan at BBC Wales, Cardiff.

The editors of *The Sunday Times* and of the *Spectator* could not have been more helpful. I would like formally to acknowledge their permissions to reproduce the material that appears in this book, first published by them. Equally, I would like to acknowledge similar permissions from Heineman for excerpts from 'Report on Rugby' and Hodder and Stoughton for those from 'Side-Steps, A Rugby Diary 1984–85'. I trust that, by accident, no-one has been omitted.

Finally, I would like to thank my wife, Mary, for reading the proofs, an unusual task since she was there when the earliest articles were first written.

Preface

All readers of what follows who are not Welsh, and some who are, should realise that there is no truth about Wales. All Welsh writers are governed by background and by the confusions of change in class and language in the first place, and by the forms of self-dramatisation they choose, or neurosis subsequently chooses. This accounts for liveliness, wit and, alas, dishonesty in those cases where the force of the observation is denied. There are historians, novelists, dramatists, poets, politicians and broadcasters who will deny it. They will claim to speak for the nation. These people are known as 'professional Welshmen', although there are women, too. They may be detected by the wilful, if variable, persistence of accent; by references to 'Mam'; by being Marxist while middle-class; by insisting that male voice choirs are singing well when audibly they are not. I would like to think that this selection from journalistic pieces written from the early Fifties reflects a different attitude. Most of them were designed for an English or otherwise foreign audience, although the last third of the book is a recent sort-of-diary which belongs to compatriot readers of the *Western Mail,* the editors of which, by the way, are to blame for the book's title: it was their choice for my column there, not mine. My view of journalism was expressed, though, in a column written in a Californian night-club for the *Sunday Times* in 1966:

Travelling Man

Gliding down Sunset Boulevard in a white Thunderbird convertible, the sun low behind the trees of Beverly Hills, seems a proper occasion to reflect on the miseries of the

11

profession of journalism and the emotional sacrifices it demands of those who practise it. Writing about Liverpool or Westminster or the aspirations of Scottish nationalism or Welsh, will do almost as well in bringing home the truth that the journalist is a kind of Flying Dutchman, condemned forever to wonder the earth. (A sad concept made uncomfortable and exhausting by jet airplanes.)

Hollywood, the automated dream factory, heightens the sense of necessary detachment that afflicts so many of us. Celluloid is a removal from life: the printed image helps along any twitch of alienation owned by actor or directors who create film. There are even television performers who need to see themselves on the screen from time to time to make sure that they still exist. So that here in Beverly Hills when the journalist romances about a romance, mythologises a myth, he can (with confidence) feel as far removed from life as lived as if he was on the moon. In California nowadays he is not very far from the moon, either.

What makes Hollywood even worse is that it's scarcely possible to see it not for the Los Angeles smog but for the evocative haze that hangs over boulevards like Wilshire and Vine and Sunset, and drifts along the Strip. From the age of seven, from our penny seats in the Regal Cinema, the names have had an incalculable (and no doubt deplorable) influence.

At school we could draw a street map of Hollywood when hard put to it to remember the ground plan of a Cistercian monastery. The map chartered the imagination and soon became peopled – and then was (wildly or movingly) annotated – by West, Fitzgerald, Chandler, Schulberg. Why, in this very bar only the other night Frank Sinatra himself did or did not punch, was or was not punched. And look who's just come in, not perhaps as gorgeous in life, but still, but still . . .

All this is a hazard extra to the ageing journalist's problem with the experience of *déja vu,* of having been everywhere and seen everything, having felt what he was going to feel the first time round, so that second time round he inclines towards the alleys of the bizarre. That's bad enough. What is worse is to have the sense of *déja vu* before actually witnessing the scene.

Big Sur is familiar. Here, as described, quail stroll along lawns beneath lemon trees. The flower of the pineapple guava grows like a crimson butterfly but with black antennae. A light breeze blows from the Pacific hundreds of feet below. China lies across the water. The mind has seen it all before, which wouldn't matter for the traveller free to feel that this is one of the loveliest places in the world, and leave it at that. The journalist is not such a traveller, poor thing.

One stops off at the body show on the Strip, observes a show-titled "Campaign Headquarters" – the set done up like a polling station with Stars and Stripes, hears the girls introduced as "The incumbent Patty Brown," "The Republican challenger Ronnie Reagan." You may decorate your car with stickers reading "God is Alive and Living in Argentina" or "Batman for Governor."

Eating a meal surrounded by the gilded extravagances of Californian rococo, a man dressed as Nero plays a fiddle in my left ear, while his sidekick, a shade anachronistically, plays a piano-accordion on the right. Yet the reality scarcely measures up to the hillarious and savage fancies of Nathanael West or, more recently, Terry Southern in "The Loved One." Art always catches an earlier plane.

These difficulties a journalist can live with. Frequently anger or scepticism or delight will sufficiently diminish their inhibiting effect. What is more difficult, and the heavier penalty, is the matter of detachment.

It's possible, though sentimental, to make a virtue of this, for the travelling man to see himself as a kind of Philip Marlowe figure, the lonely fellow searching for truth in a hard world. "Down these mean streets a man must go who is not himself mean," as Marlowe's creator put it about these very Hollywood streets. American journalists are sometimes given to romanticising themselves in this way.

But there is a higher sentimentality available to the

journalist suffering from a bad case of the Flying Dutchman. What happens is that he arrives at a place, among a group, perhaps coal miners, perhaps actors, perhaps a political conference. He watches, he notes, he interprets – they act, they decide, they control. He departs, he writes, he arrives elsewhere in a new place, among a new group. Meanwhile the group left behind go on being what they were, and so do the new group. He feels removed from the apparent homogeneity of the cultures he describes or any community since he belongs to a peculiar culture whose definition is difficult to catch at. He's always that chap standing in the corner, whispering to one or two, when his isn't the face pressed against the window pane.

Yet this, too, is a piece of sentimentality, since it contains the illusion that the life he observes and describes is homogeneous, when it is, I believe, a form of insult to call any society that. The people who make up the community described regard themselves as separate. They are Flying Dutchmen who don't fly.

It is probably an illusion to believe that the incipient neurosis of journalism is schizophrenia rather than, as one had been taught, paranoia. The truth probably is – and it's hard for the reporter full of self-pity, among splendours, far from home, to accept it – that he is just suffering from the human condition. The only difference, indeed, may be that someone pays his fare. To suffer it.

Sunday Times, 19th June 1966

Such a view cannot quite hold when writing about one's own country and its people, especially when some of those people are or become friends. If I am right in thinking that Welsh writers more than most are writing about themselves, then the matter is quite confusing. For example, I hear today that the terrace in Morriston, Swansea in which I spent most of my youth with my parents and grandmother and three brothers with no hot water or bath, two or three to a bed, is about to be swept away by a collapsing slagheap. There in the late Forties I upset my parents deeply by saying that I would not, when I graduated, be a schoolteacher. I would, I said, be a writer: a free man, the phrase being father of the man. No one they said, from Morriston, had ever made a living as a writer, which was true. They had struggled so that I would have a steady income, be a tidy middle-class fellow, a teacher. My mother had been a cleaner in a teacher's house. I also recall that at University College, Swansea, several of us who came from Welsh-speaking families in the district took against members of the Welsh Society Gymdeithas Gymraeg ('Gym-Gym'). This was because they seemed to us to be trying to impose on a liberal university society those cribbed, hypocritical, chapel values of the Welsh community. I even wrote a chorus we'd chant:

> Un dau tri pedwar pump chwech saith
> Let's get the hell out of the old hen iaith.

Yet by the late Sixties, discovering that the Independent Television station in Wales was governed from London, I invented a campaign to seize it by compatriots which won the day. It seemed important to do so. And in the early Eighties I was honoured to accept the Chairmanship of the new Welsh Union of Writers and left it because of serious illness. I thought the latter task useful partly because I think it a pity if Wales were to be defined only by the Welsh language. What is said in a country can be as important, if not more so, than the language in which it is uttered. These grave, troubling matters, however, are not as relevant as the hope that this collection entertains.

Mork
March 1988

I

PEOPLE

Saunders Lewis

By washing his hands of the National Eisteddfod, Saunders Lewis, one of the most distinguished Welshmen of the century – in the Nationalist view the greatest Welshman since Owain Glyndŵr – has made the last possible gesture of disassociation from organised Welshness.

That the best and most famous Welsh poet, playwright and scholar should have nothing more to do with what is popularly thought of as the power behind poetry and drama, if not scholarship, in Wales is a restatement of Lewis's paradoxical position in Welsh life, of the almost fanatical idealism which has characterised his career.

He has been the Roman Catholic leader of a predominantly Nonconformist political party; the ex-Army officer at the head of a band of pacifists; the most brilliant Welsh teacher of his generation who in his own country could not find a place to teach in; the Welshman who went to an English gaol because of his Nationalism and had his job taken away from him by Welshmen; a man of all the talents but that for compromise, who began his career as a lecturer at a Welsh University College and is ending it lecturing at a Welsh University College.

*　　*　　*

John Saunders Lewis was born in 1893 in Liverpool. His father was a Calvinistic Methodist minister; his maternal grandfather one of Wales's most famous biographers. At

Liverpool University he took a first under Lascelles Abercrombie, immediately volunteered for the Army, was commissioned in the South Wales Borderers, wounded in France and, towards the end of the war, served in Greece under that uncrowned King of Scotland, Sir Compton Mackenzie.

He returned to the University, until in 1923 he became a lecturer in Welsh at the new University College of Swansea. Three years later, after establishing a reputation as teacher, poet, scholar and orator, he founded the Plaid Cymru (Welsh Nationalist Party) and became its first president. The philosopher had come down into the market place.

Lewis's vision was of a Wales that no longer existed. His Wales – he has recreated it movingly in his plays – was a gentle and civilised country, its culture homogeneous, its literature the oldest and among the greatest of the European literatures. It was also a Roman Catholic Wales.

A man with this vision could not help but find the contrast between the golden days of Wales and the impoverished Wales of the nineteen-twenties intolerable. Everywhere, it seemed to Lewis and others, the interests of Wales were being subordinated to foreign wishes; the major political parties were obsessed with their doctrinaire squabbles when an historic European culture was dying. Lewis's new party demanded: ". . . not independence but freedom. And the meaning of freedom in this matter is responsibility. We who are Welsh people claim that we are responsible for the civilisation and the ways of social life in our part of Europe."

* * *

Many notable Welshmen supported their articulate young compatriot. Many more were sympathetic to the Plaid's cultural arguments but found the party's economic programme absurd, considering economic devolution anachronistic and unreasonable. It has never won a seat in the British Parliament. What its supporters have done, by persisting in their extreme and rather impractical nationalism, is to create a situation in which a watered-down version of their policy, like Lady Megan Lloyd-George's present campaign for a Parliament for Wales, can gain public support and cause the Labour Party machine much trouble. By functioning as a revolutionary cadre, but without arms, and as they claim, infiltrating influential places, schools, university, pulpit, the stage, journalism, they have done a great deal, if by no means all, to bring about the revival of interest in Welsh language and culture within Wales and in Welsh affairs outside, which has been so marked a post-war development.

*   *   *

It has been known for Nonconformist ministers in Wales to speak of Roman Catholicism as if it were the work of the Devil. Therefore, when the leader of the mainly Nonconformist Plaid became a convert to Roman Catholicism there was widespread uneasiness; the conversion emphasised the difference between Lewis and his followers. His Wales was not their Wales; his life even was quite unlike theirs.

He had a highly cultivated taste in wine; among wine merchants in South Wales he is regarded as a connoisseur. Yet total abstinence was the traditional doctrine of the chapels from which the Plaid drew its support. Lewis liked cigars – in the context a curiously aristocratic trait. He was passionately concerned to raise standards in Welsh literature and always considered it from the highest standards of European criticism. Inevitably he found much in Welsh writing wanting and never minced his words in saying so. The more parochial of his followers, for whom it was enough that a work was Welsh for it to be perfect, were baffled or angry at his intellectual honesty.

In time, the pressure of these incompatibilities became intolerable, and in the early years of the war Lewis resigned his presidency of the Plaid. The simple reason given was that he considered his Roman Catholicism hindered the progress of the

21

party. This, however, was not the first time that the people to whom he had devoted himself had behaved curiously towards him.

In 1936 Saunders Lewis and two Nationalist colleagues, the Rev. Lewis Valentine and the Welsh short-story writer, Mr D. J. Williams, tried to set on fire a bombing school which the Air Ministry had begun to build in the Lleyn Peninsula. Although the men admitted their offence, the jury at Caernarvon failed to agree on a verdict; throughout the trial there were large Nationalist crowds outside the courthouse. The trial was then removed to the Old Bailey, where the Welshmen refused to plead and were sentenced to a year's imprisonment.

Lewis's speech in his own defence at Caernarvon was charteristic of him, lucid, reasonable and persuasive. He drew the court's attention to the other proposed bombing schools, at Abbotsbury and Holy Island, which the Air Ministry had *not* built after highly-publicised protests:

> Will you try to understand our feelings when we saw the foremost scholars and literary men of England talking of the "sacredness" of ducks and swans, and succeeding on that argument in compelling the Air Ministry to withdraw the bombing range, while here in Wales, at the very same time, we were organising a nation-wide protest on behalf of the truly sacred things in Creation – a Nation, its language, its literature, its separate traditions and immemorial ways of Christian life – and we could not get the Government even to receive a deputation to discuss the matter with us? The irony of the contrast is the irony of blasphemy.

When the conspirators were released from prison the Rev. Lewis Valentine resumed his pulpit; Mr Williams, who had been English master at Fishguard Grammar School, became the Welsh master there – and Saunders Lewis was dismissed from his post at University College, Swansea.

This extraordinary behaviour had serious results for Lewis.

For fourteen years he found nowhere to teach, and supported himself and his family by his Welsh-language journalism and his plays, neither of which earned him much money. His journalism during this time is regarded by many Welshmen as having been the finest in the language, as his verse and plays are recognised as being in the highest tradition. But even during the lean years he would not write in English and still does not. He reads as little English as possible; the influence of the English language in Wales being so great, he believes it has to be resisted positively; and so mostly he reads Italian and French.

*   *   *

Since 1943, when he stood unsuccessfully as a Welsh Nationalist candidate in a University of Wales Parliamentary by-election, he has cut himself free from politics, although he still believes in the Plaid Cymru policy and is willing to comment, usually scathingly, always with great humour, on movements such as the "Parliament of Wales Campaign." He regards his excursion into politics as a necessary duty which has now been performed; he has finally returned to his scholarship, which has won him a European reputation if little recognition in England.

In 1951 he was appointed senior lecturer in Welsh at University College, Cardiff. He lives now in Penarth, on the outskirts of Cardiff, among the decaying Gothic Palaces, the Rhine Castles and the Chateaux of the long-dead coal millionaires – a lonely eminence in Welsh life, respected as incorruptible, as the supreme idealist, the genius of modern Welsh literature, the man whose life with its promise and tragedies is the solitary exemplar of his argument that Wales is a European nation, and of the predicament of small cultures.

Saunders Lewis, a frail, small man, persuasively eloquent, even *tête à tête,* is, in the words of a friend, "an omniscient sort of joker."

The Observer, Sunday, 8th August 1954.

Lady Megan Lloyd George

This, at last, was the end of the evening's five meetings, the time 10.30, the place a Welfare Hall, the candidate blue-eyed, small and slim in a comfy suit with, as they say, blue twin-set, angora Dutch bonnet and zip-up boots, delivering her peroration with that air of innocent concentration that Vicky has captured, almost the little girl playing schoolteachers. Then applause, the brisk, busy return to her seat; the chairman's appeal to "send Lady Megan back to *Westminister*"; a shout of encouragement from the auditorium and the candidate trips to the edge of the stage, waves and smiles; and the applauders and the applause drift out into the black, drizzling night. A man runs on to the platform. During her speech he has written a Welsh poem in praise of Lady Megan. "Read it to me," she says. He declaims it and is rewarded with a smile so dazzling that he is clearly stunned. "Isn't that lovely," says Lady Megan to me, "he's written me a poem." Her eyes are wrinkled-up with delight; the whole face clenched in a fist of gaiety.

Outside in the rain, it's handshakes all round. People have come a long way to see the famous daughter of the fabulous man. A miner shakes her hand for two whole minutes saying over and over again: "Well, well, well, Megan Lloyd George, *shwd i chwi, merch?*" The smile is now impish and disappears only when a woman asks her to autograph a snapshot of David Lloyd George's grave at Llandystymdwy. Beside the car another little crowd waits to shake hands, on some faces that wrapt, detached look of men who intend to mention, in passing, to grandchildren that they shook Lady Megan Lloyd George by the hand. "What did you say?" *"Hwyl fawr."* "And what did Lady Megan say?" *"Diolch yn fawr."*

Driving the 16 miles back to Carmarthen Town, slowly – "I've had one accident and don't want another" – I reflected that, before this difficult, tense campaign began, some of her friends had been whispering that she wouldn't take much part in the struggle. After all, even is she doesn't look it, she is 54.

This is her seventh campaign. And the constituency *so large, too, so* tiring. Between ourselves – *knowing, informed and wrong* – Lady Megan won't be doing very much.

There are tales of tempestuous arguments between candidate and agents over arranging the fixture-list of 100 meetings. Lady Megan likes her own way; but so, if less dramatically, do agents. But whether or not she wanted to take so furiously active a part as she did, she did. That evening, like all other evenings, except Sundays, the car left the hotel at 5.30 for the journey into the interior. Already there had been a lunch-time meeting with farmers from the "bible-black," whisky-golden county; interviews by journalists ("I'd love to ask *you* a question"); and the, at first, speculative and then gradually confident working-out of an attitude for a speech about defence.

In the car a series of fluent statements in reply to questions about things Welsh, industry, the Liberal Party and then, in the middle of somewhere, her first meeting, applause for the entry of the gladiator from 60 people, half of them men, nearly filling a small hall with its tiny stage. "A few words" from the chairman . . . "great honour and privilege . . . bearer of a great name . . ."; a speech in Welsh about Suez and coal lasting 25 minutes, cheers, handshakes; outside again, sympathy expressed for a wet dog and away on the seven-mile journey to the next chapel vestry, discussing the effects on the county finances of the new equalisation grant. At this hall – high on a hill, anthracite small-coal on the path, a horse champing the grass in the graveyard – people sat on window-sills and stood on the steps outside in the cold. Scheduled to speak for 15 minutes, Lady Megan spoke for 30 in her best form; better even, I thought, than at Carmarthen Market Hall on Aneurin Bevan's night, the occasional sentence in cut-glass English interspersing the Welsh of the north; passionate about the "criminal folly" of Suez, now ironic and now angry about the Tories, the stabbing finger a revolver-barrel firing-off the rhetorical questions. *Pwy? . . . Pwy? . . . Pwy? (Who? . . . Who? Who?).* A Nationalist asks a question in the form of a speech and Lady Megan answers with such sweet earnestness that the absurd but persistent image of the little girl reciting a poem of her own composition returns.

In the car the driver, very stern, said: "We're over half an hour late." "Oh, but I couldn't leave them. They were so wonderful," the full blaze of charm directed at the driver. He glowed. A brief dissertation on *Titus Andronicus;* on her bilingual dog; on national feeling's not being Nationalist feeling; and then another crowded hall. Dissident notes here. The unspoken question was articulated, not directly, as on another night ("Why have you sold your birthright?"), but unmistakably: "Tell me, Lady Megan, what party did you belong to when you voted for the nationalisation of coal?" The answer, slow and firm: "I am a radical, like my father before me. The Liberal Party is no longer the home for radicals. The home for radicals is the Labour Party. You say I have changed. It is not *I* who have changed."

We were late leaving there, too. It was while *en route* along unlit lanes to the fourth meeting that Lady Megan gaily expressed her fatigue. It had been midnight when she returned to the hotel the previous evening; it was to be midnight the next evening. And even though it was only to be 11.15 this evening, there was to be a discussion, over a lager, of agriculture until 12, the candidate still absorbing and providing information, all her faces in turn appearing, while I at half her age was being counted-out by sheep. But it was while the car was slowing down outside hall No. 4 and the committee-men were sprinting from shelter through the rain that Lady Megan asked the great question: "Why to I do this? Tell me, why do I do it?" A minute later the applause, the quick laughter for the joke and then the grave, attentive faces for the denunciation of Suez.

The New Statesman and Nation, 2nd March 1957

Emlyn Williams

The President of Wednesday's session of the National Eisteddfod at Rhyl will be a Welsh-speaking Welshman who has become his nation's most successful playwright and actor without ever competing in or even appearing at its senior national congress. On August 17 he will, back in England, attend the rehearsal of his new play "Someone Waiting," in which he will also be producer and player. So his presence at Rhyl will remind ambitious Welshmen that their own language offers no rewards comparable to those to be won in England. Collier-tenors, dairyman-declaimers and preacher-poets when they hear the light, precise voice of the white-haired man on the platform will be thinking. For whether he likes it or not or whether they like, officially, to admit it or not, Emlyn Williams has become for his own countrymen the contemporary symbol of success, typifying the Welsh boy of humble origin who wins fame and fortune across the border. Returning, if briefly, in triumph to his own people, he will find a true welcome springing from an unaffected admiration; in a nation containing so many entertainers some may feel that there but for bad luck, missed chances, poor health, or simple indolence, go we.

*　　　*　　　*

George Emlyn Williams was born at Mostyn, Flintshire, in 1905, into a Wales different from that made familiar by other writers. In the North he was away from the unsightly slag-heaps, the derelict valleys, the strikes and militant industrial bitterness of the South. The country around his home was pastoral; the squirearchy still survived. Nearby was a Catholic monastery, and not far away was the English Border. This difference in background made the Wales of Emlyn Williams' plays in many ways strange to the people of the South. The accent was different and they felt that the quality of the life portrayed was untypical and baffling.

Two things, however, the South Walian could easily recognise. One was poverty and the other the determination to fight poverty through education and application. The young George (for so he was known then and still is in Flintshire) revealed very early that he possessed useful weapons in this fight. Before he won a scholarship to Holywell County School, he had already gained one prize, that of the Flintshire Sunday School Union for an essay, written when he was eight years old, in Welsh, on the minor prophet Jonah. He had also shown that he was different, the schoolboy games of his brothers and friends did not attract him.

*   *   *

At the County School he showed his prowess and determination quickly. He acted in Welsh plays and wrote an unpublished novel. He needed more practice in speaking French so he called at Llanassa Abbey and when told that some of the monks could help, he was given entry for conversational exercise; he worked there in the evening after school for a whole year. He was rewarded in time with scholarships; one in Switzerland, one at Oxford. There his College was Christ Church, a house for long much favoured by the aristocratic and wealthy. It was a big change from Mostyn.

His parents always had suitably Welsh ambitions for their son. His father wanted him to be a teacher, his mother a preacher. At Oxford it was made obvious that the dark, intent young Welshman was to become neither. He joined the O.U.D.S. and took part in their Shakespearean productions. Even in a small part in "Love's Labour's Lost." G. E. Williams, Ch. Ch., as he appeared on the programme, was conspicuous and took the eye of the one London critic. He also wrote a play; "The Vigil," is marked by its strange quality of poetry and imagination.

From Oxford, Emlyn Williams went to London and made his first appearance on the professional stage in 1927 in a small role in "And so to Bed." At the age of 23 he played at the

Embassy Theatre in his own play "Glamour." In the same year he appeared in the French play "Thérèse Raquin" (in French) and two years later, he further proved his polyglot capacity in the Italian "La Piccola."

For the next twenty years he was continually on the stage or making films. His adaptation of "The Late Christopher Bean" from a French to a Welsh setting with a superb performance by Edith Evans was highly successful. He was Angelo in Wallace's "On the Spot," Danny in his own successful thriller 'Night Must Fall' and Branwell Brontë in "Wild Decembers," and Lord Lebanon – his favourite part, it is said, in his first film, "The Case of the Frightened Lady." He seemed most at home in sinister surroundings, with something morbid round the corner.

In 1937 he worked at the Old Vic. His play "Spring, 1600," had shown his enjoyment of the Shakespearean scene. In 1938 he was the brilliant schoolboy in another of his long-running plays, "The Corn is Green," which won for him the award given by the New York Critics' Circle for the best foreign play of the year. He drew on his Welsh background for "Druid's Rest" and "The Wind of Heaven" and deserted it in "Accolade," which did not have the success to which he had become accustomed. He has directed, written and acted in a notable film with a Welsh setting. "The Last Days of Dolwyn," and has appeared in a number of other films. For the last two years he has experienced the most remarkable success of his theatrical career with his representation of, and readings from, Charles Dickens. This has won him the acclaim of critics here and in America. A recent revue sketch in the West End has had fun with Mr Dickens enacting Mr Williams.

*   *   *

At 48 Emlyn Williams has the white hairs of age and abounding energy of youth: middle-age seems to be eluding him. No business man has governed the affairs of a major industry with a more iron will than Emlyn Williams has conducted his own career. While he was touring with his excerpts from Dickens's novels he was learning "Bleak House" by heart, and sleeping usually only four hours a night. For most of his life, he has been acting in his last play while writing the next; he works with fluency; but he can work anywhere.

His work has been criticised for lack of important comment of life. But Williams does not set out to be a preacher; that was a profession he avoided when he preferred the grease-paint to the gown and cassock. The solemn view that a play which is theatrically effective cannot be a very good play is not shared by him.

*   *   *

The background of Emlyn Williams's most ambitious plays, "The Corn is Green" and "The Wind of Heaven" and of his film "The Last Days of Dolwyn," has been the countryside of his youth. This gives them freshness and authenticity. His theme is often the devotion of women towards gifted boys or men. "The Corn is Green" is an essay in gratitude to a woman-teacher. He does not need the periods of rustication which are often considered necessary to the creative writer. Wales is in him; he does not have to go back and look for it.

Like many a great player he has been limited by lack of height. He is not tall enough to play the classic parts which have become the modern tests. He has had to create his own roles and to restrict himself in other plays to characterisation in which the "thews and big assemblance" of a man do not matter.

When Emlyn Williams appears at the Eisteddfod this week,his people can express their awareness of many achievements. One of these is to have put Welsh acting firmly on the English mat. Until he acted professionally and began to write his plays with Welsh backgrounds and Welsh characters there were few really Welsh Welshmen on the English stage. (Sir Lewis Casson, it is true, was educated at Ruthin, but Dame Edith Evans is London Welsh.) There are now Welsh actors of many talents; Emlyn Williams has contributed to this, either directly or indirectly, through his work and influence. Richard Jenkins, now widely known as Richard Burton, has come from a mining background at Pontrhydyfen in South Wales and combines, at the age of 28, starring in Hollywood with service of the "Old Vic"; he is to play "Hamlet" at the Edinburgh Festival this year. It is significant that Burton had his first professional part in Williams's play "Druid's Rest." His career has much in common with that of the boy from Mostyn, for he too went up to Oxford with scholarships and then passed to a stage career with quickly won success.

* * *

So Emlyn Williams has given a lead where the Welsh, with their natural vivacity and richness of performance, may increasingly follow. Perhaps the most striking feature of his life has been his eagerness not only to idolise Charles Dickens, but to re-create the master at his reading-desk and in the flow of his dramatic monologues. For Dickens was the voice of Southern England and especially of London. It is the man from North Wales who has reminded London of its legacy by showing with such far-ranging skill the form and pressure of the master himself, the pomp and pride of the Dickensian prigs and bullies, and the glorious absurdity of the Dickensian drolls; his memorising of the Dickens texts is amazing, for he is really acting, not reading them. His supreme feat was to put the vast panorama of "Bleak House" on his one-man stage. It may be thought that it is the macabre in Dickens which draws the best from this specialist in the sinister. But he revels in the laughter too.

Next month he returns from the dais to the theatre. He is only midway in his career: the best may be to come.

The Observer, August 1959.

Aneurin Bevan

The hills where he made his first speeches and one of his last and where he will be buried and where the wild, melancholy sound of Welsh hymns is heard this week-end, are the bleakest in South Wales, even if they are near the Beacons. Their scars are deepest. In winter the grass is grey and in spring not much greener. Ponies and combative sheep abandon them for the streets in search of food. Over the hill from Tredegar, industry is at its ugliest, the smoke billowing out of the gash in the earth that is Ebbw Vale. When the rain falls, as it did the day Aneurin Bevan died, it seems an impossible alchemy that anyone or anything should come out of such a place with gifts great enough to dazzle the world. But it happened and it doesn't need much of an exploration of the mining and steel towns to grasp that, in spite of the dead grass and the slagheaps and the smoke, alchemy was unnecessary. The hero was his own people.

The more vulgar images of a valley in tears when the news of his death came were, as one would think, untrue. The death was expected. But the sadness was of a kind which would probably seem peculiar in parts of the country where heroes seldom embody with such extraordinary fidelity the attitudes and history (and in their talents express) the exacting character and dreams of place and people. When kings who were loved by their people died it was, I suppose, this kind of sadness, except that this people retain, as their king recommended, the bump of irreverence.

'Of course, when he bought that farm, we were a bit troubled. A gentleman farmer seemed a Tory sort of thing. But then we thought he was entitled to it for all he'd done. And then we thought – Would anyone think twice if anybody else who'd done as well as he had bought a luxury yacht, let alone a farm. Shows you how straight Nye was compared with the rest that we should think such a thing.'

'I could never understand the fuss they made about that

"lower than vermin" speech. Aneurin was quite right. They were lower than vermin. Any crowd that could let the things happen that happened here before the war are lower than vermin, let's face it.'

'I think he'd have had a good laugh about what the papers are saying about him today, especially the *Daily Express* and *Western Mail*. I remember him saying once that if he ever got a favourable mention in them that he wouldn't dare show his face in Tredegar.'

'During the war, it was a funny thing. I mean, we were fighting the war like everybody else. But we thought Nye was wonderful attacking Churchill like that. Great. After all, don't forget, Churchill was no bloody hero down here. He was no friend of the miners. I'm not saying he was just a war-monger – fair's fair. But Nye was speaking for us. He always was."

'He was never clannish about Welsh people. He just was Welsh, Tredegar Welsh, anyway. He never lost his accent, either, never got out of touch. Mind you, he liked the good things in life. Why not? So do I. I know that we didn't see much of him in these last few years, but we didn't mind. We were proud of him. Anything Nye did was all right because it was bound to be all right if Nye was doing it.'

'Any road, how can they say he didn't do anything for Wales? What about the National Health? Look at the difference that's made down here. And take when the Eisteddfod was here. The council gave them money, which they were entitled to do because of some act Nye passed. He cared about things like that, see. He wasn't just a politician.'

'All this nonsense in the papers about him being wayward and brilliant and a phrase-maker, as if it's a terrible thing to be. What did they want? Some dry old stick? It lifted you up just to hear them talk whatever he was saying. When he was younger he was a bit more fiery, I suppose, but the times were more fiery, weren't they?'

'People who used to work with him in the pit say he was like a tiger underground.'

These random appraisals offered around Tredegar's

enormous clock and in the pubs and clubs and cafes in the places around could be heard in most other towns in industrial Wales. I don't know anyone who didn't feel that Aneurin Bevan represented him. At meetings in Swansea or Cardiff he was welcomed with the same family enthusiasm and almost an equal sense of pride as at those on the hillside above Tredegar. After his death people have talked about him as people do in Welsh parlours after funerals freely, as if they'd known him well, and wanted to fix him in their minds by praise.

'It wasn't just that he was a collier's son who became a Cabinet minister, though God knows that was enough. It's that he was always a collier's son in his heart. He knew what we were thinking because he was one of us. Do you see what I mean? He was a sort of underdog like us, but he was a topdog underdog.'

'And he could speak. To have the gift of words, to hold the meeting in your hands. Those are the things, boy.'

And inevitably, the more sophisticated forms of praise, reflecting sometimes unconsciously, the general thesis of the superiority of the Welsh over the English. This gift of words, for example, which in Wales is often held to be different, from, and superior to, any question of the meaning of words. The sound is what matters, the grace and charm and fire of the words, whatever they may mean. Men who stride the hills like bards of old, should not be brought down to the level of flatland people. Poets and preachers, the men with the gift, should be listened to and praised and followed.

But isn't there here a danger of Messianism? Not when the gift is used as a defence against precisely that. Inextricably confused are the notions that all men are equal, but that some men have superior gifts which ensure them insights into the nature of things while yet remaining equal and part of the people among whom they grew up and, being Welsh, suffered.

And, of course, the opinion that it was the obtuseness of the English, their placidity, their over-weening lack of imagination which prevented Aneurin Bevan becoming Prime Minister or Foreign Secretary and making the country dynamic and gay in his own image. Or was it impossible for any man to become these things who retained so purely the ideals of his people?

New Statesman, 16th July 1960

Richard Burton

'The hero of the poem,' wrote John Dryden pompously of Anthony in his *All for Love,* 'ought not to be a character of perfect virtue, for then he could not,without injustice, be made unhappy; nor yet altogether wicked because he could not then be pitied.' Pitying Richard Burton may seem one of the more difficult exercises in puritan analysis. When *Cleopatra,* the most expensive of epics, opens here next week, whether his Marc Antony is good or bad he will be the most famous actor in the world. What more could the 12th child of a Welsh miner ask than to be immensely rich and certain to be richer? Not many such have a large share in a Swiss bank.

He is as handsome and attractive to women as any man could wish to be. His presence is as commanding, his voice as powerful and subtle as any in his profession. His Cleopatra – Miss Elizabeth Taylor, in case anyone has been away from the newspapers for a year – is one of the more glittering prizes of our time. Miss Taylor dotes on him. (Eliza to Burton's Higgins rather than Cleopatra to his Antony.) Yet, for all this, his friends, many of whom still stubbornly try to persuade themselves that the playing-out of *Cleopatra* in the private lives of hero and heroine must be cunning sales-talk, begin to weep in their beer. They believed the romance of the golden boy's career would have taken a different course; that at 37 he would now be the greatest actor on the English-speaking stage rather than the press's most celebrated lover in a year of stiff competition.

So poor have been the films that Burton has appeared in,

that it is difficult to recall quite how brilliant was his achievement and promise a decade ago. Then he dominated the Old Vic. His melancholy and passionate Hamlet with its unusual masculinity was probably the best since the war. As Coriolanus and Iago, his disciplined fire made it clear that he was an actor who could maintain the classic tradition of the English stage in the idiom of the present.

That promise had been there since he had been very young. Like Dylan Thomas, he was a memorable schoolboy actor. Burton even appeared in the West End – in Emlyn Williams's *Druid's Rest* – while he was still at Port Talbot Secondary School. As an adolescent he had the curious, brooding air that characterised his maturer acting. Not that offstage he was as amiable an adolescent as he was later to become the most agreeable of actors. The adulation of Port Talbot schoolgirls and his manifest talent turned his head in the direction of theatricality. It was after he had been to Oxford, briefly, and the Royal Air Force that he became the entertaining drinking companion, the uproarious, generous and extraordinary modest boyo, with the Welsh gift of being at home in all places.

That a miner's son should have become a celebrated actor so young requires some explanation, and the explanation goes some way to accounting for his present apparent squandering of his talent. The Afan Valley village in which he was born is locked away in a bend in the river and is celebrated even in that gloomy valley for the peculiar, wild melancholy of its inhabitants. They are given to the harp and the drink. An impressive viaduct dominates the village which, as the local joke has it, is just as well, or where else could the natives jump from? Burton, whose name was Jenkins, was brought up by one of his sisters since his mother had died when he was young. He went to the secondary school, but left when he was 14 to work in the local Co-op for two years. He then went back to school because he was adopted by a teacher of English, a noteable figure in Welsh drama, at that time, Philip Burton. It was his name that he took. His help accounts for the early success.

One of Burton's most attractive features is his affection for his family and his home village. He has built houses for his brothers: one is called Camelot. There is nothing spurious, as there could be, about this feeling. It isn't just that he visits the local rugby clubhouse – he was a good rugby player and follows the London Welsh club in London, enlivening the duller matches by taking Miss Taylor along. That would scarcely be any sacrifice. But he'll also visit valley schools, when asked to present prizes to children, children whose parents have mixed views about his current behaviour, pride in his success battling with a nonconformist censure, tormented in turn with local affection for his wife who comes from over the Bwlch mountain. These warring elements he contains within him. But there was another characteristic common to all who were brought up in that place at that time: a fear of poverty, and the sense of life's uncertainty that poverty breeds.

When Burton first became celebrated in London he bought a house in Belsize Park. He split it up into flats, not because he was greedy for money, but so that he would have some income when, as he expected, the unbelievable miracle of his career would end; which event he expected hourly. The great sums of money offered by the cinema were bound to attract him, and they did. Only for people accustomed to money is more money irrelevant. At times he would rationalise his abandoning the classic stage for the silver screen by promising himself that one day he would have a theatre, a company, or something, of his own. He banked his fortune.

But the desire to be rich beyond the possibility of disaster scarcely accounts for him making so many bad films. Actors have made good films and have still been rich. (Not that he is as good an actor on celluloid as on the stage: his energy and passion do not communicate even when the ghastly lines permit the possibility.) Other aspects of his Welshness are probably a better explanation.

Welsh romanticism has a startling arrogance. Ideally, it likes its heroes to die young; the dream is of the golden boy of natural genius who effortlessly conquers the English world.

The romance lies in the ascent. Exercising the power is boring, requiring diligence and consistency. Early death is attractive because it rules out the chance of solid middle-age. The Welsh have all the talents, except for being 45. What to do with all that talent is the perennial problem. Dylan Thomas, thus is the perfect hero. This arrogance – an arrogance that masquerades as modesty – infects the performer because this is how he sees himself. Perversely, pleasure lies in the waste of talent. If you can't die, at least you can assuage the gods by pretending. Burton is an intelligent and self-aware man and understands his inheritance: he may thus defeat. He is not an old man. His current behaviour reveals how freshly his romantic instincts are preserved. It may be that if he returns to the stage seriously he will show that his great talent equally is intact. Otherwise he promises to make the subject for another cinema epic more like *All for Love* than *Cleopatra*. Burton has more to offer than the role of the heavy in a personal melodrama.

New Statesman, 26th July 1963.

Geraint Evans

Paumgartner, the founder of the Salzburg Festival, dying, is held to have cried, 'Eevans, where is my Eevans. Where is Mozart's only Figaro?' It has been reported that 'Eevans', as Sir Geraint, our knight of the opera, is known throughout *Mittel Europa,* when told this tale, burst into tears, and why not? Presented with the anecdote, however, our hero replies: 'First I've ever heard of it, though it would be nice if it were true.' There are quite enough conductors ready to express the view that Geraint Evans is the incomparable Mozartian of his time. 'He sings' as Solti put it rather dryly, 'all the notes.' He doesn't need apocrypha.

Last Friday the 50-year-old Welsh baritone whose dramatic, almost Italianate features and bull-like frame are, by reason of his appearing so often on television, better-known to more people than any other British opera singer, celebrated a quarter-century of appearances at the Royal Opera House by signing *Don Pasquale*. But Don Pasquale is a shade too pathetic an old fellow for Sir Geraint's resonance and theatrical gaieties. It was his Figaro which first made his reputation abroad. One performance in the early sixties established Evans as the best of his time. What was peculiar about his performance in that hothouse of the super-ego was the quality of his acting. Wächter, Jurinac and the rest might merely plant themselves at the footlights and sing beautifully; the scarcely-known Welshman would be representing the raging, uprising servant Mozart intended. Later he was to emphasise even more his understanding of the revolutionary element in the role by using, for example, a sword rather than a measuring rod in *Se vuol ballere,* where he determines to teach Count Almaviva a lesson.

For his Falstaff he has been, from time to time, quite heavily criticised on the grounds that he over-elaborates, even vulgarises the role by excessive broad gesture. To which his reply is that since he is aware that audiences – ignorant of Italian – often miss the sense, not to mention the nuance, of the libretto, he is trying to provide the sense in action. Unlike many singers (and critics) he thinks an opera is improved by being understood.

In the same way at Covent Garden he's been known to interject a joke or two in English into a German performance of the *Magic Flute,* if only to rouse a House glumly gaping at what the Master intended as comedy. He's pretty good, too, at handling the earnest critic. In the late Sixties one such expressed surprise and scholarly interest in an unusual *Don Giovanni* where Sir Geraint played Leporello to Tito Gobbi's *Don,* neither of them being exactly in the first flush of youth. Giovanni was represented as a broken-down seedy roué, his servant Leporello mocking his sexuality, the pair of them comprising a nasty duo. Was this some interpretation based on a new understandng and insight? 'Not really,' said Leporello Evans. 'Tito was older than Dons often are. I am older. I played to him. If it looked seedy, perhaps old men behaving like that look seedy.'

In the hysterical, sometimes ludicrous world in which he has worked Evans's calm is so striking as to be a puzzle. The rages and petulance, the ostentatious randiness, the jealous protocols of bouquets, the snarling about fees that make so many opera singers wearisome, are missing. Even the antics that distinguish so many of his fellow-countrymen are so much absent in him that one can ascribe his character either to saintliness, which is improbable, or, more likely, to an incurable puritanism. He works like a man who managed to escape going down the pit, but never had the opportunity, through being poor, of a higher education. Really, he could not have been born at a worse time, in Cilfynydd, just as the Rhondda was falling into a decline of unparalleled industrial sadness, the unemployment rate soon reaching and staying around 50 per cent, until the figures fell because the people moved away out of despair. His mother died young. At 15 he was dressing windows in Pontypridd with one small talent that seemed of little account: a voice that could make the floor tremble. Came the war, a sympathetic teacher in Hamburg where he was serving in the RAF; a total transformation; within three years he was on stage at Covent Garden, the Royal Opera's Figaro at the age of 26.

To make so much of puritanism in a man notably gregarious and funny, a raconteur who has had roomfuls entertained with his anecdotes from Salzburg to San Francisco, may seem far-fetched; and largely it is restricted to his work-ethic, his faith in transformation through industry. His tolerance, which is wide, suddenly stops at the idea that there is virtue in idleness. He once met by chance a middle-class university drop-out who subsequently was acquitted in the Angry Brigade trial, not the kind of person Sir Geraint would normally meet, unless he happened to be a member of the Welsh Language Society painting-out signposts near his house on Cardigan Bay. On the one hand stood the working-class knight saying work is good; on the other the bourgeois member of the Claimant's Union attacking the system, the folly of work. For the opera singer it was not a matter of politics – he claims to have no politics – but a matter of whether one was a layabout or one was not.

He has, though, none of the puritan's greed for money. He earns an enormous amount, is among the dozen best-paid singers in the world. For his first *Figaro* at Covent Garden he earned £10. There now, as at Salzburg and the Metropolitan, he earns at least a hundred times that amount. Yet he has never, unlike some, been a taxdodger and it is said that when the Harlech Consortium of which he was the key member won the television franchise for Wales, he completely forgot to invest in it until friends brought the oversight to his notice. And among opera singers he is one of the few who feels that fees for the most celebrated singers have grown dangerously high for the profession's health, which would sound hypocritical coming from anyone else.

There are, of course, colleagues who find him just too good to be true, who will try to put down his generosity with his money and, more importantly, his time, to a subtle assumption of power over a generation of singers. His willingness to hear young singers, to encourage foreign opera houses to engage the astonishing new crowd of British tenors and sopranos – and not only the Welsh – baffles them. Or if it's not that he wants that kind of power – how, after all, can it just be kindness of heart? – then the other glib explanation is that he must be insecure and want to be loved. Who isn't? Who doesn't? Encouraging rivals does seem on the face of it a curious way to express insecurity.

Whatever the motive, his capacity for work is phenomenal. At a time of life when most men will settle for a draw and give the mind a rest, he could be observed singing in a recording studio with Klemperer his familiar role Guigliemo in *Cosi Fan Tutte* while learning for the first time the role of *Don Alfonso* in the same opera for the Covent Garden production. (On stage he could also be observed prompting the baritone singing his old role when the latter suddenly dried.) Immediately the Covent Garden production was on stage, he began learning in German Berg's *Wozzeck* (for Salzburg) which he had previously sung in English. Simultaneously in Cardiff he was preparing TV programmes in Welsh as well as his familiar arias in German, Italian, Russian, even English: unlike some other famous Welshmen who won the Harlech contract he has kept his promises and made more programmes than it was thought possible a commercial station could transmit.

Television suits him, and he television, which is unusual since opera singers generally are given to the hammiest of facial and bodily gestures. But in Evans's case it is explicable because he has devoted so many laborious hours to mastering the techniques of 'playback' and camera movement. Like many another autodidact he is a passionate proselytiser. Not usually an eloquent man, he grows persuasively articulate when preaching his sermon on bringing opera to the people. Television can do that; therefore he learns about television.

Perhaps opera singers should be more absurd than Sir Geraint, should not live in Orpington, should not, if they have a small yacht, keep it in Cardigan Bay but at St Tropez, and if they have a Mercedes not have one that's six years old, and not have been married for 25 years to a clever, pretty woman from their small coal village. Perhaps they should join the gang at Lake Constance and live it up. People like him make it possible to defend the enormous subsidy to Covent Garden. Opera of the kind he sings, in the way he sings it, is not a bastard and faintly nonsensical art-form, but one of the higher manifestations of the human spirit available, worth the money.

New Statesman, 16th February 1973

John Tripp

When a Welsh poet is buried more than the earth is disturbed. For those who were his friends and his fans, John Tripp's early death means much more than the passing of a fine writer and inspiring entertainer.

42

The fear, after mourning, is that no one will now occupy that space he made his own, a territory in which the brave, free spirit sets down the condition of the Welsh people and place in memorable language. Obituaries of admired pals are peculiarly difficult at the best of times, whatever they might be. With someone as powerful in his smoking, drinking, hilarious presence the task is more anguished since it is hard to believe that, when we all meet, he will not be there. He was always there and impossible to miss. But we did our best and it went, more or less, like this.

At the Cardiff crematorium Glyn Jones and Roland Mathias offered solemn and sensitive appraisals of his life and work. Since John Tripp had been an agnostic – we learned that he had lost his faith at a Sunday school class at Ararat Chapel in Bargoed, quite characteristically – we still decided that it was proper to sing *Cwm Rhondda*. Didn't the hymn, after all, own qualities as much social as religious?

We, that is the Welsh Union of Writers, then held a long wake at The Gower, a pub in Cathays, Cardiff, swiftly organised by the poet and playwright Nigel Jenkins. I have never known a more moving occasion. Nothing so distinguished it as its gentility. This quality would have astonished the late poet since there was seldom, if ever, an event at which he was present not made famous by some outrageous gesture. In the course of six hours there was only one incident which might have struck him as appropriate.

A choir, Cor Cochion Caerdydd (the Cardiff Red Choir), performed very well. The choristers hail mainly from Caerphilly. Towards the end of their tribute they sang the *Internationale,* which enraged one of John Tripp's friends in the audience. No doubt he felt that the song's associations with the antics of the Comintern in Germany in the 'Twenties or the Hitler-Stalin pact, not to mention Soviet Imperialism, was news that had not yet reached Caerphilly. He threw sandwiches and beer at the choir, which switched swiftly to the Welsh National anthem.

The other five hours of the evening were occupied by an

array of Welsh actors, poets, novelists and the poet's editors, Ned Thomas and John Osmond, all reading his work and offering anecdotes. Few men have created as many tales as John Tripp.

Chris Mills met him recently in the street and asked the poet how he was doing. "I'm on a diet," said John. "What kind of diet is that?" "A whisky diet." "How is it going?" "Very well," said John. "I've lost three days already."

Robert Minhinnick read a poem he had written for the occasion, from which a few lines read:

> "And, creature of the great indoors,
> It was strange that I should see you last
> Walking down the Merthyr road
> That ravaged sheepskin
> An affront to Whitchurch decency."

I offered a tale of my own as an illustration of the poet's boundless charm and kindness. When recently I was only a few hours out of a cancer operation at St Lawrence Hospital, Chepstow, a nurse came and said that there was a man on the phone insisting on speaking to "the chairman" – his mode of addressing me lately on account of the Writers' Union. He said that his great friend Jean Henderson was going to drive him to visit me. I suggested he might leave it until I was fitter, partly because I thought the other patients might find the visit alarming. I regret now that a memorable scene was lost. He then sent me a poem about myself – he wrote many poems about his friends.

Comparing his departure with the last Welsh poet of his standing – in the English language, that is – I wonder how he would have pondered on the decorousness of the day compared with the strange going of Dylan Thomas.

On the journey from Southampton the Thomas coffin was taken on a wrong road and was heading for Cornwall while the mourners headed for Laugharne. At the BBC radio studios in Park Place, Dylan Thomas's friends asked that the shutters in the room be drawn before offering their tributes, or so the tale goes, even though no window looked out of the place. Many of us were puzzled about that at the time.

They were very different kinds of poets, John Tripp and Dylan Thomas, but they shared a melancholy, a sense of innocence gone – John's was a vigorous, earned, urban lament, alive with wit. He could move his audiences to laughter as much as tears. The onanism of ideology was alien to him; he was at the whim of no fashionable cultural or historical fancy.

One of his short stories from 1970 was read at the wake by Robin Reeves which gave a perceptive account of a Welsh academic who made it in the big time. His poem *Inquisition* about the divide in Wales on the matter of language was read at the wake.

To be a free man is exhausting and John died at 58, yet writing as exhuberantly as ever. Those of us who admired his work are going to miss that gift for the demotic, that warm, compassionate eye cast on the way we live now. I think the best we can offer the memory of a man who so much banked his treasure in the hearts of his friends, is to carry on his battle against the Establishment in all its forms.

His only enemies were those in power who for a multitude of reasons deny freedom – and occasionally they were landlords who observed the licensing laws. We lack his talent, but even had we it, I can hear his voice say that the good will always lose, their virtue triumphant only in a wake.

Western Mail, February 25th 1986

Carwyn James

How strong the custom is in Wales, which is nice, for women to buy rugby books for men. I was bought Alun Richard's study of Carwyn James today in Swansea by a friend: it was my fifty-fith birthday; Carwyn whom I had known since the mid-forties was coeval. I had been booked to stay in the hotel in Amsterdam in which he died two weeks after that sad end. I changed hotels. Two weeks before he died we had exchanged drinks and cigarettes in the BBC Club in Cardiff. He and I were the only two people we knew who still smoked untipped Senior Service, a legacy, we thought, of our service days, his Navy, in my case, RAF. We always would agree that there was no point in smoking unless fags had quality: they had to be a real smoke. I went into a village in the Wye Valley lately and asked the tobacconist for Senior Service. He told me: "I used to sell a lot of them, but not any more, because my customers have all died." Carwyn died before I could tell him that tale.

It was playing Carwyn in a schools' match in the 'forties that made me realise that there was a class I could not aspire to. In the 'fifties, when I was writing about rugby for *The Observer* I would report as often as seemed unbiased about his revelatory performances at outside-half for Llanelli and the manner in which he was creating an exuberant and delightful style of play. People who admire his intellectual gifts and his subsequent achievements forget how dazzling a player he was for so long. Like his inheritor, Barry John, he was never tackled; neither would he demean himself by tackling. That Llanelli team of the 'fifties understood rugby. Their Carwyn was a prince: no one must touch him.

During his playing career Carwyn would call around and drink a cup of tea with us in Swansea. He was not then the gin-and-tonic man he later became celebrated as. We would talk more about poetry and Welsh nationalism than rugby. In the late 'seventies he agreed to be my guest, or oppo, as we put it, when I had a BBC Radio arts programme and was keen to launch a new Welsh magazine *Arcade* with some publicity. An audience expecting some forceful analysis of the game were briefly puzzled at my references to an Arcadian culture, and Carwyn's quite brilliant response with quotations from Welsh poetry, ancient and modern.

The last time I saw him, a few weeks before he died, he asked me if I had remembered a chat we'd had in the 'fifties

about what we wanted to do with our lives. I said I did. I had
said that I'd like to write a few books that might make people
laugh and see the world as we saw it. And he had said he would
like people to play the sort of rugby that would give pleasure
and see the game as he saw it. As he wrapped his sad, eczema-
troubled hands one in the other, and looked so unhappy, I said
he'd made it.

Side-steps – A Rugby Diary 1984/85

Goronwy Rees

What folly it is to think that there are no new experiences
left. One thing I never dreamed possible was that one day I
would see two close friends depicted on television, played by
an actor and actress.

Yet, so it was the other night when Goronwy Rees and his
wife Margie, were represented as key figures in a drama about
Marxist Russian spies Sir Anthony Blunt, Guy Burgess and
Donald Maclean.

How they would have fallen about at the film as, I hope,
their children will when they have overcome their proper
anger. Goronwy and Margie were given to laughter: it was
one of their many charms, even when they had a lot not to
laugh about.

It was inevitable that the actor and actress in the BBC film
would not look like Goronwy and Margie, nor talk like them,
or behave like them; but not that they should be so unlike.
Margie was one of the most attractive women I ever met, her
voice as distinctive – even rather of the style – as Lauren
Bacall's.

She was hightly intelligent. In the film she seemed a pea-
brained sweetie. In the film Goronwy was a plump man who
seemed unsure, even frightened. In life he was, to his cost, slim,
elegant, charming and brilliant, a man of reckless courage.

Of all the eminent Welshmen I've known, he was the most

fascinating and, in terms of the conflicts of our century, the most important in his interests. Many maintain that he threw his great talents away: he didn't and I don't.

Since some will not know of him, his career, briefly, was this. He was born in Aberystwyth in 1909, son of a famous Welsh preacher. He was Welsh-speaking, which became important later on. He went to school in Cardiff, played rugby and then became the outstanding scholar of his time at Oxford.

He was a Socialist who lived in Berlin, came home to be an editor at the *Spectator,* where he wrote possibly the best, certainly the earliest, anti-Nazi journalism. Friendly with Guy Burgess and many of the rest of the Communist crowd – since they were mostly homosexual they were known as the Homintern – but volunteered for the Royal Welsh Fusiliers when war broke out.

His Marxist pals were against fighting since their hero Stalin had signed a pact with Hitler. When Hitler invaded Russia it became a different war. All this he had described in his two majestic volumes of autobiography. The BBC film suggested he was a Communist Party member and had been briefly a Soviet spy: neither claim is true.

As far as Wales went, in the 'Fifties he was persuaded by that Welsh *eminence gris* Dr Tom Jones to become principal of the University College, Aberystwyth. He fell out with the Establishment. He offended them as, for different reasons, he did the London Establishment, by publishing anonymously in *The People* an account of his friendship with Guy Burgess.

In this he was aided by Keidrych Rhys, the editor of *Wales.* Guy Burgess had by now gone to Moscow, telephoning Goronwy and Margie en route.

In London several were afraid of what Goronwy might write next and about whom? After all, hadn't Colonel Rees been General Montgomery's side-kick, been a senior Intelligence figure himself? In passing, almost, he had written the first and best novel on the matter of brainwashing – *Where No Wounds Were.*

He told me how his anonymity in *The People* had been unmasked. In the 'Thirties, before he married Margie, he had abandoned one affair with a famous woman novelist – he is the central figure in her best novel – for her friend, another writer. The latter, 20 years later, was to shop him because he had abandoned her. Time is surely long in affairs of the heart.

I came to know the Rees family after I had supported his Aberystwyth cause in 1956 in *The Observer*. In London in the 'Sixties when I worked at the *New Statesman* and *Panorama* we enjoyed ourselves in their company with their friends Richard Hughes, Arthur Koesler, A. J. Ayer and so many others.

Since I was often working in Central and Eastern Europe their experience of the Nazi and Stalinist tyrannies was as illuminating as any on offer. (Sir Freddy Ayer has written in protest at inaccuracies in the BBC film).

In the late 'Seventies, just before he died and just after Margie had, Goronwy and myself went on a journey to Berlin, Vienna and Geneva, his old haunts. We were making a film for HTV Wales which Aled Vaughan had proposed in the teeth of the opposition from two members of the Aberystwyth Establishment on the company's board.

In Vienna we saw a performance of the Brecht-Weill *Mahagonny*. Goronwy was moved since he had seen the premiere so many turbulent decades earlier. He had known Bertolt Brecht and translated his poems. That night he told me that Anthony Blunt had been the Fourth Man, and named a Fifth.

He talked about the Communists he had known. His view was that anyone who remained in the Communist Party, or even as a Marxist, after the Soviet putsch in Prague in 1948, let alone after the Hungarian uprising of 1956, no longer qualified as a human being.

The next day in Geneva he swore me to secrecy about Blunt. We were on our way to hear Margaret Price, Ryland Davies and Anne Howells sing in Mozart's *Cosi Fan Tutte*. An unusual couple of Welsh days, we agreed: a long way from Aberystwyth, would you say?

By that time Goronwy had become unpopular in certain

Welsh circles. He was hostile to political nationalism. In his view also, Wales would be a healthier place if the language died, even though it was his first language. It was one of the few subjects on which we differed.

He was scornful of people who made a cause of the language when it wasn't their first language. This he saw at best neurotic, at worst opportunism. I think his vehemence was partly due to irritation with some troglodytes at Aberystwyth, but also because the language cause had not then become a non-political affair.

He used to maintain that Saunders Lewis had once said that it wouldn't be all bad if Hitler won if that meant the Welsh language surviving. In Goronwy's view the battle must always be against the totalitarian, whether Fascist or Marxist. His insights had certainly been learned the hard way.

One of the pleasures, away from his company, of meeting Goronwy's contemporaries at Oxford where he was a Fellow as well as bursar of All Souls and generous with his hospitality there, was their jealousy of him. Two Labour Cabinet Ministers could scarcely speak to him, so sharp was their envy of his mind and style.

There was puzzlement at his lack of ambition since he probably had the sharpest intelligence of any Welshman since David Lloyd George.

He's described his view of himself as a "bundle of sensations" in the philosopher Hume's terms. His curiosity and fastidious, private integrity baffled a lot of people. The BBC play exhibited surprise that Margie called him 'Rees.' This is a common trait among West Wales's women, yet Margie was English.

His five children also called him Rees, still do. I always found it curiously charming and characteristic, a trait of warm, affectionate distance, a signal of healthy independence; and independent he certainly was. He could look on tempests and not be shaken, even if they were often of his own making. He was as indifferent to the might of English Establishment pursuing him as the Welsh; and amusing about both.

His final derisive view about the row at Aberystwyth was that it was due not to his *People* articles, nor his drinking with students, nor his bills at the off-licence, nor local wives' hostility to Margie being English, but something fundamental.

When he sold off some property in the interests of the college, he called in neutral, alien, estate-agents and solicitors to deal with the sale, rather than locals. That was too much for the Cardigan Welsh. At least that was what he told me, laughing.

Western Mail, 20th January 1987

Wynford Vaughan-Thomas

In the last year of his life Wynford and myself used to play what seems to the stranger a macabre game. We would ask what each would say of the other in an obituary since we were both suffering from the same affliction: cancer. One thing he knew I'd say – it was his favourite compliment about his friends – was that he was: "a life enhancer". He offered one thought for his own epitaph: "time will not wither nor custom stale that infinite variety act which is myself". I said I thought that would leave too much an impression of the frivolous when he was nothing like as frivolous as he would pretend.

Wynford the brilliant raconteur and country-lover was well known – as man as celebrated socially as he had been, as a war correspondent, famous nationally. And then there was the man who knew all about wine, who would climb Cader Idris in his sixties, when not riding a horse along the narrow length of Wales.

In private circles he was the author of fine limericks and delightful erotic verse. I was always impressed, too, that when he used our house on the Welsh border as a staging post children as well as adults were excited at his coming: his stories had a universal appeal. The spirits in any room lifted when this sprite of a Celtic past pitched up from some fresh adventure.

There is not a lot to say when a man in his early seventies arrives in state of joy one day to announce that he had been breathalysed on perhaps the only day in his life when he was quite innocent, because he had driven down a one way street in a fury because all he had been offered at a wedding reception was a small glass of sherry.

We met 20 years ago this month. Although we had been born in the same town, went to the same Swansea Grammar School and although we were in the same business we were strangers. I asked him as I did close friends, Aled Vaughan, Richard Burton, Geraint Evans if he would help with an idea I had to win a television franchise for Wales and the West of England. He at once dropped his connection with a David Frost enterprise for London Weekend and then astonished me with industry. His enthusiasm was familiar. So was his radio fame. But here – he was then 58 – was a stunning physical as well as organisational effort.

He won the day after dramatic and hilarious episodes many of which we laughed over in Wynford's last months. Since in 1967 both he and myself were BBC people it was not surprising that Sir Huw Wheldon, and old friend, should meet us in our victory week at the Saville Club and seeing me first should say 'Judas'. And then meeting Wynford in the bar say 'Judas 2'. At the very first board meeting of Harlech Television, Wynford was in form so characteristic as to be unbeatable. We always sat next to each other and he would keep his diary decorated beautifully with drawings of churches and seals and dolphins. The company was in trouble. Our victory had dislocated the Stock Market, The licence to print money in commercial television had run out.

I was arguing to stick to our grand programme policies: after all I had written them. Wynford launched on a dazzling anecdote. At the Battle of Anzio, he said he had won fame as a hero by shouting as he ran after the deserters "come back you cowards". "I suggest we do the same here," he said. As it happens he was brave at Anzio but he liked to tell a tale against himself if it suited him.

Inevitably in working with people who have great public repute the reality of character comes to look different. It is seldom the acquaintance improves an image. For years every meeting revealed a new Wynford. One day when we argued about a company matter Wynford proposed a drink elsewhere. As usual we talked evasively. Then, out of the blue Cardiff sky he began to sing an aria from the Marriage of Figaro, in Italian. The rest of the day he offered samples from all the Mozart Italian operas. What was so impressive and endearing was not so much the astonishing display of memory but that he should so have wanted to learn the libretti.

In the day-to-day work of the television company, when Aled Vaughan inspired a brilliant station, that remarkable energy and capacity to beguile encouraged tough fellow workers in hard times. The public might have seen a boulevardier. A few of us saw a different Wynford.

His life had been changed utterly by being one of that first group who went into the Belsen concentration camp. After that horror he could never be solemn, could not ever take himself seriously: that was the end. His delight in the physical world which he could so sharply express in broadcasting more than in his books was undiminished. The gravity of the work of his early years was gone. If you knew Wynford at all well that knowledge of what had changed him was always with you.

My last chat with him just before Christmas was typical. He was delighted to think that the central character in Kingsley Amis novel 'The Old Devils,' was based on him. He told me, with great vigour and joy, a wonderful slanderous tale about a celebrated Welshman whom we both detested and swore me to secrecy. He also reported that he had been coming along well with an earlier plan to devote much of his time to playing on the piano composers of the 17th century.

It is going to be very hard for a lot of people for a long time not to open the door and see him there and have him greet you as if life had been a desert since he saw you last.

The Daily Telegraph, 25th February 1987

Margaret Price

Margaret Price, the Blackwood nightingale, is the greatest singer in her generation in the whole, wide world. At which firm statement some, perhaps, will cavil, reciting in their minds a litany of Miss Price's cosmopolitan colleagues and rivals.

Here they will say, is a case of patriotism run wild, of acquaintance, even friendship and doting admiration causing the columnist to lose his marbles. Such is not so. There is evidence, after the prima donna's recently concluded performances of Bellini's *Norma* at the Royal Opera House, that the English, like French, Germans, Austrians and Welsh have at last accepted her pre-eminence.

It is true that the *Observer's* Mr Peter Heyworth went only so far as to write that Margaret Price is merely the best British singer of her generation. The opera critic of the *Spectator*, Mr Rodney Milnes – a man whose knowledge and judgement I always recognised as superior to mine when I was his oppo at the *New Statesman* – would not have this. The word 'British', he proposed, should be removed. Mr Milnes wrote, "Miss Price's voice is a phenomenon-full, voluminous without ever being blowsy, creamily round, absolutely even in tone throughout a range of over two octaves and without any discernible break between registers: an excitingly fruity chest voice is called into play without a hint of change of gear. There is never any question of her singing anything but dead in tune. But the way she uses her voice is something else again: her musicianship is such as to reaffirm the truth of the old cliché that the human voice is – or rather can be – the most expressive of all musical instruments. The pliancy and grace of her phrasing makes you gasp in wonder . . ."

This fabulous voice and career was launched in an unusual manner, one I was lucky enough to observe. In 1963 at Covent Garden Teresa Berganza fell ill just before a performance of *The Marriage of Figaro*. A Miss Margaret Price would replace her in the role of Cherubino. The young singer, scarcely in her twenties, thrown into the company of some of the world's most famous Mozartians, had then a small voice, but brought down the sympathetic house with her beauty and courage. By chance in my diary I find the ticket stub and dinner bill for the evening. The stall were £2.10s each: for Norma last week the same seats were £40. Dinner then was £3, now £40.

Later we were to learn that here was an unusually intelligent, even intellectual singer. Her tuition by James Lockhart was immaculate. She sings in Russian, German, Italian in a manner to fox the natives. Whether in grand opera, in lieder or in folk song she is unmatched, her progress so unforced that there is no reason she should not sing for as long as she wishes. She reminded me the other day that Lotte Lehmann had sung until she was 70, and looked forward to doing the same. She has pretty well given up smoking so there is every chance.

It's a fortunate blessing, too, that examples of her art from an early age are recorded both on record and film. Recently Sir Geraint Evans and myself were looking at a television programme we had made together in 1968 in which Miss Price appeared. She looked ravishing, while singing Lehar, moving down the staircase at the Opera House. More, she and Sir Geraint sang the Pamina-Papagene duet from Mozart's *Magic Flute* so perfectly that Sir Geraint was unusually moved to say that he had never heard it better sung, but that he hadn't realised how well he himself used to sing.

There is another quality about the Blackwood Nightingale that sets her apart: her outspokeness. No other international singer is quite so frank with conductors, however celebrated or with impressarios, however powerful they suppose themselves to be. Partly she is awesome because she is a perfectionist and expects others to be when often they are not; partly her bravado helps the impression along. It is hard to think of another singer – or indeed accompanist – who would carry on with a performance when the lights had failed on stage as did Miss Price and pianist Anthony Hose with Lizst's tricky *Petrarch Sonnets* at La Scala, Milan.

Many leading conductors like her friends, dote on her.

Carlos Kleiber and Claudio Abbado would, I'm sure, like her to sing everything. With other conductors her progress has been stormy, but, as with all people of her kind of repute, I suspect some of the tales are apocryphal. Is it really true, for example, as a fellow Welsh singer present swears was the case, that at Saltzburg once at rehearsal, irritated by a famous conductor's tempi, and convinced that long ago that the conductor had performed for the Nazis, Miss Price interrupted matters by strolling to the footlights and saluting him with a Seig Heil?

About her own life she is very frank. She speaks openly of her melancholy and frequent unhappines; is not sentimental about her childhood. Her ebullience is a persuasive disguise. She laughs a lot. Her generosity is not easily forgotten although friends have found it difficult to remember the way home after a special fish soup she makes with champagne.

A few months ago she went to Cardigan to give a recital to help raise money for a piano at the local school. Mercifully, too, unlike some of our celebrated compatriots, she has none of the manner of the 'professional' Welsh, has no need for that authentic phoniness, or is it phoney authenticity which is so nauseating with some? She is herself, and sings in Welsh like an angel.

For her native audience the sadness is that, living in Munich, Margaret Price is seldom in Britain, although she will be singing here this year more than at any time in the past decade. And quite why it should be so warm a feeling to have heard someone it is possible to talk of in the same breath as Galli-Curci, Patti, Melba or Callas, is hard to explain, but there it is.

Western Mail, 17th March 1987

II

BBC TALKS

Early Talks

I

I was a spoiled child, I'm happy to say, made much of by
women. The day after I was born in Swansea in 1929, Wall
Street collapsed. The catastrophic consequences of that event
included the triumph of Hitler and a World War, the
depression in South Wales and, poignantly for me, the collapse
of my parents. Matters were not improved by my being to read
before I was three, both in Welsh and English so that, for
example, I was able to read the obituary column in the Evening
Post of my sister who was a year younger than myself.

We were, in the early Thirties, a privileged family. Ours
was the largest house in Treboeth, a Welsh-speaking village on
the edge of Swansea. We had a swimming pool, a tennis court,
two bathrooms. When a plaque was unveiled to Gwrosydd, a
neighbour who had written that fine song Calon Lan, my
father did the unveiling. The annual fete was held on the lawn;
my mother was the lady bountiful. Armstrong-Siddely was the
only car around. Evan Walters a painter of repute who
brought Augustus John to the house recorded our childhood:
his painting of my mother captures her beauty. But I was never
much part of that household – my elder brother – we were four
sons – was more so and, I suspect, felt its collapse more deeply.
I spent my time with mother's family across the road, an
incomparable crowd.

Heol Fach it was called, a row of cottages, condemned as a
slum before I was born, occupied almost completely by my

mother's grandmother's family. There was no water; there was no light. They drank tea all day long made with water from a well; when it was dark, they talked by candlelight. With that passion both for truth and mischief, which were important influences, they would talk about my mother and father. There were semantic difficulties. I would call my great grandmother, who couldn't speak English, Mamgu, which means grandmother. I would call my grandmother, Mam, which didn't leave much for my mother, except Mum. And then there were the sisters of my great grandmother and the sisters of the my grandmother and my mother's four sisters. I was the toy.

Whether the memories of early childhood are true or are the merging of subsequent anecdote with the half-remembered, it is impossible to say. I think I recall waking up in hospital at the age of three when I'd fractured my skull falling-off the roof of the house and being pleased to see everyone looking so pleased I was alive. But it may be I remember being told they were pleased. The dreadful day when my father's brother, John, after whom I was named, was killed driving his car into a cliff at Caswell, I do remember, because his children were my friends. But even there the memory is confused by my father telling me that his other brother had died alongside him at Salonika in 1918 when they had been through four years of the Great War together through France and the Balkans. There was a lot of death in my childhood.

In the small room in Heol Fach where my great grand-mother held court, with a fine dresser, which I now have, and with big fires, because although the men, who were all colliers, were usually out of work, there was always coal, I would listen to them describe my mother and father, as if it were a fairy tale. They were known as Charlie and Saretta, that being the affectionate merger of her names, Sarah and Esther. He was always presented as the ogre; the Lord of the Manor. She was one of them who had left school at the age of 12 and had gone as a serving girl to my father's household and then had married him. I think now that they didn't realise I was listening, since I was very small; or perhaps, since they spoiled me so much, that they were snatching a hostage in so small a place. They were certainly successful.

One of my uncles there had a boxing academy. Its stage was an old colliery which my father's father had owned. The ring was poised above the shaft. Every Saturday morning we would go, a crowd of midgets, inspired by Farr and Peterson, and our own uncle Ronnie who was to be the European champion, and dance about. One day – I was seven then – we met and trotted along to the ring to discover that a wall had crumbled and the ring and our gloves had all fallen 400 feet into the darkness and the water. The distance was so great we couldn't even see the ring floating. 'Lucky', my uncle said, 'we weren't on the night shift'.

We can never escape from our childhood, from family, from the society which nurtures us, but I don't have all that much time for people who make those factors excuses for themselves, whether they are Marxists, or poets like Philip Larkin, or Freudians: Free Will does count, self-pity not attractive. In that context, I offer these anecdotes from Swansea until the Nazi blitz. Though I'm not denying Freud's point that men spoiled by women in childhood think they can do what they like for the rest of their lives.

When I was nine it was held that I was a good singer and a rugby player. My mother's young brother, Bryn, taught me how to play football: he took me to see Wales play at Swansea. Suddenly he went away. He had TB. Then he was dead. He was 19. It was the first time that I could not believe something. He had spent – and I can see now how boring it must have been for him – weeks playing football with me. And he was dead. I was at Brynhyfryd Elementary School where the choir was famous, singing at the National Eisteddfod. Being in the choir was fine. In the crowd singing 'Where're you walk', 'Nearer my God to Thee', 'The Holy City' and 'Jim Cro Crystyn', a pleasure. Now it was decided that I had to be the soloist.

It sounds absurd that any child of nine should have any prescience that a bad time was starting but I do remember thinking it. There was a concert at the Patti Pavilion in Swansea, a large hall. I had to sing the solo. It was, as you might guess, 'Where're you walk' and the 'Holy City'. Very firmly I said to my mother that I didn't want to do it. I now see that, out of some unrealised dream of her own, she fancied me doing it. She even went and bought a gramophone and a recording of La Boheme. It was the first opera I had ever heard – and that was influential, too. Nevertheless, standing there before an audience of some two thousand people and singing away, still seems to me the beginning of an inexplicable aspect of my life. Having such a distaste for public display, I was to make my life out of it.

What had happened was that I had become an enthusiastic Christian. While I might go with my mother's family to the Welsh chapels of Mynyddbach or Morriston, I was also the soloist in the high church in Treboeth built by my builder father and his father. The language of the Bible and liturgy entranced me. Humility seemed to me the message. Self-parade was wrong. I went to church four times every Sunday, twice during the week, even persuaded a curate to be a spare scrum half. We played cricket illegally on putting greens and once on a bowls green.

The collapse of the family coincided with the declaration of war. My brothers and myself spent summer holidays in Llandybie in West Wales where my father's family had come from, pigs hanging out to dry over the fire and the slate floor, where the men farmed in summer and worked in the anthracite slants in winter. It was a farmhouse rich with tales. There were the three colliers who had gone poaching on the Towy under the bridge at Llandeilo. They had a dog. They had dynamite. They lit the fuse. Flung it. Before it reached the water, the dog ran back, the stick between its teeth. One survived. And then there was the tale of the agent for Alfred Mond, Lord Melchett, who after the General Strike, had walked into the Gents at Ammanford, put a stick of dynamite under his bowler and, as my uncle said, met his Maker headless.

In the middle of all these cheerful explosive anecdotes, and us scrambling like apes over quarries and being taken down coalmines, putting coins on railway lines, smoking Woodbines, buying the first Beano, my father arrived in his long motoring coat which I was subsequently to wear for ten years. On the drive to Swansea he said we would have a surprise at home. He also said he would no longer have a car and that civilisation was ended.

Some ten years or so later when I was a college student and needed to have jobs in the vacation, I was to be a builders' labourer on the land where we so often played cricket illegally. My wife has a letter – an enormously long letter, which is another weakness friends have borne patiently – in which I describe sentiments felt at being part of an outfit tearing up the land of my childhood. But people were moving from slums to come and live here – some of them my aunties – on this council estate within sight of Swansea Bay. There is also a long account of my uneasiness that I was working next to an Irishman in charge of a powerful drill who was prone to epileptic fits so that I had to be wary as he occasionally would misdirect it. I always seemed to be in strange company in those jobs, until I appreciated the universal lunacy of the human race. One summer I was working at tying electric cables to girders high above furnaces in a steelworks in the Swansea Valley with a sinister figure fresh from jail, saturnine, bald and terse, who took me dog racing. We made a small fortune backing dogs at long odds. Each race was unusual. In the first the favourite slowed down: Leo's friends had put lead in its muzzle. Our outsider won the second because it was not the dog it was supposed to be: the lights had dimmed, surprisingly, as the race was launched. The last race was the triumph. Two dogs taking a bend rolled over and over. Ours ran through. A whisper like a breeze went through the crowd. 'Those dogs that fell over', Leo explained, 'had chewing gum between their toes'. I asked him why, with this gift of his, he bothered to do the dangerous job were were doing? He explained that if he didn't have a job the police would wonder what he was doing.

The idea of the world as chaos was bound though to be governed by the liveliness of the memory of the Great War at home. The Great War in Pictures, that terrifying record of the European tragedy, was graced by my father's accounts of what it was like at Paschaendale and how all his friends had been slaughtered. In the garden we would dig trenches – I find this hard to credit, but we did – and childishly try and re enact the battle, throwing lumps of mud at eath other. How can one, as a child, behave like that, and have a deep hatred of war? Yet we did, organised in battalions. The play acting was soon to stop because the bombs in Swansea were to be real ones.

The surprise was to see my mother lying in bed with a new son or brother alongside her. I said to her she looked very pretty, and she said she was sorry but I would understand one day. My father had to sell his yard in Swansea docks; his building firm. In the time before the house had to be sold – this was the Wall Street Crash reaching to Treboeth – the Nazis began bombing the town.

The first night of the Swansea Blitz we were all together – Evan Walters was there – rushing around the garden with our buckets of sand dousing incendiary bombs. The second night when so many people were killed my father and Evan had gone down to the town. That night a high explosive bomb landed in the garden and killed our next door neighbour. Although later I was to see horrible deaths in another war, the sound of that bomb is a governing memory, perhaps because I recognised that my mother's hysteria was due to her conviction that my father and Evan were destroyed in the conflagration we could witness of lovely old Swansea. When they returned at dawn, very drunk, blood on their clothes, with stories about the terrible things they had seen, and to see how her rage turned to joy, then I suppose my character was formed. I didn't mind that we were now going to be poor. I had been happy where we were going to be poor. But when the house was sold and the furniture they cared for, I did think I would try and take care of them. As it turned out, I did.

II

Ruin lay around us in our adolescence in Swansea during the War. There were the old ruins in the shallow valley, the defunct copper works, long dead iron mills, the coal and slag tips like mountains of the moon. And now the town destroyed, that we walked through every day on our way to the Grammar School, rubble still in heaps after the Blitz. Because the old school had been demolished it wasn't possible to go to lessons most of the time. Sometimes you went to school in the mornings, sometimes in the afternoons. Since from the ages of 11 to 14 I was devoting all my time to rugby football or, in season, to cricket, this was a good arrangement. For three years I thought of nothing else – except that I was now head choirboy in the parish church and being paid 2s6d a week, an important promotion although I think I enjoyed being allowed to read a Lesson as much as the pay. There are pictures of myself as captain of rugby teams, the visage grim. And then, suddenly, all was changed. What that elixir tasted like, what potion worked that it was literature and history that instead were to excite me, I simply cannot say. Not that it is very beguiling: explanations of behaviour cannot compete in interest with behaviour observed. But for what it is worth, I suspect that it occurred to me that while I might, on account of my size and generally ox-like construction, be a hot shot as a player in *our* school, there were these characters we played in Llanelli, Ammanford, Cardiff and Newport, who were of a different order of talent. So that while it might be alright to play for fun – as indeed I did until a nasty injury at 20 – there seemed no point in taking a game seriously enough to train. It was the best decision I ever made because it led by suddenly paying attention in class, to my entering the Sixth form of that school – which was like entering a palace equally constructed by the Marx Brothers, Aristotle and Walt Disney. I cannot believe that there have ever, within or without, the state system, been better teachers than I enjoyed and, in history especially, I was particularly fortunate since many of my comrades did not share the teacher's and my obsession with Central Europe, and so wouldn't come to school. My lessons were tutorials. I find it hard now to credit that it was such a wild place, but did set down an account of it, only partly fictionalised, a long time ago in the New Statesman: Here part it.

'Anarchy is reigning in this school' said the headmaster, who in the make-shift classrooms of the bombed buildings was a kind of Vasco da Gama, a man continually making exciting discoveries, arriving with a flourish at the scene of bizarre activities. Often, being in the sixth form, we could avoid seeing any master for days on end. Being a small group we could fight a guerilla campaign, as a unit we had more flexibility than the larger younger classes, and of course more confidence from years of wartime training.

One winter we stayed a whole week in a small, attic room making toast and smoking. If Vasco hadn't got to hear and how we never knew, that a notorious character-he was notorious for selling part of the central heating system to a scrap merchant in the town, and the flowers from the gardens in season – that this boy was taking a bath in the next attic room to ours, we should never have been caught. Confronting this boy in the bath with a great shout of 'Bathing. Bathing. You don't come to school to bathe' his nostrils were attracted by the smell of smoke. We heard his shout of 'Smoking' clearly before he came running into the room. He was a great shouter, with a wild smile. Usually rushing into a room he would shout out the nature of his discovery two or three times and then smile wildly. It was as if blinding intuition had suddenly made plain the pattern of his life's work.

We used to take a detached view of his behaviour. Detachment at that time was fashionable because we were all a bit shocked from bombs falling or it might have been through reading Isherwood. We saw ourselves in relation to things and to active people like Vasco. In the mornings we used to fight our way off the school bus where anarchy certainly reigned, past hooligans who had their feet hanging out of the windows and younger boys and girls sticking hatpins into each other, struggling out of innocence and go and stand on the great wasteland among the blitzed ruins of the town. Someone would make a long speech about death and scuttling rats and so on and how he stood in relation to them. The important thing was not to listen but to see yourself in relation to him and to the ruined, romantic town. Some days we went to the billiards hall. In school we used to write detached poems which were, measured with a ruler, longer than Paradise Lost. Again it was important that no-one should read them.

The activists, the people who prevented life from coming to a dead stop, the boys who got into trouble, were a different group. They and we, and Vasco, had our best moments when we were given a classroom, a tall, narrow room high in the building. Activists used to hand from the windowsills. ('You don't come to school to hang from window sills') One clear spring day when the daffodils in the long grass were in their full glory (before the boy in the bath sold them) two activists broke up the spare furniture and stuffed it up the chimney. We forgot about it and went about our business. A week or so later, one afternoon when detached poems were being written and the activists were kicking a rugby ball at one another, Vasco rushed into to the room, ran at speed to the fireplace and thrust his hand up the chimney. We observed closely as he struggled and with a tremendous shout of discovery, pulled down the leg of a chair. 'Chairs up the chimney' he cried. Pieces of chair tumbled down and suprisingly large lumps of soot. He waved the chair leg in the air. 'You come from broken homes' he shouted. 'You are the unsung victims of the war'. His smile was wonderful to see.

This fruitful chaos was matched equally chaotically in my home life but in a melancholy way. For a while I'd lived with my elder brother in that Slav like commune in Treboeth occupied by my mother's family. Under heavy pressure the council had put taps in the cottages: there was water. Now, though, that I had become an intellectual rather than a football player, reading was difficult since the wind through the walls blew out the candles. One night the wall of the house fell down, so I moved to Morriston to live with my mother's parents. At which point, the war being over, my parents returned from East Anglia where my father had been helping the Americans build aerodromes and where, on a visit, I once saw Crosby, Hope and Glenn Miller plain – my hero Sinatra was not there. My grandfather had just died, his last remark being to me. 'There's a fag in my pocket', he said. I presumed he wanted a last smoke. Not so. It was for me. He had been a melter in the steelworks, a teetotaller, a Rechabite. His funeral was a wonder, the two choirs of the town uniting at the graveside. So it came about that my parents slept in one bedroom and three of us brothers in the next bedroom with my grandmother, who always wore cabbage leaves around her head at night for her headaches: that she had them did not surprise me. Another brother slept, with a squeeze box, in a room barely big enough for him. It was always cold and I was always angry because my mother had to go and scrub floors to help us make our way. I used to write small paragraphs for the local newspaper. They paid.

But during the day it was all poetry and the Treaty of Kujuck Kainarjdi and driving friends crazy by reciting that key work Browne's *Religio Medici* – 'As for the world I count it not an Inn but a Hospital: a place not to live but to die in . . . Methinks I have outlived my self and begin to weary of the sun: I have shaken hands with delight, in my warm blood and Canicular days . . . the World to me is but a dream or mockshow and we all therein but Pantalones and Anticks . . .

But however glib they are, these theatrical displays in early years, I'm sure they direct enthusiasms, so that when the melancholy is earned, the words are available. Or is it that the words, or, the Anticks say of Shakespeare's or, worse, Webster's characters truly colour a view and guide one's own antics.

Reading now, for the first time in 35 years, the diary I kept at 15 and the stuff I wrote for the school magazine then,. I can't think there's much I can derive from it which could help the young listener keen to make writing his trade. Pomposity and plagiarism seem the main characteristics of my work at that age. A week went by in May 1945 without a diary entry: It resumes: 'I apologise for this pause in an account devoted to a true portrait of my contemporaries and in the interests of posterity', followed by the scores of a cricket match we were playing in. There is some theft from Blake in the poems. Thus, of the Swansea Valley tips: 'Unnatural hill who made them'. I can't quite place the plagiarism in the next one – is it Edgar Allen Poe – although I may have been sending someone up:

> Within the valleys deep and brown,
> And on the shadowy mountain's crown
> The tired light is dying down;
> And earth and stars and sea and sky
> Are tired of sleep as I
> Am tired of you . . .

There is even in the same copy of the magazine a libretto I wrote – and I only mention this nonsense to encourage a young listener to believe that there is always hope – in which three clowns dressed in black, white and green – the other two also became professional writers – sneer at each other. One song – and weren't we so amusing – goes:

Could you O purest white serene
Glance at your noble wrist so clean
And tell me how much closer to Heaven
Am I than I was at two twenty seven
     To which the other fellow replies:
What care you O ebony black
You gormless brainless useless hack.

How much I borrowed, I cannot remember and don't think it matters. Publication creates confidence; confidence helps the style along: print makes the word a piece of sculpture.

In school they tried to persuade me to stay on a year and go to Oxford since I was fairly young and had done well in the exams and was regarded, to my embarassment, as a big shot since who else but my hero Dylan Thomas had both edited the magazine and won the Cross Country cup. Perhaps if we hadn't been so poor I might have, but I doubt it. I'd been in school long enough. When later, in London, I was to observe the harm Oxford had done to so many colleagues, I was glad I had gone to the University College in Swansea.

Not that I could have guessed that the same wonderful anarchy was to prevail there as at school. I was in training. On my first night, a 17 year old among ex-Battle of Britain pilots, the heroes of the bombing war, even Colonels no less, I was detained at the police station in Cardiff after a college rugby game. In no time I won fame for being banned from the women's hostel; had started a newspaper and had defined forever my distaste for authority, I knew that freedom was all that mattered. It was heady stuff. And I was in love and walking the 5 miles home most nights to our crowded, cold and miserable house.

Rip Van Winkle and Oblomov are the senior citizens in the spiritual rest home for those of us who – in my case for 50 years – find it very difficult to get out of bed in the morning. The arms of Morpheus have always offered the firmest of embraces. Who could compete? There is an even more pretentious way of putting this common trait. It is held by some possessing that Celtic gift for making a strength out of frailty, for decorating a weakness, that when Welsh or Irish men – not women, oddly – howl as they leave the womb, they are offering merely the first expression of a life long howl that their comfort has been disturbed. Some forever regard it is the first and most unforgivable demonstration of feminine infidelity. I think that attitude unkind. For all my scepticism of all ascriptions of general characteristics to any people of a race or nationality, I do think a crossness at being born accounts a lot for the fact that I've been late getting up every morning of my life. It certainly is not that I'm reluctant to face the day – once up that is. Indeed my enthusiasm for any coming mischief has been a source of much trouble to my family and friends.

In school or at university – where I missed every nine o clock lecture for three years, some given by teachers as distinguished as Kingsley Amis and philosophers Rush Rhees, W. B. Gallie, Karl Britton – there it was not so much of a problem as it proved in the Royal Air Force. In the three months I was at OCTU in the winter of 1947 in East Anglia there was snow falling or on the ground every day. The personnel, as we were known, in our hut were composed of university people and men, many Polish, who had served as NCOs in aircrew during the war and were now seeking commissions. We were needed in Korea for that horrible war. The NCOs being generous men and perhaps aware that I wasn't doing the cause much good being late on parade, offered to help. They would bring me breakfast and make my bed. Naturally I refused these kindness at first. Then a friend, Alan Simmance, had a fine idea. Since I had edited a college newspaper and magazine, why didn't I seize the Course magazine? We talked and saw the power of the idea. If the magazine belonged to our hut and I wrote profiles of Course commanders pointing out that they possessed a genius akin to Napoloens, Von Richthofen's, you name it, then we would be the favourite sons. And so it was that in the evenings I wrote while they played and in the mornings I had an extra hour in bed. But it was they, in the end, who went to war, and many of them who had survived the World War were killed. I was taken off the draft in Korea at the last minute

It was noticed that firing Bren, Sten or any other guns in the heavy snow I was unable to see targets since my spectacles were covered. Eyesight damaged through those years of reading by candlelight had ironically become a saviour and I was sent instead to the 505 squadron in Bristol where pilots flew at the weekend and life in the mess was luxurious and any talents for farce and anarchy was now given every opportunity. It was the beginning of the happiest ten years of my life, indeed of anyone I've known in the neurotic worlds of journalism or writing of any kind.

But that old characteristic which was to bring me the only nickname I think I've ever had – 'The late Mr Morgan' – had survived the period of comfort in the RAF Mess. I was now a shift worker on the Melting Shop floor, in front of the spectacular furnaces, of the Abbey steelworks in Port Talbot. I was late for every morning shift in the 20 months I worked there.

That I was there is not as surprising as it may seem. Certainly there was nothing in it of any desire to identify with the working class, Bevanite socialist though I was. I was after all working among relatives and men who had come from West Wales as the old steel mills closed. Some of the older melters had worked with my grandfather. And anyway I have never cared to identify myself with any group for emotional reasons to which I don't naturally belong:

converts create more difficulties for themselves than any they hope to solve.

What had happened was that I had married a girl from Cwmafon near Port Talbot. At that time, in the early Fifties it was difficult, for arts graduates of the University of Wales to find jobs except in schoolteaching or those trainee schemes offered by Marks and Spencer, ICI and so on. My wife had tried one of those at Marks and Spencer and didn't much care for it. But the prospect of us being on the dole together was less fearsome than it might have been because an event had occurred in my last weeks in the RAF so exciting that even now 28 years later the memory is as fresh as the water in the stream I'm lucky enough to look out on as write. The quality of the excitement shows how modest, how naive, how innocent we were then.

What happened was that I had sent a short story to the New Statesman. Ever since I had been 16 that magazine had been my secular Bible, not only for its Left wing politics but for the quality of its critics and its occasional writers of fiction. Obviously at the time I wasn't aware, as I was to be later, of some weaknesses in the paper's attitudes. I was star struck about it, as I was about some other people alive, like Aneurin Bevan, Dylan Thomas and P. G. Wodehouse and the unfortunately dead, like Mozart and Stendhal. Returning one afternoon from London to Bristol feeling quite pleased with myself since I had recovered some secret documents – I was a sort of intelligence officer – which I'd left in my brief-case in a taxi, I was met by my wife with the news that Kingsley Martin, the editor of the New Statesman, wanted me to visit him. They were publishing my story. Later, when I was to be on the staff of the paper my view was inevitably to change about Kingsley and some of his colleagues, but the delight of that day ensured how the rest of my life would go. One way or another, I was never going to take a job proper. I was going to try and write.

And so it was back once more to a small cottage in South Wales, this time to my wife's home. It was less heavily populated than my own families' cottages and the fires even heated the house but there was a new excuse for staying in bed. Because I was writing in the New Statesman, the Observer asked me to write for them and because of all that a dashing young producer at the BBC in Cardiff, Aled Vaughan, who remains a colleague and friend, asked me to do a weekly radio programme. After two years of laughing and typing in and around the BBC and the steelworks, I was earning enough to give up my £6 a week in the melting shop and return to live in beloved Swansea. The idyll – I almost pronounced it idle – continued.

That, by the accident of being able to put a few words together and more have been able to read them in a tolerable voice, should produce a life of such delight then, as now, is a matter of wonder to me. In Swansea for five years, we would stay in bed until 10 or 11; in the summer we would either play tennis in the afternoon, or cricket on the beach at Rhossili or Oxwich Bay. In the evenings we'd work

The shades of the prison house of conventional success were soon to gather about this growing boy, but that was an enchanted time. I read the other day that Kingsley Amis who was the most amusing member of what he calls 'the set', refers to this period with a sad nostalgia. Everyone's work was going well, although none, rightly, as well as Kingsley's. My parents even had been 'given' – marvellous locution that – a council house in the non-industrial part of the town. There is no town quite like Swansea for looking out on from a hill – just before lunch: no spirit – unless there was rain about – could not but be uplifted. Life was not to be worse in the future, but it was to be different. The age of innocence was soon to end.

Early in 1957 I was telephoned by a producer on the BBC Panorama programme, Charles Wheeler. It sounds hard to credit, but I had never seen a television programme. Would I meet him and the crew in Llanelli and do a film report about unemployment. I went and talked to a few people I'd met because I'd been writing about them and offered a few sentences to the camera. So it came about that the first person I ever saw on television – I'd arrived late at the Amis' who had a telly – was myself.

Within a few weeks I was asked to do a similar sort of thing for an amazing new programme. This was the Tonight programme as its producer Donald Baverstock, accurately forecast to me on the telephone, would 'transform the face of the whole thing, boy'. As it turned out the director I was to work with was the purest talent the BBC possessed: Don Haworth, a working class man whose demonic sense of anarchy was to make him not just a great director of documentaries on film, but an Italia prize winner for his radio plays. Our sense of socialism and comedy coincided. We had an uproarious time raiding British communities in the interest of truth.

That old distaste for self-parade, a hang over from my boy soprano days, made me turn down television invitations to move to London. When though, Kingsley Martin and John Freeman asked me to come to work at the New Statesman we packed our bags, very reluctantly, as ever drifting into the future.

IV

Dylan Thomas used to tell a story of a visit he made to the home of W. H. Davies, the tramp poet about whose verses Thomas could in private be unkind. 'What is this life if full of care /We cannot manage to pay the fare'. Mrs Davies began a long recitation of the countries the wayfarer had visited while the tramp wayfarer himself sat with a smile on his face as Dylan Thomas reported of such self-satisfaction that he looked like a cat that had got at the gin. 'Spain, Ecuador, Italy, Alexandria . . .' the litany went on until the proud wife stopped. There was a silence broken when W. H. Davies said: 'And Japan'.

Two unfortunate attitudes to the journalism of the

travelling man are also summed-up in the tale. In fifteen years of metropolitan reporting I visited most countries, from China to the Yemen, even. The audience can take a cynical view; so what do journalists see? Journalists can say, so what: Haven't we all. I mention this because I saw a survey among undergraduates reported in which a high proportion said they wished to be television or newspaper reporters because 'you see the world and meet famous people'. To which I would say, for separate and complicated reasons, so what.

Certainly you do get to meet famous people and some are not worth meeting. For me it has been a lasting, useful delight to have been able to talk about the character of European socialism with people I stood in awe of: Aneurin Bevan, Pierre Mendes France, Milovan Djilas, Willi Brandt. It was no less the case to have conversations in Moscow, Shanghai, Prague, with unheard of citizens who were in their different ways as illuminating in an understanding of the world as anyone famous. And it maybe a comment on the present state of journalism, or the country, that it could sound pompous to say that although I drifted reluctantly at the end of my twenties into London and the big time of the smoke, that I had a genuine passion to communicate through word and picture my sense of the world's injustice.

The delights of the new life for a while staved-off the difficulties. Don Howarth, the late Xanthe Wakefield and myself, with a film crew, would maraud in Britain for the Tonight programme like bandits. We would ring each other in the morning and ask what town we were in and be careful to leave it before the citizens saw themselves on the screen. If I was unlucky enough to be in the studio – an exercise I disliked – the general air of hilarity would be constant. I recall opening a programme interviewing a man with concrete teeth and asking him whether he had a concrete kettle. Was his bed of concrete? At that time, I read in my diary, Don Howarth and myself were working on two strategies. The first was to leave this enormously popular and genuinely creative programme for Panorama, the second to upstage the producers by my adopting bizarre techniques, like not asking questions, just saying 'really', or 'hmmm' and concluding: 'Who asked you for your opinion'. The programme which began with the interview with the man with the concrete teeth ended with my interviewing Franz Josef Strauss about nuclear war in Europe, during the course of which he snatched my notes from my hand, and I snatched them back, and he snatched them back again. The Marx brothers have never been far away. We made our escape to Panorama and no one would speak to us in the BBC bar for a year.

The case was that I had entered in the late Fifties the trade of television journalism at the time of its greatest excitement, novelty, wealth, and impact on society. There's a remark of Addison's when he was in Lloyd George's government that, in Downing Street then, you felt in the morning that you could have everything you could lay your hands on. When, as I like to recall, one behaved like that but in the interests of representing a point of view that otherwise was not expressed, how could I not have thought I was engaged in educating not myself but the people I had sprung from.

Many lazy animals, given they possess a strong constitution, when pointed in the right direction, run like crazy for a while, and for ten years I did a case of dynamis drift. In scores of cities I seldom bothered to sleep. That schoolboy obsession with central Europe was given full play. In most communist countries, including China, we made the first political films and saw the inside of jails in Yugoslavia, Poland and Rumania. In Peking in 1964 we were invited inside and the government there took offence when I remarked, meaning well I think, that life inside the gaol was little different from life outside. Colleagues were sometimes sceptical about the urgency of some these trips. What a remarkable coincidence they would unkindly suggest that there would quite so often be a new or brilliant production of the Marriage of Figaro, or the Magic Flute or Don Giovanni in Berlin or Vienna or even San Francisco and Chicago when it was vital to be in those cities, or, at worst heading somewhere when production lay on the route. There was even a Figaro at the Bolshoi where I sat in a row otherwise occupied by members of the Viet Cong. It was a bizarre and poignant experience in the intervals of listening to the most civilised and life-enhancing musical masterpiece produced by the Western world, to be talking about villages in Vietnam where these men lay burrowed on the outskirts while the Americans, to whom I'd been attached, had tried to blast them to pieces.

We remained, though, my wife and myself as naive as ever. When I occupied my office at the New Statesman with its gorgeous view of Lincoln's Inn, I was genuinely shocked to find my colleagues – John Freeman, Paul Johnson, Barbara Castle, Anthony Howard – were all Oxbridge people, many public school boys, representatives of groups we had made such serious fun of. Socialism clearly was not about class. They were very tolerant, though, of the fact that I seldom came to the office partly because the paper could not afford its staff to travel often and the BBC were paying for my wanderings about which I would write for the Statesman. It never occurred to me either that there might be people at the BBC who might object that I might one day be writing socialist propaganda in the magazine while presenting myself as on objective reporter on Panorama. To myself I just seemed valiant for truth.

Along with the dynamic drift and the naivety went an enduring lack of interest in material possessions except for books, gramophone records and the acquisition of restaurant bills and opera tickets. Mammon also works in mysterious ways. I simply had no sense that I was one of the best paid journalists in Britain in my early thirties. If visitors would admire our large house in a fashionable part of the town – we had a son now and needed more room – I would say in all innocence that it was handy because it was on the Central Line half way between the BBC and the New Statesman, which was inexcusable, but I thought I put this lack of the material imagination, ambition even, to poverty in adolescence. Others I know feel the converse drive, deprivation later demanding the material to compensate. It may be one decides unknowingly one day when young that it is better to live inside one's head because that is at no one's mercy. The silver apples of the moon, the golden apples of the sun, grew all year long at home and abroad, until a sudden congress of disasters brought the party to an end.

I was in Vietnam with my wild friend, the director Jo Menell and the cameraman Ernie Christie who was later killed. We had a lucky escape there. Jo had persuaded me to come to a night club owned by the Prime Minister Marshall Ky where he maintained, accurately, an 8 year old girl torch singer was to be heard. At one in the morning we left and found a fight going on in the street between American troops and the local police – the white mice. In a jeep sat a girl wearing a large golden clock on her chest. Her boy friend was one of the soldiers being beaten-up. He was arrested and so she asked if we would mind keeping her company while she drove home. She was a New Zealander. Jo refused since we had arranged to go to an opium den, also owned by the Prime Minister, to make the final arrangements to catch a plane to do an interview with him at his house in Darlat the next morning. The plane was leaving at five.

This seemed to me bad manners so we drove to her place near the airport where a small battle was going on. She drove the jeep into a ditch where it stuck in the mud. We cowered for a while, myself wondering how I would return to Saigon in time to fly to the interview, forgetting I was actually at the airport. An ambulance came along the road, stopped for me, and so I rode back among the wounded, in time to drive back again and fly to Darlat in a DC3. Aboard were the three of us, Vietnamese troops, and a police chief sitting on a throne in the centre of the fuselage. We were all filthy. As we approached Darlat there was an explosion in the plane. Two clowns began firing towards the rear, almost tearing off the tail, so inexplicably that we had no time to film this lunatic event, The plane swaying, the pilot managed to land. The police chief's coffee thermos had exploded.

We saw, as everyone did there, many dreadful acts of cruelty, but I had to come home suddenly because I heard my wife was gravely ill in hospital. Amazingly she recovered, but then her mother had a serious stroke and came to live with us, and within the year my mother had cancer and was dead. And I had left the BBC because of a suggestion that American behaviour in Vietnam was not as I had seen it. A period of confusion was to begin.

Fiction, as these five talks have taught me, is a much superior form of autobiography; wearing a mask, as I think Wilde wrote, is the only fashion which reveals truth. The absence of a mask, it seems to me, leads to deceptions arising as much from affection, duty, concern for others, as for one-self, so that I've been lately reading my favourite auto-biographers of my own time, Paustovsky, Ben Hecht, Ford Madox Ford, V. S. Pritchett and Goronwy Rees with a new puzzlement. Which lines does one read between? The image of myself I've presented is I gather unrecogniseable to those who know me well. Where I see myself as this troubled, secretive, introspective failure concerned with the human condition, they see a reckless, ebullient, self-indulgent joker. I only mention this as a warning against the truth of auto-biography, and also to explain what may seem curious: that I so disliked my brief period of celebrity on television when I had the experience of gifted mimics like Timothy Birdsall and Stanley Baxter imitating me. Some colleagues, I know, liked that kind of thing, liked being recognised in the street, offered the best seats in restaurants. There are television groupies. Actors, quite properly, enjoy it. The ambiguities of my response take some sorting-out and I certainly don't propose to give a gift horse a sharp crack in the teeth, not having chosen to look it in the mouth.

Curiously, it was though, in the period of my life, my late thirties, early forties, which was a dark time, when I made what I suppose will be the best remembered contribution to British television. The films of which I'm most proud – in Vietnam, in Czechoslovakia during that moving Spring, in Moscow, in South Africa, of Munich the last days of Cambodia the portrait of Lloyd George – will lie there. There still exists a snobbery which prevents these artefacts being taken as seriously as they were meant.

If you will bear with me, I'll explain the strange circumstances in which a successful television company came to be invented. I had fallen-out with the BBC, very reluctantly, over the treatment of a film I had made in Vietnam. Two senators had been flown-in from Washington to attack the film in the studio while I was at my wife's bedside in hospital. My film was true; moreover, my dismay at American behaviour was based on a love for America, a nation whose culture had shaped those of us brought up on the movies of the Forties, on its wits. Here was the emblem of freedom destroyed by its savagery. Since I had spent many months of my life explaining the inadequacies of life in communist societies, I didn't care for the kind of figures in the BBC who were suggesting that I was against American behaviour in Vietnam because I was left wing. One man who would have no part of that was Huw Wheldon. I told him I was going to leave and join colleagues who were departing from Panorama – Jeremy Isaacs, Philip Whitehead, Jolyon Wimhurst. He suggested that instead I might consider being Controller of the BBC in our home country. It was a flattering suggestion but, I explained to Huw, I was congenitally incapable of having a job. We then had the usual entertaining conversation in which he said I was quite wrong about him in a profile I'd done in the New Statesman suggesting he was interested in power. Nor me, I said.

What he had done, though, was put an idea in my mind. For ten years, apart from visits to parents and watching Wales play rugby, I'd hardly been to my own country. Within days I'd met old friends who had been at the BBC, all of whom were involved in organising bids for the franchises of independent television companies which were about to be renewed. Some were for Scotland, some for Yorkshire, some for the new London contracts. Mooching about in a state of some emotional confusion, with so much sickness in the family, sad about the BBC and the New Statesman, I sat down with a piece of paper.

My method of work has always been a matter of fun to others. For some reason they find if hard to believe that staring at the sun, playing tennis, or working on a new drink, a list is being drawn up in the mind. Myself, I put it down to a combination of training in mathematical logic and air force organisation, that these lists of elements are formulated. Anyway, I have this document setting out what seemed to me necessary to seize the franchise for television in Wales and the West of England. My serious motive was that there should be a television station in Wales run for and by Welsh people. I had the idea that programme people should hold some sway. I wanted to try and preserve a spirit which had meant so much to my life in television in my own early, exuberant days. I wanted, too, Wales, to be a European country with comparable standards.

So the battle plan drawn up I rang first Richard Burton whom I knew and Wynford Vaughan Thomas whom I did not. Wynford was in London and we met. With that enthusiasm I was at once to admire, he abandoned his other television enterprise. Wales was our country. I explained my plan. Richard was in the South of France, filming. I flew to see him. He was his usual generous self – indeed, offered to pay for the whole enterprise until I explained that it was not that kind of thing, but more political. In the end, it didn't do him much good which I regret being so kind to myself and those that followed, when all he was being was patriotic and generous. Not that he was overjoyed one night when he and a friend lost to myself and his wife Elizabeth Taylor at snooker. snooker.

When I came back from seeing Richard, I then went to see Geraint Evans at Covent Garden and Stanley Baker on location in Hertfordshire, and was very pleased at winning their support. Wynford, meanwhile, following the order of battle, had gathered together some other Welsh people and through his friend, the late Martin Cadbury, a group of Bristol businessmen, known to none of us. Since no-one except myself had dreamed of applying for this franchise, they were all, Wynford reported, a little bewildered. I had, meanwhile, rung my friend Aled Vaughan at the BBC in Cardiff, asking if, were we to win, he would be in charge of programmes in Cardiff. To my delight, he agreed. My difficulty was that there was going to be a putsch in Greece and perhaps a war in Israel and my feet were itching.

Letter from a Pub

Who would dare decorate a film set for an English village like this: we have a castle built in the 12th century, ornamented later with Elizabethan windows. Oliver Cromwell used it as an ammunition depot to guard against the Royalist Welsh half a mile away across Offa's Dyke. The Moat Society preserves the moat, now rich in daffodils in the sun. The coach house stands. The view some 400 feet down into the Wye Valley is one of the most spectacular in its gentle way in Europe. The river not quite visible in the balance of the lower hills, the trees antique and abundant.

The French writer Albert Camus, said that he knew people for whom a landscape could compose the mind; I think I'm one such.

The village is St. Briavels, named after a mendicant cleric who came from Aberystwyth some 1400 years ago, and moved on to Brittany. The public house is called The George, built in the 17th century. Ten years ago, a lintel in a fireplace was discovered to have been either a Celtic cross, or some memorial to the Norman baron of the village in 1070. Inventive research has it that it was stolen from the graveyard of the church across the street – the church being first built in 1066.

There is a tunnel between the pub and the church. Here, we scholars observed, was a case of that old Celtic connection between drink and God, briefly interrupted by the Methodist revival. That interruption is over. The George has resumed its historic role; one that may not or may be common to many pubs. Here it may be defined as the intelligence headquarters, the GCHQ of the territory.

The George is important to me. I work at home a lot in a house down the old Roman road – Mork Lane – between the church and our ford. Mork, I learnt in the pub from the orchestral conductor Vernon Handley – a scholar of language – means the extremity of an estate, rather like the German mark. So, if I'm working at home I've been mooching up to the pub most lunchtimes for gossip with whoever's around, and especially with the proprieter Roy Welsh and his wife Deirdre. Roy has just sold the place, being of an age to retire. Deirdre was once a dancer in Las Vegas, and was on stage with Frank Sinatra. Roy Welsh – he is 63 – is good on the matter of the publican's craft. He has a gift much like that of the actor, the artist, the financier, the football player, but which is more rare. Can we, now that he's retired, analyse the gift.

At heart the good publican has to be a chameleon. He is formed by his public. He knows with whom to be grave, with whom to laugh. When a wit is there he'll be witty; when a customer is suffering, he will put on his funeral air. With a ruffian he'll be rough.

Roy was brought up in the trade: his father was both a publican and a lay preacher in Wales – a combination which must be unique. Roy went to elementary school at Pandy in Gwent where a fellow pupil was the Cambridge Marxist Professor Raymond Williams, whose nickname – mysteriously – was Shaver.

At the age of 14 he went to work as a page boy in a hotel in Abergavenny. During the war he appeared onstage, having moved on, as a member of the Swansea Little Theatre, and was tempted to become an actor. He chose, though, to reserve his performances for the smart hotels he ran or owned in the home counties where he flourished, before coming to our village to create an unusual theatre of his own in an antique, very pretty pub.

We all know about looking into the future pot and seeing the world as it is not, so that when one of our company, Douglas, says that if you want to know anything about anything in the whole world, you only have to step into the bar at the George scepticism does assert itself. Yet, in all sobriety, the evidence does suggest that there is something in it. The customers are attracted by Roy – I exclude the American, German, Swedish tourists who come in summer. The steady customers include accountants, conductors, road sweepers, ex-miners, farmers, painters, lawyers, football players, surveyors, and wives who are teachers, pianists, computer operators, bed and breakfast proprietors, and then of course the doctor and his Irish wife.

So, what is to be learned at the George? Last week I needed to know what hat size I took. I was being presented with a prize and my head had to be measured. And so I raised the question which puzzled the company as much as it had me, not though for long. Paul, who is a surveyor and a leading bell-ringer in British churches, thought he had the answer. He went to his car and brought in his 100 feet tape measure. His opinion was that you measure the circumference of the head and then you apply the calculation on pi. Pi it seems is a symbol which is equivalent to a ratio of 22:7. I'm not proud of this ignorance. Anyway, Paul's wife had with her a pocket calculator which works out the complicated mathematical stuff to do with pi. We learned by this process that my head size was 7 and five eighths, at which of course the whole company wanted their heads measured, the pi calculated. And so the lunchtime passed in an orgy of head measuring.

What the question the week before was – what must be done about the rats in a neighbour's house? A council worker and a football player had ferrets – they would sort it out. As the chat went on I mentioned that last year I'd been down in West Wales, cut off in a cottage doing some writing, when I'd heard an odd tale about rats. An old man there said he had lost some duck eggs. In his opinion rats had carried them away – more, they had done so using a cunning technique. One rat would lie on its back and his pals would place the duck egg on its stomach. They would then entwine their tails and drag the laden rat to their lair. My friends in the George at St. Briavels thought this a piece of Celtic fancy. The truth is that the duck egg is placed on the stomach of the rat, but the comrades merely pull the laden one by the tail. They take turns until all the eggs are stolen in an interesting, labour-sharing way. Like so many, my friends think rats suffer from having a bad name.

As it turned out, their day's ratting and ferreting, or however one puts it, was not a great success. The Jill ferret was on heat, so the boy ferrets – the hobs – paid all their attention to her and squabbled, and ignored the rats entirely.

The week before the question was more dreadful. Two young men drove their car into the wall of my house. I called the police and fire brigade and the doctor and the ambulance. Arc lights were set up. There was glass and blood on the flagstones. The car was so crushed that the fire brigade found it hard to reach the youngsters for all their struggle. They were in agony, their heads and legs smashed. They were going down to the River Wye to fish. Their friends in the car behind them were with me trembling and aghast, as was I myself. There've been so many crashes lately on our dangerous roads. The boys did not die but are still in hospital, and likely to be so for a while. The wall had to be repaired so who'd know who. In these matters the George has an incomparable expert: Irene who works there as a barmaid at lunchtime.

Irene's mother keeps a pub deep in the Forest of Dean, called the Rising Sun. We've often wondered why it should be called that since it was built to meet the needs of the coalminers in the forest. There are so many pubs called the Miner's Arms. Irene and myself differ on the question. Her view is that the Rising Sun is so called because it's what the miners saw when they came off nightshift. Mine is that it was what they saw when they went down the pit in the morning.

Irene is an unusual woman to find behind a bar. Not only for her wit and radiance – she will not accept drinks from anyone. Her intelligence in the GCHQ sense too is priceless. She found someone to mend my wall. It seemed only proper that he was a Morris Dancer who had just been promoted to be the horse. I hadn't realised that if you were the horse then not only did you not have to exhaust yourself with so much dancing about, but you won the greater share of the applause. You do learn a lot by living in the country.

The George naturally is not always dramatic or eccentric. If you have an income tax problem there's the accountant to help. There are prosperous entrepreneurs who support the Labour party. But we try and keep away from complicated cross-patch politics. Internal feuds do exist. I conduct one against dogs, and am restrained in the interests of peace and goodwill from making a citizen's arrest on their owners. It has been suggested I stop offering the thought quite so often, but if I want to drink in a kennel then I will go and drink in a kennel. We tolerate each other's obsessions. To tolerate the Welsh is regarded as a gesture, the nearby border having a troubled history. And then there's the George as a place simply to discover what's going on. Someone always knows what match is worth going to see, what opera is on in Bristol or Cardiff.

Since I wander about a lot, it was just by chance and meeting Douglas and Yvonne, that I learned that the tenor Robert Tear was giving a concert the next evening in Monmouth. Of all British or Welsh tenors, Mr. Tear is the greater lieder singer. And so we went and heard a fine recital. He sang one of my favourites – Schumann's LIEDERKREIS. It was the kind of music – romantic, songs of love – that the Wye Valley lends itself to. On the drive home I made an effort at the Moonlight Song since it was such a night, and the poet had written of the bright stars and heaven kissing the Earth, and the soul spreading its wings to fly home.

By the time we returned to the George some seven miles from Monmouth, I had moved on to a most anguished lyric. I should explain that Yvonne is a music teacher but that Douglas is my Scottish accompanist whenever we give, or rather rehearse recitals in the pub. We've been working for some time on transposing familiar airs into an atonal scale, an exercise which causes, I suspect, more curiosity than pleasure. This Schumann song is about the exile who dreams of home, and given that we were returning to the Forest of Dean, it did seem appropriate, if in bad taste. It goes: 'My father and mother have long been dead; how soon will the day come when I shall rest with the forest above me?'

The tone changed back in the pub because I needed to sort out with Freddy, who was a tiger moth pilot, how we were going to divide a pig I'd bought the day before from a photographer friend who was just off to Afghanistan. The pig had been roaming wild, nurtured on brambles and barbed wire. It struck me as a bargain. It proved to be like a pig of childhood – fat, succulent, a taste my son had never known in his young life.

But coming back to the point about Roy Welsh being an impressario as much as a publican, it strikes me that the life of a pub does have many characteristics of a play. The curtain comes down at closing time. The dramatist of a theatre finishes his play; life has to go on for his audience. They do not have the comfort and ease of the tragic ending. So it may be that the theatre of the pub is observing certain dramatic conventions. We're all playing a part, preserving a surface courtesy, using the place as a means of escape. It isn't the drink then that is the means of escape but the polite observances of the chat, the jokes, the exchange of news, the desire for information. If that really is the case, how remarkable that we're all so civilised, and more, that we should so wish to be.

Letter from a Farm

An urban man, I live surrounded by farms, in the morning I look out of one bedroom window and there the cows are in place, black and white, as still on the slope of the hill as the toy cows of childhood. Why they don't move, I don't understand, knowing nothing and caring as little about animal life. When I look out of the other window, I see the farmers' chickens, One of them joins me on the lawn when the sun is shining, hopping over the dry stone wall; we present an odd scene. I sit in my canvas chair reading, to my left sits the hen, to my right our cat, Siani who is almost nineteen years old and not nice. In her old age her voice has grown contralto and querulous, her black hair is turning brown. I'm told that if she were a human being, she would now be 95 years old. I can believe it. But it's when I open the front door in the morning for the postman that the country opera begins. Across the narrow road is an orchard, inhabited by sheep and their young, I hadn't known that lambs were born at different times of the year; they are. This seems to make a sheep cross. When they see me they run to the wall and shout. There is a school of thought which maintains that they are showing friendship, that they are glad to see me, merely saying good morning, in their tuneless way. Until recently, I was prepared to believe this generous interpretation but by accident came to do some research into sheep, on a different farm. If I seem to digress, it is not the case.

Under my house there flows a minor tributary of the River Wye. It moves through the land and ponds of another farmer to the east of me, a trout farmer. A while ago, I was asked to write something about the Wye, and went to its sources in Plynlimmon, the mountain range in mid-Wales. My stream travels through a tunnel under the house which children have swum through. On the slopes of Plynlimmon where the Wye rises, I was attacked by sheep, I had to jump over a fence to escape them. I asked their owner why this should be, why animals held in the popular imagination to be so docile should be so fierce. He said there was a good reason, the land was so poor, the sheep needed to be fed by the human hand therefore the human being was the provider. When he turned out, as in my case, not to be a provider, then the sheep were cross, there-fore, they attacked. Later, I discovered from an account written by a traveller in the eighteenth century on the very same Plynlimmon slope that the sheep then had behaved in the same ferocious way. This discovery about sheep led me to construct a very urban joke. If this talk has a theme, it is the weary relationship between the townie and the countryman, the countryman's view of him, the tension between those who delight in the loveliness of nature and the farmers need to make a living our of land and natural things.

The joke was this, I inverted a composer. I pretended I had discovered discovered dog eared manuscripts in Alsace. The composer was called Schwenk, he was a dog lover, he was bald and wore a wig of dog hair, Schubert and Rossini couldn't stand him because, he smelled of dog. He may even have invented the Alsation. His father had played billiards with Mozart, but was a countryman who died when he fell out of a tree. I wrote some songs and my friend Norman Kaye, with whom I had written a serious opera, wrote some music. This absurd work was performed, its inspiration, along with my dislike of dogs, lay in the sheep who shouted to me in the morning. I won't quote the whole of the sheep duet, but just offer enough to convey the flavour of farm life. The verse goes,

"Our lamb is led to slaughter,
She is our dearest daughter,
And who gives a damn for a lonely ram
And you're daft and asleep as a lonely sheep."

The revolutionary chorus which is frequently reprised in any performance goes,

"No more the skewer,
Kebab no more,
Ram and ewe shall rise
And to the lamb's surprise,
The dogs attacking sheep, will die."

A neighbour when he heard this song, sung on the radio, rang me to say that he had parked his car outside a pub nearby, called the Orepool, the ore being mined there and that when he returned to it, a jacob ram had rushed at the headlights and smashed them and that he had needed to jump into the driving seat or the beast would have attacked him. But, even among the sheep and ram communities it seems there are class distinctions. The kind of ram or sheep that will attack you is upper class, accustomed to being spoiled and fed, there are sheep like the rest of us, walked over, left to fend for themselves, not feeling too good most of the time, the kind of sheep we count at night to sleep. The farmers, my neighbours who surround me, have a hard life, mine is not as easy as I think they think it is. They live in beautiful houses, mine is the newest out of four, built in 1740, skipping to my taste nicely, from their Jacobean to my Georgian. Winter is very wet always, and last time we had heavy snow too, for three weeks. They are at work all day, just the family with no paid help, they seldom have more than a day or two holiday a year. When lately there was, as they say, a virus about, I took the medicine and stayed in bed a day. They carried on working and were in the end laid out longer, because they felt they had to go on working for the cows, or the lambs or the fish, would not be all they should be, they might even die. One of them offered me a parable, that must be universal. A visitor comes to a farm and asks the farmer how he's doing? He says he's doing well. He has this idiot who comes at five in the morning and takes out the herd, and then feeds the lambs and then looks at the silo, and brings the animals in, and milks them and then does the books and falls asleep exhausted at eleven at night. The visitor asks the farmer if he can meet this idiot, this sad case, the farmer replies, you're talking to him.

My neighbours do not qualify as the spoilers of the countryside. Not so far way there are farmers who have put up hideous buildings for all our local objections. The territory the Wye Valley is designated as an area of outstanding natural beauty, but there are farmers who have erected dreadful looking factories. They are above the law. The colour of most peoples roofs is governed, as is the use to which you may put a barn.

The farmer may do as he pleases. In our difficult landscape, difficult from a farmers point of view, we do not suffer the horrors of East Anglia; wheat, grain, rape, do not grow here. Hedges remain hedges, the birds still sing. I have a warbler, a dipper, even a kingfisher in the stream. What makes even the nicest of farmers unpopular in our territory is that they do not pay rates. Why should they not, the arguments goes, when they're all doing so well out of the Common Market. Those familiar with the political history of the farmers rate exception, who know that it was a necessary relief in the collapse of prices in the thirties, wonder why it should be so sweeter benefit when times have been good. In the new countryside farmers tend to keep each others company, partly over the rates matter. They have common interests of course, and yet I detect a bizzare social development. Perhaps farmers keep together in the country, because country people don't care for them too much. A profound political issue is raised by farming, farmers' subsidies are acceptable, the subsidies for coalmining create uproar. Will expensive food be needed more than expensive coal. When there is over production of both in Western Europe.

That argument is more neglected than the concern between the country lover and the country worker. Here I find myself in a peculiar dilemma. I'm not a tourist. I'm not much of a naturalist, except that I love where I am. My wife has to remind me of the names of the trees in the garden even. Throughout the winter, when I've been on my own a lot, I have been tense with anxiety, not only about the old cat, but about a plant called a plumbago. If I give it too much water it might freeze to death, if too little it might die of thirst. That's the kind of countryman I am. And so, when one reads of the debates between the National Farmers' Union and the Conservational, which side am I on? One day the question will be answered no doubt. In the meantime, I think, an uneasy curiosity is all that is possible.

For example, last evening we had a problem. I saw several dead trout floating down my stream from Chris Grooms' trout farm, I rang him to tell him so and asked if anything was wrong. To be honest I don't mention it when live trout swim down. At one time we had an unusual debate at home here, my son proposed fishing for the trout in our stream, I said that he shouldn't because they were like pets. You wouldn't want to treat Siani the cat as something to catch. Who, he asked would want to eat a cat? The trout were being killed by a small gang of mink. They had been gathering under my house and had moved early to attack the trout in the lakes next door. It seems that, once they have killed them, they eat very little of the fish. My neighbour had been to buy some very powerful bullets, the name Nobel, of the peace prize was on the packet, and he was going to spend the rest of the day watching out for them. I'm often woken by the sound of gunfire. Many gunmen in the forests are pursuing grey squirrels currently, since they are killing so many young birds. At which, suddenly as I see and hear my neighbour blast a mink apart with a heavy Nobel cartridge, it strikes me that my dilemma in this small house, is more than a matter of farmer or conservationist. I used to have to use Bren and Sten and other guns when I was holding is Majesty's commission. I'd been in wars and think of guns as wars.

When I was a townie the countryside was a sweet thing, I spent a lot of my childhood on a farm in West Wales, a poor one, but a farm very like that in Dylan Thomas's Fern Hill,

> And then to awake, and the farm, like a wanderer white
> With a dew came back, to cock on his shoulder: it was all
> Shining, it was Adam and maiden."

That affectionate memory is alive. The importance then it strikes me of being in the position in which I find myself is one that may be valuable for anyone interested in politics. I used to make pretty shrewd attacks on farmers, I think, and would still about the fat cats in the East of England and their city friends, but more to the point is that experience induces a deep sleep in idealogy. When the balance is considered between need and the ideal, where I am it becomes more difficult to parade a conviction. The experience has a general importance, making the marxist, the fascist, who wish to force their will even more ludicrous than otherwise they might seem. In that way, living in the countryside and having a look at the stars at night and wishing the dogs would not bark and hearing the stream roar in season and brooding on whether the trees are going to fall down or not, and what is the name of that flower, comes to make some sense. What would be a disgrace is not to recognise that I am a very lucky man. Very few people who work in the country think they're lucky, they think they are pretty hard done by, and if your try and tell them differently, you are a fool. Nature makes venerable oaks.

Letter from a small Television Channel

What a pleasure it is to celebrate an artistic experiment that has worked, a fresh display of aesthetic exuberance. And for a Welshman how much more so when it is something that has happened in his own country. I'm talking about a new television channel, S4C, Sianel Pedwar Ec as it is known, the Welsh language equivalent of the British Channel Four. A new, entertaining and serious Bohemia has grown around it and in, of all places, the docks at Cardiff. Those docks, which held the ships that carried Welsh steam coal to the world, now house a nest of artists and technicians who are selling their films at home and abroad. The Coal Exchange, a grand building that once saw fortunes made by coal owners, where David Lloyd George sold knighthoods, now houses film makers. Under gaudy umbrellas on the pavements near the water sit animators, directors, playwrights, men and women peddling ideas, watchful about contracts: and here comes an actor dressed as the Pope, blessing all in sight as he passes through the bar.

At which I think I had better, as they say in the House of

Commons, declare an interest in this Welsh language television channel. One of my greatest friends, Euryn Ogwen Williams is the Controller of Programmes. I am writing some plays for the Channel. Many of the film directors, editors, dubbing mixers were colleagues when we were all at Harlech Television. For several years I wrote documents and appeared before Parliamentary Committees giving evidence in the long, often troubled, discussions which led to the government establishing a separate Channel for Welsh-language programmes nearly three years ago. There is a review going on currently about the future of the experiment: I doubt if anyone believes there will be changes made, if only for the negative reason that no one is looking for trouble on the language front in Wales when there is trouble on several other fronts. Therefore the prospect looks good for all those independent, freebooting, arm-chancing writers and directors and actors whose flowering is the excitement in Welsh broadcasting and whose example is of a general British importance.

Most of the programmes that are transmitted in Welsh *are* made by the principal broadcasting agents, BBC Wales and HTV Wales. They provide the news and the current affairs and most of the soap operas. You could say that they fund S4C, except that in fact the taxpayer is paying because the commercial television companies have their levy on profits reduced in order to chip into the S4C kitty. The overtly political programmes therefore, whether domestic or international, belong to the BBC and ITV. There might be an exception now and then where questions of balance are obscured. Let's suppose, say, a Welsh Marxist were to do a film for a freelance company about the Soviet victory in the Second World War; it would not need, I take it, to be balanced by a Welsh Fascist considering the Nazi fate.

Most of the work of the independents, though, is imaginative and artistically creative. I find the atmosphere in which they flourish peculiarly interesting because it reminds me of the time in the Fifties and early Sixties, when I reported for the BBC Tonight and Panorama programmes. Everything in the whole world seemed new and possible them, and not, I think, just because I was young. It was a time much as one of Prime Minister Lloyd George's colleagues put it: when you got up in the morning you felt that everything was yours. That timidity that seems to have grown, that invasive self-censorship, that absence of mischief and wit, even that absence of money, which presently inhibits much broadcasting has not affected what I see of the work of the new school in Wales. Those I work with sparkle like mountain streams.

Give us, then, you may say, an example. What do these fine words mean? This week offered one as characteristic technically as you could wish. The director Richard Watkins, a man in his Thirties from Swansea who used to play rugby for Grenoble in France, has made a portrait of Dennis O'Neill,the new opera star, the internationally celebrated tenor. Dennis is from West Wales and speaks Welsh. I watched the film with the director. It is still in a rough cut state. Having made a few films about opera singers, I have never seen one as good as this. Its merit lies not only in the tenor's honesty but in its original techniques. Joseph Losey's *Don Giovanni* and Franco Rossi's *Carmen*, both fine films, might have been even better, and certainly would have been cheaper, if they had known of the cunning devices of Richard Watkins.

The problem in films of opera singers performing always was that they needed to mime – perfect sound was not possible on location, we all thought. Few singers were good at matching facial movement to a pre-recorded sound track. In this film of Dennis O'Neill what the director has done is have the Welsh National Opera orchestra and their conductor Julian Smith record their contribution. This is then re-played on video to the conductor on location. He then conducts the singer from the video replayed. To give an example from the film, Dennis O'Neill is singing the opening tenor aria from Donizetti's L'Elisir D'Amore. For all you can tell, here is this simple, rather daft farm boy sitting in the hay in Tuscany. In fact he's outside a farm cottage in Gwent. So precisely does the conductor match the beat of the singer from the video on a small set in the farmyard, that the tenor's performance is perfect. One would expect it to be perfectly sung. Dennis O'Neill is the most Italianate of British tenors. What the technique offers though is something unusual for an opera performance on film. It has a physical immediacy as great as in the opera house. That distancing which spoils so many opera performances on television is absent. The technique permits as powerful a presence as you could wish. In another sequence, when Dennis O'Neill sings Calvaradossi's first aria from Tosca, even watching sitting in a small cutting-room, looking at a rough cut with that scratched sound of a cutting-room, my hair crackled as it can do in a great performance in an opera house.

As important as the quality of performance, though, is a vital fact about the Welsh independents. They work on small budgets. Their profit *is* small, but they have a talent for cutting costs. Richard Watkins' film probably cost much less than half it would have cost the BBC, perhaps even a third of what it would have cost an ITV company. This is partly because the expensive tenor eschewed his normal fee and took a gamble on the film selling abroad. But that isn't the main reason. Rather it is the exercise of an ingenuity in all aspects of the production. Thus, at the Metropolitan Opera House in New York as little costly filming as possible was done when Dennis O'Neill was singing there, but performances were reproduced in a church in Cardiff docks around the corner from the Coal Exchange. You'd never think it.

Richard Watkins is just one example. Other directors, Gareth Wyn Jones, Stephen Bayley, Karl Francis and Will Aaron, and so many have made films in Welsh which, subtitled, are selling in Europe, even in America. In the Cardiff Coal exchange, John Cross has equipment for dubbing which I'm told is as good as anything in Europe. But it isn't the importance of this flowering for Wales which may matter most – indeed within Wales there are a few cavils, a few doubts expressed among those not interested in aesthetic matters.

The BBC in London, for example, is now of the view that independent producers and directors should be encouraged. Cost is a factor in this novel judgement. I don't think it should just be a financial factor, though, that weights. Just as important is that passion a fracture can engender, a move away from bureaucracy, from that defunct element in management which inhibits ingenuity. But the independent of quality has to be a gambler. His work always has to be the best. Not everyone has the temperament to risk himself, or herself. But those who do will tell you that they are part of a new movement, and are full of beans. For them the new channel, S4C, is a liberation.

But if their experience is a lesson for British broadcasting, a means of recapturing that spirit of the late Fifties and early Sixties; within Wales there are, as I say, a few doubts about S4C. When the Channel was set up there were jokes. One went that the channel would cost £20 million a year. Half a million people speak Welsh. If they were asked would they rather be given £400 tax free or have their own Channel, how would they vote? That kind of vulgarity has passed. But people do ask why only 100,000 watch? Travelling about Wales looking at the condition of the language, I think I may have found an answer.

In the nature of things most people making the programmes are middle-class. Several of them do not speak Welsh but use translators. How much then is the channel helping to meet that need, the survival of the Welsh language, which led to the successful political campaign whereby it was created? I was very struck recently to discover that whereas 30 years ago 14 of the Llanelli rugby team spoke Welsh, now only three do. In the part of Swansea where I come from only a quarter of the famous Morriston Orpheus choir now speak Welsh; when I belonged to it in the late Forties, three-quarters did.

So it could be that a state of affairs is being created where by the Welsh language becomes a middle-class matter. Certainly the question concerns people in charge of S4C. Most Welsh people who are not part of the Welsh language industry cast a cold eye on its more self-regarding manifestations. The language can become a bourgeois device for self-advancement, whether in education, Government ministries or, even, in broadcasting. I think myself that it would be a pity if all those in the Welsh language industry were not to recognise that they are alienating working-class people in Wales from their own country and language. There is a trait in some of the Welsh middle-class, a kind of tribalism, rather like the Italian or Irish family mobs in Chicago, except that they use jobs rather than guns as weapons.

Because just as the rise of the free-booter on S4C – as indeed on Channel 4 in London – is valuable for broadcasting vigour, so, in a very odd, paradoxical way the defence of the Welsh language through film and drama has a useful lesson for the English. The decline of the Welsh language is described as due to the power of English. The Welsh language channel is part of a resistance movement. Now, with the greater power of the American language, English is threatened. American commercial television erodes the English culture and language. Thus a circle may be being created. It would be some irony wouldn't it if Euryn Ogwen Williams' small Channel in Wales were to help save the old enemy. Whatever happens, though, on that grand cultural or political level, it is enough for now to delight in this new nest built for singing birds. It may not, after all, as we so feared, be closing time in the gardens – and docklands – of the West.

Letter from the Far West

There is a familiar kind of migration, the one in which birds follow the sun. Humans likewise pursue either the warmth of fortune, or at least escape from the cold of poverty. In West Wales now, I think, there is a new kind in that lovely country along the Towy and the Teifi Rivers, and north to the bogs and beyond to the thinner grass and air of the mountains, and further west to the sea, that's so wild in winter, there is a migration of people which says much about the state of Britain in general, and the condition of Wales in particular, difficulties and comedies are created in equal measure. Migration is a sensitive subject, it divides us. Taking a grand view, you could say that those who object to the free movement of peoples are totalitarian, small, closed minds, in love with frontiers, passports, ideally with armed guards patrolling, and those who do not object are open, big, optimistic souls, who like to leave doors unlocked That definition may be a little unfair, but not by much.

The truth is that most of us are migrants. If we look closely at our own cases, the results are surprising. My wife, for example, is half-Irish half-Welsh. Her grandfather Madden came from Waterford in Ireland to work as a coal trimmer in Port Talbot docks during the Welsh coal boom at the turn of the century. She in turn, is a migrant from a village in the Afan Valley to London. My family were migrants in the last century from the very part of West Wales I am describing. They settled as small farmers and as carpenters on the outskirts of Swansea. Several of them fought the company of soldiers sent down from England to put down the agrarian insurrection, the Rebecca Riots 150 years ago. One, a namesake was put in Swansea gaol, but so the history goes, so fierce was his father, that the soldiers were afraid to arrest him. That has been the historic pattern in the part of the country I am describing. A background important to understand in complicated new movements, as the 20th century comes to an end.

I learned about them for an unusual, even ludicrous reason. I was living for a while in a cottage in West Wales, a ruin elegantly rebuilt almost on the banks of the River Teifi, on the borders of the old Cardigan, Pembroke and Carmarthen counties. I was alone most of the time writing a book, and the book, the irony took some time to occur to me, was the biography of a Welshman whose family had left a Welsh cottage almost exactly like that which I had borrowed. That family, the Humphreys, had migrated to Chicago ninety years earlier in search of a fortune they did not find. They left poverty in Wales only to find it 3000 miles away, but more violently. Their son though, he found a fortune alright. He became a colleague of Al Capone and succeeded the Italian as America's leading gangster. He was a man of wit and style, and a murderer. 'Treat your crooked neighbour as you would treat your crooked self' he would say. He was believed or so I claim, to have invented the laundering of money in business, even the slogan 'Vote early, vote often' in Chicago politics was his.

The experience of writing about this son of Welsh speaking parents in the Welsh countryside they had abandoned increases my natural wariness in describing the peculiar state of affairs that now obtains in the west. Until recently, only two kinds of English people have been arriving in numbers large enough to be noticed in the hamlets and market towns. There were those buying second homes, their popularity varied according to how much they were friendly, and to how many groceries and other goods they bought in local stores. And then there were the communards, the hippies, those infected with the American peace and other movements of the 60's. These often lived in tents, tepees or broken-down outhouses. Few worked, and unemployment figures in the district grew higher even than expected. The locals knew them as the Blackfoot tribe, this being a part of the world where people usually wash and wear shoes. The Blackfoots were not popular. What is happening now is a more general settlement by the English middle-class. I am not suggesting that all migrants are English, indeed the cottage I borrowed belongs to a member of the Welsh-speaking intelligentsia in Cardiff, prosperous enough to have a second home and spend money on it.

For all that, the English influence grows. It can be seen in shops, pubs and restaurants. The tourist trade burgeons, indeed the University of Wales is appointing a Professor of Tourism. I should like to share his inaugural address. Will he I wonder, offer menus. In the village where I was staying most shop-keepers were English.

The Welsh do not seem too happy keeping shops or restaurants. Perhaps there is a vulgarity in selling goods to people. It could scarcely be that we can't count. Perhaps it is a sensitivity of nature that inhibits us from serving people. Some tribal sense of superiority. I used to pass some time playing a rather silly joke on shop-keepers; writing books alone can make anyone lightheaded! I would pretend I could not speak English. My Welsh is in fact, very poor, with six year olds I am a veritable Demonsthanes, the Immanuel Kant of the infant class, with anyone older I run for cover. However, the English shop-keepers were not to know this, since they spoke hardly any Welsh at all. I soon discovered which were hostile to their neighbours, which friendly. On balance, most were unfriendly, but perhaps because they thought I was playing the fool.

What can irritate is that migrants owning shops and hotels and cafes of the tourist trade, often don't bother to learn any Welsh at all. This is laziness often, when not indifference. Discourtesy is another word. Since much of the Welsh spoken by the Welsh is itself, simple. Thus in a shop in Newcastle Emlyn a cheerful market town on the Teifi, I asked for a pound of cheese. 'Sharp?' asked the lady. 'Yes' I said in Welsh. 'Real Sharp?' 'Yes' I said in Welsh again, 'Real Sharp' is clearly the Welsh for strong cheese. It's not hard to conduct that trans-action in Welsh. I wouldn't be so bold as to offer grave observations on an historic if relatively small, novelty in migration patterns if I was relying only on my perhaps, eccentric research methodology. Those who know confirm what I detected.

The Welsh writer, John Osmond, has done some serious work. He made a film for HTV Wales about it. The root of the matter lies in property as so often. What is happening which is leading to a movement more important perhaps than tourism or shop-keeping, is the changing pattern of farming. It's remarkable how important farming still is in Britain, or is it that I think so, because I spend my time in the countryside.

Here in West Wales it is the case though that farming styles have a direct and important consequence for people who live in cities, the people who want to be away from traffic and the smoke and the cracked pavements and the rubbish that is not collected, and the litter and the noise. Because farms are not prosperous enough, land not good enough, they amalgamate. Sons and daughters may not want to run them. They then leave the district, having sold out to a neighbour. Outhouses are freed, even cottages, barns are available for conversion. They are cheap. Families can sell up in an English city and move west, following the sun. They have some capital now, they may grow vegetables for income. They may breed rabbits and then there is pottery.

This is not the movement of retired people, as say on the north Wales coast. The Costa Geriatrica. These are people who in their phrase are 'leaving the rat race'. They are vigorous people wanting to make, again as they say 'a new life'. The most important thing about them from the point of view of the native inhabitants, is that they have children, 'so naturally they have children you say, what's so special about that'. What is special is the question, 'What language will the children speak in school?' 'Will they become part of the old and still surviving life of the far west? Or will the old life change and became an English one?' There are English schools where ten years ago 5% of the children were English, and where the proportion now is 50/50. People who know about these things calculate that in six years time, 40% of the total population of the county of Cardiganshire, or Ceredigion as we know it, will be English.

Welsh people find this hard to believe. This after all, has been the heartland for centuries. This and the counties hard by. This is not Cardiff or East Wales where Welsh can be a style or a job. So what seems to happen in the schools in the accounts given me by teachers and others, is that when the children are very young, say 5 or 6, Welsh is the language they use, among English children, but as they grow older the balance changes and English increases its sway, even among the indigenous Welsh speaking children, and this is among just the children who go into the school at 5. When migrants are older, say 10,

103

when they arrive in West Wales, then the English influence inevitably asserts itself more strongly because the children are confirmed in their Englishness. This state of affairs, which distresses those Welsh for whom the preservation and vigour of the ancient language is so important, becomes more complicated when you listen to some of the arguments of the English, for example, if the migrants had not arrived, many of the small schools would have had to close, since so few Welsh children were in some hamlets. Isn't it better to have the schools open in the district? And I do know migrants like my friend Janet Dubé the poet, and her husband Steve, a journalist, who are learning Welsh and they are as busy and fruitful in the life of their place as any born there. They, and others too, have nourished the countryside, but there are problems in life and this in West Wales may be one of them, with no solutions.

Considered though as a form of migration that will grow as people wish to leave cities throughout Britain, what to return to the beginning, does it say about a new kind of exodus? It could be seen as part of that element of the great migrations of the past, from central Europe to London, from Europe and now South America to the United States, of the Irish to England. That amalgam of a desire to prosper to be free. Certainly the migration to the far west expresses a desire to be free, not as in the past of political tyranny, but of the tyranny of the urban life. It could also be though that it just as much expresses the other traditional wish to seek a fortune. The difference now is that the fortune is re-defined as the escape from wealth, from the material, from a consumption. So that after all, here we still have the birds seeking the sun. It is the sun which has changed, not the birds and the flying.

On The Family

For everything under the sun, we're told, there is a reason. So what can be the reason that so many of us are statistical freaks; that our lives so often seem to bear small resemblance to what we read is the prevailing condition of mankind in our time? Or is it just me and the people I know? I'll sketch out that background, so that you can judge. It's true that I live on my own, writing in a house in the Wye Valley on the Welsh border, solitary more perhaps than most people are. My neighbours, whom I see a lot of, are a mixed crowd, farmers, window-cleaners, surveyors, doctors, sportsmen, retired people of all kinds, some young and unemployed. When I go out to a city to turn an honest penny I do so with members of the hysterical professions, television producers, film directors, journalists, poets, musicians, broadcasters, politicians. Most of my family live in London where I find myself now. Not a typical life, you might think, but what life is typical? The main difference, I suppose, is not having a nine-to-five job, having to impose one's own discipline in work, but that is not relevant to what has suddenly struck me as peculiar in my acquaintance or friendship. In important ways we don't seem to belong to our time.

We live, as we all know, in an epoch in which civilisation, not to mention capitalism is crumbling. Clearly it must be, or we wouldn't be told so quite so often and with such formidable evidence. Unemployment is an omni-present concern we know, yet we do know there, that, distressingly, indifference among the employed is notorious, for all the hypocrisy offered pollsters. Nonsense, you may say: the people you know talk of little else. Clearly I keep the company of a lucky, frivolous or gormless crowd, the sort who fiddle while Rome burns. Let's suppose so. But what about, then – and it was this that started me thinking in the first place – what about that key institution, that corner-stone on which society rests, and which, by its crumbling, leads all to crumble: to wit, the Family.

The evidence of collapse is familiar and distressing. One marriage in every three, we read, ends in divorce. Children suffer. That liberating inheritance of the Sixties, the single-parent family, creates, we hear and know, as much poverty and misery as it does freedom and joy. The family of the past or of current television advertisements, that close circle of loving dependents, is no more. That it may never have been quite like that at any time in history is neither here nor there. The case is held to be that it is no more. Metropolitan restaurants, we read, are crowded at weekends with fathers seeing their children briefly, wracked with guilt or counting their blessings. The wretched ex-husband or ex-wife seek solace where they may, sceptical if wise but usually not. Of such is the statistical reality and I found myself nodding properly in agreement while someone in close touch with that reality was parading this dismal analysis. The institutions of marriage and family, the speaker concluded, herself a morose single-parent, had then collapsed in our life-time. Automatically, I concurred, and then driving home thought at first, how true, and then thought again.

In my mind's eye I counted the fifteen people I mostly see, friends, colleagues, neighbours. Two are divorced, one man, one woman, and each twice, which might suggest an independence of mind which makes for an unusual example. In the past there was a friend or two who were separated but that was rare. Separation is not quite the same thing since that often may be tactical as much as serious, even to do with income tax. Separation is, in *relation* to divorce, like playing poker with buttons not money. With these minor and statistically absurd exceptions, all the others are married, living together, their children mostly of an age still to be at home, or, if away, frequently returning. What can this mean? Is my experience freakish even, so much so as to be without any significance? Or is life not as it seems?

Each of these families is very different in class, prosperity, profession and politics, so that there is no explanation in any common ground. And as we'll see, it's not a matter of my liking family or domestic life particularly, so that there is no common interest there. To consider briefly some of them will help explain my puzzlement. For example, I'm engaged with an accountant neighbour in trying to help two families who live in council houses nearby to set-up a factory to go into business. One neighbour makes a small, chancy, but not bad living selling parrots in the vicinity. I wouldn't have thought that there was much profit in selling parrots: I was wrong. Parrots are much in demand if you know where to find them: he does. But he and his friend also have a talent for buying, repairing and selling second hand cars. However, since they have no collateral, no bank will bother with them. Each has a family of small children who sit around on the lawn while we discuss, with another friend, a surveyor and who has two daughters who live at home when not at university, how we can manage to find a factory nearby and begin work. That's that lot of families.

There is another group of families I see much of, the members of the executive of the Welsh Union of Writers. We are in touch much of the time. We meet every two months at each other's houses. Since we live far apart, and the union is poor, and since we drink a little when we meet, we tend to sleep where we meet. There are usually children in the house. This means, since I tend on account of my age to receive privileged treatment, I find myself, some child displaced, in a bed among dolls or teddy bears. These are the houses of journalists, writers, poets, the women radical or feminist or both, members of families, defying the statistics. So what pattern can be deduced even in this world of parrot-salesmen and radical writers, all family people?

Or let's even take the most accident-prone profession of all, one of snares and temptations which would tax the family life of saints, were they permitted such: television. I've spent 30 years in or around it. Yet even here friends I stay with, the one running a station, the wife a star of the silver screen, remain domestic, the children at home, a grandfather present. It really is most peculiar, the kind of peculiarity which creates an uneasiness in the end not, I guess, about the national statistics but about oneself. Is there some general rule lurking here if only a finger could be put on it? Like crying to like; or the attraction of opposites.

It is true that I was brought-up in perhaps the largest family known in the Western world. It was not so much, as the sociologists have it, an extended family, as more a kind of pyramid. In the row of cottages near West Wales there sat, wizened, eating bananas, my great grandmother. That there was no electric light or water in the cottages didn't surprise her: she had been there since 1842. Her children and their children and their children, myself among them, crowded around. I had aunties like other children, had cats. It came as a surprise to me, going to school just before my fourth birthday, that there were people in the world who were not relatives. Inevitably funerals were frequent so that they came to seem as much a part of the pattern of entertainment as going to the cinema, lacking, for a long time, all morbidity. Not much English was spoken which helped make the English world and the rest of the world, in time, an object of passionate curiosity. More to the point, it also by being so powerful a demonstration of family life, made family life something that belonged to the world of childhood, a factor unnecessary in the adult world. Or is that romanticising? As if to say, sure, yes, that's family life, and it was fine, let's try something else. Or it may be over-crowding makes for a wanderer? Lack of heat and light indifference to domestic comfort? That hasn't stopped me being married to the same wife for 34 years, but that is separate from domesticity.

In all this, of course, I'm putting to one side aspects of family life like the fact that what is delightful in one's own child is tedium in other people's, because there is a serious point on its way. While I may like my own family, I dislike the idea of family. There is more, though, to be said against families than mere judgements based on acquaintance since, equally, while some families are unpleasant others, as we've heard, are nice to know. The argument is against the fact of family as a closed society, one locked against the world, a source of self-regard which, given power, becomes an agent of nepotism and corruption. This is worth bearing in mind when society in general, or propagandists urging the virtues of the supposed past, deplore the way things are now.

I used to notice, when I moved away from the tribe in which I had been brought-up, and would return with tales of London and then America and the Far East and the Nile, and talk of strange peoples and presidents, the chat at home was much the same, of this uncle, or brother or distant cousin, all content that life was much as ever, except for a birth or a death, a new job, or no job, a new preacher, the team not doing so well, usually. This was a sweet world, without ambition. Naturally it contained within it particular dramas. No one can quite escape the force of Stendhal's remark in that fine study of his *On Love*: 'The imitativeness of our early years makes us acquire the passions of our parents, even when those passions poison our lives'. But mine was never a family with much ambition beyond us going to school.

What is bad about families is when they become themselves the morality, every action justified because they are carrying it out. This understanding is different from that awesome argument the philosopher Hannah Arendt who died recently used to use about families in Hitler's Germany: that people would carry out Hitler's murderous orders because they needed to look after the family. Less cruelly, we've all seen families fix jobs for relatives in private or public corporations, conspire together against the interests of better qualified people to look after their own. Gangsters, and politicians, create families of special interests in order to protect their own. In public life there are agencies designed to limit corruption against the general good. They don't always work as efficiently as they might, but they do express a sense that there is a justice in an open society where every-one has a fair chance. Yet, often, when families, whether aristocratic, middle-class or, when what little power they exert offers itself, working class conspire for self-advancement, this, alas, is thought to be a worthy expression of the affection of blood looking after blood. Doesn't seem much different to me. So that if, in this peculiarly fastidious sense, the function of family is the enemy of an honest society, and so diminishes the true freedom of each member, what's so special about families?

These speculative fancies I offer only to show that I don't happen to mix with people with families because I care for families. What then can be the explanation of the fact that life so markedly works against the statistics of our civilisation? I don't think there is one. I just wonder, though, if there aren't a few other general understandings about the condition of our time which do not match our experience of life about us.

On Money

'The rich' said Scott Fitzgerald to his fellow American novelist Ernest Hemingway, 'the rich are different from us'. 'Yes', replied Hemingway, 'they have more money'. Hemingway, the tough-guy romantic is held to have had the better of this exchange with the spiritually more romantic Fitzgerald. I think not. A few days ago I was talking to a friend of a friend and he said he was moving out of Britain. He had bought a small chateau in the South of France. My friend asked him how he could afford it; what had it cost. 'Cost? I don't know, I never asked'. We were, which is saying a lot, struck dumb. The rich, Fitzgerald might have said, *are different* from us because money does not exist for them: *we* impose its value on their gilded lives.

Hemingway's supporters may argue that this acquaintance of mine is a rare case. The rich who have made their money are a different lot. I wonder. Which attitude, for example, does this episode in a day in the life of the actor Richard Burton exemplify. Richard was as rich as most; had earned his money and spent most of it. If I was working in any city where he was working, he would lend me his Rolls Royce and his chauffeur and I thought no more of it than that it was a very comfortable way to move around.

One day early in 1967 I went down to stay with him and Miss Taylor at St. Raphael on the Cote d'Azure. They were filming there. I had a scheme to launch a bid for a television franchise for Wales. His support, I thought, would help swell a progress. With his usual wild generosity he wrote out a cheque for £3 million to help the cause. I explained that it wasn't *like that*, but needed to be a cultural-political campaign. All I wanted was a letter. Late in the evening after scores of photographers and journalists had gone – it was the day it was announced that Miss Taylor had won an Oscar for her performance in *Who's Afraid of Virginia Woolf*, while Richard had not–it was decided that we would have a game of snooker. Richard would play with his major domo, myself with Miss Taylor. She had never played before. 'We'll play for a thousand francs a corner,' said Richard. 'No we won't,' I said. 'We'll play for 10 francs.' It was a boring game since it struck me that out only chance of winning was to adopt dirty tactics at which, I'm sorry to say, I was expert. Miss Taylor followed my instructions. Our opponents lost their tempers and grew rash. We won. And so here we had this famous actor in a rage throwing down his ten francs, when only six hours earlier he had been signing a cheque for three million pounds of his own money. Had I been interested in the subject at the time, I would have reflected that money can mean many different things in the life of a man in one day. What would Fitzgerald and Hemingway have made of that?

I've come late in life to this interest in money and what I have to say may seem, therefore, child-like to practically everyone who has had a long struggle with its practical rather than spiritual or moral importance. The reasons for this are peculiar. When I was a child my parents were the wealthiest in our Welsh village. The money was lost and I spent my adolescence as the poorest child in the same community, poorest in school and college. I read that this experience can make someone either obsessed with money and material goods, or seriously indifferent to them. I belonged to the indifferent.

When I started work in my early twenties, because I could put words on paper in a certain way and read them in a certain way, editors, publishers and broadcasting organisations gave me more money than I needed. So I never thought about it, just thought about the work. So much so that although for 28 out of the 35 years of my working life I've been self-employed, it never crossed my mind to take out any insurance against sickness. So that when some 18 months ago I was struck down by illness, I realised that I hadn't been just insouciant but plain daft. I'd saved a little but thought that was for old age. At which money suddenly became a very interesting question.

Like everyone else, I've been present at a hundred conversations about it, heard who earned what, spent what, knew friends and relatives who suffered hard times, had myself a rough idea of what we were earning and spending, reported on the condition of the poor in a score of countries, spent a small fortune on holidays, opera tickets and in restaurants. But I had escaped the dominant experience of fellow citizens. I think it was Gerald Brenan who wrote: 'Those who have some means think that the most important thing in the world is love. The poor know that it is money'. And not only the poor, he might have added.

I hope all that explains the naivety of what follows. Let's put aside, though, the revelations of the great thinkers, like the psycho-analysts and the Marxists, although I daresay we'll come to those gurus who believe money has replaced both Freud and Marx as deities, as they displaced God. The mean with money may be held to be anal retentive; the extravagent the converse. Just as there is a psycho-analyst's view that Jesus was betrayed in the childhood of Judas, so there is that behaviour with money is governed by potty-training. I think all that stuff not as important as behaviour and in the last year or so, in my new anxiety, I'v been watching quite a few closely, to pick up tips, learn what to avoid. I could have read the classics on the subject, mostly French, read biographies of Midas or King Croesus of Lydia, both of whom knew a thing or two. Real life is just as illuminating and more fun.

When the word was out that my studies had begun, I was challenged to try and win a donation for charity from a well-off man who had never been known to buy a drink for anyone but himself. I set to work. Without my even drawing attention to the state of his immortal soul, nor describing the pitiful condition of the recipients and their need, he produced his cheque book and offered £100. How, I thought, he'd been traduced. What a fine fellow. I bought him a drink. He had long gone before I looked at the cheque. I saw that he had made it out to himself. So what that he may be anal retentive. How many such are walking the earth? And do they giggle to themselves?

Next I was chatting to a man, famous in the land, who felt he was growing old. He is my age. He was frightened of poverty in old age. He is wealthy, has much property. It was clear that for him, money was identified with life. Death was the absence of money; the absence of money was death. The presence of money was life; an abundance of money, therefore, no less then eternal life. In a chat over a meal this is not an easy argument to deal with kindly.

Playing for time, I launched into an extended metaphor, a useful gambit. I gave an account of walking one day in the spring sunshine down the lane from the Hardcany Castle above Prague, along the street of the Alchemists. There in their small, low, terraced cottages the Bohemians had worked to transmute base metals into gold. What, asked my friend, is the point of all this nonsense? It was a fair question since I wasn't too sure myself. The point is this, I said, Here, were these clever chaps, working away in the heat, damaging their eyesight, making gold out of Czech lead or dross. Where is the evidence that they were also trying to create an elixir of life eternal? If any body of men could have found an answer, surely it would have been that gifted lot. What chance have you compared with them? So you think it's not on, said my friend.

It's not on, I continued, and more than that why don't you give more thought to the fact that you are a camel trying to pass through the eye of a needle. At which he became threatening and offered two contradictory ideas: first that I'd soon learn about money's anguish and torments and secondly that I was too old to learn.

Once launched, as ever, on some narrow quest, some private trouble, lights shine from all around. Can you guess, asked a woman friend, what I have to do for my neighbours next month? Huh, huh, I said, which means you are going to tell me, come what may. These neighbours had left six envelopes containing cheques to be sent to five different money-lenders, Access, American Express and so on, and to one department store. The date for posting was marked on a note. Each was paying for something, the current holiday, clothes, car which the neighbours could not truly afford; each the minimum payment to keep the account alive. Their debts exceeded their annual income. This must mean, I said, in the tone of the detective, that much of their domestic chat must be given over to calculating how much to pay each outfit every month for a high-life they cannot afford. Here, with no nonsense about Prague or alchemists, was a live case of real, unreal money. Of such, said my friend, is middle-class life, even working-class life, in our time.

At which a semantic, even philosophical question intrudes. Is the passion to possess material goods quite the same as the matter of money? Goods cannot be acquired without money, but the desire *may* be a separate one. Consider the need for people in emotional distress to run to the shops. Usually it's held, and it happens to all I know, that women buy clothes, jewellery, cars, cakes even as relief from rage or upset. It also happens to men. I buy gramophone records like a drunken, if musical sailor, We all know, because the Beatles told us, that money can't buy us love: equally that spending is no substitute; but off we go. But is it the comfort or the nursing of the goods that counts, rather than the spending of the money? Excluded here are those creatures who spend because they are sad, and spend equally freely because they are happy. They are just big spenders.

At which point I confess to consulting a few texts. There is Martin Amis' novel titled simply *Money*, which deals with the American movie industry with a savage lyricism. It may be read as an insight into the manner in which money has become the American god whose disciples are busy in London. Its savagery lies in showing that in much of our society, people are bought, affections and loyalties a matter of cash, sexual love a pornographical exercise; a culture of treachery, booze, fast food, fast cars, and money. There is no other morality. Yet a century earlier writing about the same society another wit, Oscar Wilde, wrote: 'Men rage against Materialism, as they call it, forgetting that there has been no material improvement that has not spiritualised the world, and that there have been few, if any, spiritual awakenings that have not wasted the world's faculties in barren hopes and fruitless aspirations and empty or trammelling creeds'. I doubt, though, if Oscar Wilde would have been happy to see his argument succeed to the degree depicted in its hollow, rich squalid triumph in Martin Amis's *Money*.

In what way, though, does all this differ from the days of my childhood. Each week in the football season the men of the family, would fill in their pools coupons. They were miners or invalids with one dustman uncle. They understood permutations. They'd invest pennies. In the beginning they would talk of the ways the winnings would be spent. They would go to London for a week, or Blackpool. Buy a decent house. Perhaps buy a car even. The women would go to the posh shop in Swansea and deck themselves out. No more scraping, no more going out to clean for the doctor and the teacher. Was the dream money? No, the dream was a new life. Strangely, they never won and filling in the coupons came to be, almost like going to chapel, just another ritual in the ceremonies of gods that fail. Money, it seems, needs a lot of thinking about.

III

ON SPORT

Such Crowds and such Cheering

At the beginning of the 1870's there were no Rugby clubs in Wales. Yet at the end of the decade all the main towns in industrial South Wales had their team. The moving spirits were young men who had played football at school, usually in England. But in the detail of these early years there is an important clue helping to explain why Rugby football should become in Wales as it became nowhere else but in New Zealand in those early years – a national game, attracting the interest, even stimulating the passion of a whole community. The clue is the fact that dominating clubs like Newport and Swansea began as Association football teams and turned to Rugby simply because there were no fixtures for them; Rugby football was to have a clear field in the expanding and hectic industrial area.

Interest in the new game quickly grew. Big crowds began to gather at matches between the Welsh clubs and sometimes tempers were lost, especially during the South Wales Challenge Cup competition (established 1877). A final between Cardiff and Llanelly had to be abandoned because the crowd snatched the ball in pique. A leaderwriter pontificated on the scene at St Helen's Ground, Swansea: 'Swansea were losing along the touchline. Play stopped for a moment and police, officials and players endeavoured to keep the crowd back. Mr W. Bowen, the Swansea umpire, was hit by one of the roughs. A general mêlée ensued and it was decided to stop the game altogether – this is not the first time that disgraceful scenes have taken place on the St Helen's field. Let us hope it is the last.' Swansea wasn't unusual in this, of course. In most towns the crowds were desperately committed to their team's fortunes and liable to tear their hair – or someone's – at defeat.

The clubs were soon making enough money to pay players' railway fares and hotel expenses, if not more, as rumour had it. The figures of the Cardiff club are representative. In 1884–85 £364 2s 3d was taken at the gate alone (members' subscriptions, £153 8s 6d, and 'ground tickets', £36 15s 0d, were calculated separately). In 1885-86 gate-money had increased, had just about doubled, to £720 3s 9d. In 1890-91 it was £1,223 16s 10d, an increase all the more striking since in this year 'Workmen's Tickets' were first introduced; and it would be reasonable to infer that 'Workmen' would otherwise have paid at the gate. In 1890-91 there were 968 of these tickets; in the next season there were 1,678. In the next season £1,985 was taken at the gate, and in 1901-02 £2,472. Before the end of the century crowds of 30,000 were present at International matches (takings £1,600 – and what, the newspapers were beginning to ask, does the Welsh Rugby Union do with the money?), while in the first decade of the twentieth century, when Rugby football in Wales stimulated an enthusiasm even Wales hasn't known since, crowds of 40,000 and more were watching matches between Cardiff and New Zealand, between Swansea and Australia.

These were crowds composed of all kinds of people: the teams they supported represented them, mirrored them in occupation, wealth or poverty, and character. The public schoolboys of the teams' first years soon diminished in importance and Welsh Rugby became different from English Rugby. Generalization from national characteristic is, though, one of the most difficult to sustain, and anyone anxious to demonstrate from the early years of football in Wales that here, yet once more, we have a case of the Celt exercizing his civilizing influence over the brutish Anglo-Saxon, will have his work cut out. He will get there in the end, but he will have his work cut out. Small details present difficulties. The case of 'the four threequarters' is an example.

Few people would now maintain that the introduction of the 'four threequarters' into the Rugby line-up had produced any but a benign effect. In 1885 it was regarded as a revolutionary step. When, in 1886 – 'Hancock's Year' – the Cardiff Club used the system with such enormous success there were many people dubious about it. It wouldn't last. Even so talented and creative a player as A. J. Gould, the Newport and Wales centre-three-quarter, had his doubts for a long time. The crushing defeat suffered by the Welsh International side that year when they used the system seemed evidence enough that it was impracticable. (Seven years later, when Wales used it again, they were to win the Triple Crown for the first time.) It is clear now, of course, that the crushing Welsh defeat was due to the failure of eight Welsh forwards to hold nine English, which led to the four threequarters being over-run. The system was blamed whereas blame, if any, should have been laid at the door of forwards who were lighter and less skilled and less rough than the English, Scottish and Irish. But in club matches Cardiff found it a fine device. In these games they had eight forwards capable of holding nine club forwards from elsewhere well enough to get the ball to their threequarter line suffficiently often to win matches. Once the threequarters had it, swift, orthodox passes were enough to give them an overlap and a try. It was the quality of the passing which was fundamentally more important then the number of threequarters – a quality which was to win Wales many matches and great fame later – but in these matters it is the easily grasped symbol which lasts and the fourth threequarter is a useful symbol to represent Wales's first major contribution to Rugby development.

Ironically the first fourth threequarter was F. E. Hancock, and he was an Englishman. He played for Wales with success – 'He is somewhat deficient in pace perhaps, but more than makes amends for this with his dodging powers. Every Cardiff spectator is familiar with Hancock's "corkscrew runs" ' – as a critic of the time put it. A Somerset man he was, from pictures a handsome man (5 ft 9½ in, 12 stone 7 lb) with dark, shining hair, large, serious eyes and a walrus moustache. He played as fourth threequarter one day because Cardiff already had their full quota of three threequarters whom they couldn't, for merit's sake, drop. The scene is not difficult to conjure up. Someone, unconscious of his historic role, says 'I tell you what, we'll have four threequarters. Then Hancock can play.' A forward is dropped, in comes the Englishman, and life is never quite the same again.

The first glory of Welsh Rugby was thus established early – that disciplined short-passing which gave the game mobility and pace, shattered the pattern of early forward play, allowed in the light and grace of brilliant runners, and was, when forward play grew stronger, to lead to an unparalleled decade of success and to make the 1905 affair with New Zealand – a country much exercised at the same time with making the game fit for intelligent men – one of the most important dates in Welsh history since the death of Llewelyn the Last. Early, too, the Cardiff club was making a crucial contribution to world Rugby. Not that they were the outstanding Welsh club in the last fifteen years of the century. Newport and Swansea were often more successful, Newport very early demonstrating the tremendous success Welsh teams might enjoy if their forwards matched their backs in quality, especially when the backs were of A. J. Gould's quality.

The temptation is almost overpoweringly strong to recite the detail of those early years for its own sake. Resisting it, and picking our way among memoirs, memories and *rapportage*, important differences between Rugby in Wales and elsewhere stand out. Some similarities occur, of course. In Lancashire and Yorkshire, like South Wales, working men were playing Rugby. There too, matches attracted large and enthusiastic crowds. But in the north emphasis remained on the forward in attack. With a similar economic and social character – roughly speaking – Wales made a different sort of game of Rugby.

A complex of explanation suggests itself. Grant the argument that in Scotland – and to a lesser extent England – the form of play came to be equated with a certain *ethos*, with the

122

Spirit of the Game, due to the influence of the public schools, then in Wales the *ethos* did not have the same force, so that it seemed less morally damaging to alter the form of play. Men came to the game with no preconceived and rigid notions. They played as the spirit took them. In the early days, too, the Welshmen, being smaller, were continually being swept aside and mauled by their opponents: some compensating devices were needed. The big men had to be dodged. It isn't too fanciful either to look for an explanation in the Welsh cast of mind, in its celebrated cleverness and admiration for cleverness. The reaction of English and Scottish Rugby supporters in the 'nineties and later to the brothers James and to R. M. Owen bears a striking resemblance to the reaction of certain generals and politicians to David Lloyd George. Mingled with amazement was admiration and fear, the whole amalgam tinged with moral disapprobation, with the feeling that this wasn't the way to behave. And there is, too, the inexplicable but evident natural talent for football that Welshmen seem to possess. Of some of them one can only say that they have a genius for it. From photographs of men like Owen and Trew one can see that they are possessed by Rugby football as others have been by music or mysticism. (This may seem improbable to people who think of Rugby foot-ballers in terms of simple extroverts with happy, smiling faces.) But wasn't there something 'possessed' about C. Morgan's play for Wales? For these men life was football. It was something to which they could devote their intelligence and wit. Their play was a creative act. And neither Owen nor Trew lived long after they had finished playing.

But in saying that the Spirit of the Game was not as at high a proof in Wales, we aren't saying that the players were less sportsmanlike. They played in as good a spirit as anyone else, and were, if anything, less rough. Indeed, Welshmen very properly take exception to the idea that their teams have been rougher than, say, the English. Even in the 'twenties, when a lot of hard things were said about Welsh forwards, there seems every reason to believe those members of the

Welsh pack who have recently told us that they did nothing that the English forwards weren't in the habit of doing. Legendary instructions on the field like: 'If you see something black, kick it. It may be the ball,' are just better remembered when said by Welshmen. Some players certainly had little ways with them. In his highly readable and well-informed *Great Rugger Players*, Mr J. B. G. Thomas recounts how R. M. Owen won the match against England for Wales in 1902 by winning a penalty award in front of the English posts. His gambit was to pretend to pick up the ball when Wales heeled: 'His opponent,' Mr Thomas writes, 'sensing a quick heel, rushed round the scrum at top speed, but did not hear Owen whisper in Welsh, "Keep the ball in, boys." And so Owen was tackled by Oughtred while not in possession and the referee had no option but to award Wales a penalty-kick.' Men who played with Owen are full of praise for his extraordinary invention of moves of this kind, and of a kind more suitable to the *mores* of the time (like his reverse pass which led to victory over New Zealand in 1905) and for his ability in judging just when the referee was in sight and when not.

Where the Welsh did differ was in their refusal to be bound slavishly to formal arrangements and rigid ideas. There was no nonsense about *everyone* having to tackle. If a man was brilliant enough in attack, that was good enough. One of the best examples is P. Phillips, the Newport outside-half in the famous and unbeaten team of 1891-92, who seems never to have bothered with defensive play. From newspaper reports of Wales's first victory at home over England – in 1893 – it seems he scarcely tackled and barely ever kicked in defence. He was a very frail man – just over 8 stone in weight. Had the climate of opinion been such that no man should play in the International unless he could tackle, he would never have played for Wales. Certainly there was criticism of him – the ferocious tone of inter-town rivalry in Wales at that time has to be savoured to be enjoyed – some people in the Principality thinking there was huge moral virtue in tackling. (This argument goes on in Wales, only nowadays the defensive school are very much in the ascendant.) It was also said of the James brothers that their tackling was poor and, for that matter, of W. J. Bancroft, but here evidence conflicts. The explanation of this, perhaps, and of Phillips' success in the Newport team is the reply given by a member of the Swansea side in the late 'nineties when he was asked about the defensive qualities of the side's heroes. 'I couldn't tell you,' he said. 'Ever since I've been playing for Swansea, we've been attacking.'

Men came fresh to the game. No schoolteacher had told them how to play. They played as they saw fit. The only tradition was that all new ideas were welcome. And, of course, all kinds of men played, not only the large heavy men, but the small and frail, the labouring man alongside the lawyer, docker and doctor together.

Towards the end of the century Rugby occupied in industrial Wales the same position as Association football in industrial England. Swansea provides a very fair microcosm of the situation and since there isn't room to examine each side in detail, the Swansea club seems, from the point of view of the game's social history, a useful example. Particularly since it was in Swansea that the question of professionalism – in the affair of the brothers James – at last burst into flames.

Swansea in the 'nineties was a rapidly expanding community. It was still the world's most important metallurgical centre. Coal and steel and tinplate were its principal industries. Its docks were growing. The town also believed that it was a better place than Cardiff and fancied its chance as the capital city of Wales. It was then a very Welsh town. Like Newport, Cardiff, and Llanelli it had taken Rugby to its heart. Its Rugby players strode about the town like gods. The James brothers – David and Evan – were possibly the most admired. In W. J. T. Collins's phrase: 'Great advances in the science of half-back play began with the brothers James – they were the great initiators of half-back tactics.' What happened to the brothers James is an instructive saga, a sidelight on the attitudes of the time. The James family was large and poor. The brothers were labourers, and from their first appearance in 1889 the idols of the large, enthusiastic and excitable Swansea crowds. On 27th January 1893, Argus, the Rugby critic of the Swansea *Cambrian*, astonished the Rugby world by reporting the following:

'Oh, where, Oh where are the Famous Half-backs?

'To-night a committee will sit in solemn conclave to receive evidence relative to the flight of the brothers James from Swansea to Manchester when it is expected some startling statements will be made. The case of the erstwhile Swansea halves is exciting great interest throughout the whole football world, for upon its result will depend the future of professionalism. For the brothers to deny they were not induced to leave the home of their birth by pecuniary considerations is absurd on the face of it. No men would leave a town where they could get fair work and pay and fly to a far distant town in the "hope" of finding employment. Lancashire and Yorkshire people may believe such a "cock and bull" story, but we in South Wales and those who conduct the Rugby affairs of England and Wales are not to be misled by such a story. My readers would probably like to know the circumstances under which the "curly-headed marmosets" left Swansea.

'A few days prior to their sudden flight, a Swansea man was in High Street, when he was accosted by a well-dressed man who appeared to be a stranger to the town.

' "Could you tell me where I could see the brothers James, the famous half-backs?" he said.

'The Swansea man gazed somewhat at his questioner and with a merry and wicked twinkle in his eyes, replied: "Yes, I know where they are, but what do you want them for?"

' "Oh, I am a cousin of theirs and have not seen them for some years. I belong to Gloucester and have just run down for a trip."

'The twinkle in the Swansea man's eye grew merrier and more wicked. "Get along with you," he said. "Do you think

I don't know a Gloucester man from a Lancashire man, I know what you want. You want them to play for some club."

'The stranger seemed taken by surprise . . .

' "Well, eh, as you have pressed my object I think I may as well tell you that a club in Manchester is hard up for a pair of half-backs. We want a good pair. Do you think we could get the brothers James? Are they hard to satisfy?"

'The reply he received was that although Swansea people had done much for the Jameses, they were not satisfied – indeed, it looked as if it would take a lot to satisfy them.

' "But do you think", asked the stranger, "that they would be satisfied with jobs at 25s. each and which could be made worth £2 a week?"

' . . . A few days afterwards the brothers James played for a "club near Manchester". Evidence to the above effect will be given at the meeting to-night.'

The Welsh press at this time, as for much of the 'nineties, was full of the James brothers. So much so that some readers were driven to writing letters reading: 'The going-away of the James brothes had been given an importance that disgusts one. Why, had we lost half a dozen of our best men a greater commotion could not have been made. And who are the Jameses? Men not above – if even up to the level of – the ordinary labourer, and yet, because they are adepts at football, they are worshipped, aye, idolised.'

Some articles are revealing:

'I was told a few days ago on very good authority that after the Scottish International at Swansea last year they (the brothers) were simply supplied with gold by some of their well-to-do admirers. Money was placed in their clothes and they were treated like heroes by everyone they met. And yet they forsook the town which petted and fêted them, at the first opportunity. I could say something more about the "curly-headed marmosets" as to how they were treated in Swansea but it would not be advisable.'

The Welsh journalists, however, soon lost their critical

tone towards the brothers James for deserting Swansea. With quite astonishing speed there was a volte-face and the ogres on the scene became the Rugby Union; it was sinister figures like Rowland Hill and Marshall who were being so nasty to Evan and David: 'The Rugby Union have treated Welsh football as if it does not exist.' In February 1894 Argus of the *Cambrian* was looking forward to the day when everyone would see '. . . the curly-headed marmosets play for Swansea again. When the brothers again march on the St Helen's field wearing the "All White" jersey, there will be such a crowd and such cheering as has not been heard there for many a long day'.

David and Evan James, after three years, were readmitted and there *was* such a crowd and such cheering and, in January 1899, they were selected again for Wales, and, on 14th January at St Helen's Swansea, they came on to the field before a record crowd (30,000) for a match in Wales – twice as many, as the Swansea journalists fell over themselves to point out, as had watched Wales six years before in Cardiff. Even though Evan broke his collar-bone in the first five minutes, they ran, with a dazzling skill, through the English side as they pleased. The night before the match Englishmen had been boasting about how their forwards would trample the James brothers and the rest of Wales's 'much-vaunted backs' into the sod. For all that, they lost by 26 points to 3.

The performance of the marvellous James brothers was universally acclaimed – by the *Sunday Times*, the *St James Gazette*, and the magazine *Sport and Play*, as well as the Welsh press. There had been nothing so brilliant before. The edition of the Swansea *Daily Post* with an account of the match beat all the former circulation records by 6,000. Men who saw the match have explained to us that it was the most crushing defeat England ever suffered and that the men who were principally responsible for it were Evan and David James, so that it was no wonder really that they were regarded as two of the greatest Welshmen that ever trod, and no wonder that it took away the breath of the whole country when the brothers turned professional again just twelve days after this match. 'Oh, you never saw their like,' one of the 30,000 told us. This time Broughton Rangers took the whole James family – sixteen of them, including grandmother. Fortunately for Swansea, Owen, Trew and R. Jones arrived to replace 'the curly-headed marmosets'. £250 was the signing on fee.

But even after the formation of the Northern Union, Welsh club teams did not change their social character. The trek 'North', which was to have a debilitating effect on Welsh football in the decades of depression, was not made by many. The occupations for the 1908 Swansea side indicates this:

J. Bancroft: Copper-yard worker.
H. Toft: Railway-worker.
W. J. Trew: Boilermaker (later a publican).
W. Hopkins: Surveyor.
F. Lewis: Coalminer.
A. Arnold: Schoolteacher.
W. Symonds: Clerk.
R. Jones: Publican.
R. M. Owen: Publican.
T. Bateman: Shipbuilder.
A. Smith: Schoolteacher.
D. J. Thomas: Coalminer.
G. Hayward: 'Learning to be a diver.'
I. Morgan: Coal-trimmer.
H. Hunt: Haulier.
F. Scrine: Publican.
D. Davies: Dock labourer.
B. Davies: Police Constable.

The high incidence of publicans is explained by this being a trade which served as a reward for the heroes of the field of praise. In the 'twenties the Glamorgan Constabulary provided patronage. In the 'fifties, the educational system having expanded, jobs as physical training instructors at schools and colleges have tended to replace both. Each decade has its devices. Nine of the Swansea team fifty years later were, or had been, university students.

We are not suggesting that Rugby football in Wales has changed dramatically in its social character in the past half-century. There have been changes, but, for a variety of reasons, it still remains the game of the people to an extent unparalleled in Britain, although not in New Zealand. That it doesn't attract quite as many as it did is simply because professional Association football has drawn to it talents and support which earlier would have gone to Rugby. As early as 1894 a soccer match at Swansea attracted a gate of £150 and after the 1914-18 war soccer heroes began to compete seriously for the atttention of a public which earlier had venerated Rugby men. The ambitions of young men of working-class families were directed away from the Rugby fields. It is reasonable to suppose that celebrated Swansea soccer players like the brothers Charles and Allchurch might, fifty years ago, have played Rugby for their town.

The remarkable thing is, in fact, that Welsh Rugby has been able to hold-off the challenge of the two kinds of professional football and still retain so much of its original character. Miners and steelworkers are still to be found in the major teams and even more so playing for 'second-class' clubs; and still constitute as great a part of the crowd at International matches at Cardiff. The peculiar classlessness of Welsh society is the simple explanation of this, and the proportionately small size of the middle-class in Wales. Another explanation – and a consequence of this – is the close relationship between the Grammar Schools and the people. Sons of steel and tinplate workers and coalminers have been going to the grammar schools for a long time. The schools play Rugby and so the industrial villages or the suburbs where the boys live play Rugby. So that even when, as nowa-days, a Welsh club or International side may seem to contain an extraordinarily high proportion of university students or schoolteachers, this does not mean that suddenly the game has lost its popular basis. It simply means that young men who fifty years ago would have been miners or tinplate workers or railwaymen, have stayed the course at the grammar school and gone on to college. (Rugby footballers seem to be very popular applicants for university places. A new social phenomenon has emerged, too, in Welsh Rugby circles. A graduate of the University of Wales will often elect to go to Cambridge or Oxford to read for his Diploma in Education, rather than take it at his home college. Two members of the Swansea team in recent seasons have done this and both won 'Blues'.) You would imagine from this that Rugby in Wales has grown more polite, and, by and large it has, except that in the season 1958-59 there were ominous signs – forwards punching, butting with their heads in one Swansea *v.* Llanelli match, doing things they shouldn't in a Newport *v.* Cardiff match, too many late tackles in too many matches – of a relapse which a lot of people were concerned about. It isn't difficult for referees to put an end to all this, and no one would be sorry if they did.

Report on Rugby

Never Again

Between St. Helen's Ground, Swansea, and the sea there is only a road and the oldest railway in the world. Towards the Mumbles Head are tall trees; towards the town a slim white tower tells the time. It is famous for cricket as well as Rugby. As long as Rugby matches have been played they have been played there.

After this season they may never be again. When the Welsh and Scottish teams leave the field next Saturday, half-naked, swopping jerseys, surrounded by the occupational fence-jumpers, coal-tip gauchos and small boys, they may well be the last to do so.

131

Rugby in Wales, like any other way of passing the time which makes men passionate and creates power, has its politics. Like more serious politics they are enlivened by East-West prejudices. It is closing time for the stadium in the West because the covered accommodation is inadequate, and because so many of the crowd cannot see the game at all, and so many more as through the wrong end of a telescope, ant-like. At Cardiff, in the East, on the other hand, all spectators who are not dwarfs can see everything.

There is something to be said for the Eastenders. Anyone who has stood on the bank at the Swansea end of St. Helen's – the cricket field between him and the play – sees a strange game. When a man falls down on the half-way line one applauds a try: a kick ahead is a drop goal. Unless one uses a telescope the score-board is too far away to read.

Loyalists and Romantics (all men mad about Rugby are Romantics) will not have this. Recite the great names and games of the ground; talk about the character of the ground, the singing that is more spontaneous than at sophisticated Cardiff; listen to the old men who saw Bancroft kick goals from the corner-flag, and the men of all ages who have their propaganda of memories; and the spell is cast.

I march with the Western tribe for scarcely noble reasons. An institution at St. Helen's is the two very small boys in school jerseys who stand on the tanner-bank touchline and chase the ball in the outfield between line and spectator. For a long time I was one of those small boys, trotting from under the grandstand, receiving a special jocose cheer. This was during the war, when amateurs and professionals played together in some of the finest games St. Helen's has ever known.

In the touch we ran as hard as anyone. We passed the ball to the minor deities in shorts in the best style: sometimes, even we kicked it. The important thing was not to become flustered, when chasing the ball a long way, at the ironies of the crowd, and to remember that it had not paid to see you perform. After the game, delighted and inaudible, we had tea with the players; later we had their autographs.

The decision to play all internationals at Cardiff is not final; a lot depends on the improvements that Swansea Borough intends to make in accommodation. One hopes they will satisfy the angry Eastern people; or that the balance of power may be otherwise maintained.

The Observer

Excursion Limited

Call him Davy Jones. He is five foot six, of slight build: age fifty. From the bridge of his nose to the roots of tough, grey hair, a blue star. He is not a collier now but has a light job in a steelworks. He lives in his own house in the fourth Rugby valley from the left. Every other Saturday he goes down to his big town, watches one of the first-class teams; his comments are acid. Other Saturdays he stands on the low coal-tip and watches the local team run around in the scrub. But he is a member of no Rugby club. The only club he belongs to is the Workingman's, where Rugby is high politics and his, to his great pleasure, is the voice in the wilderness.

When Wales play Scotland at Murrayfield he travels up for the week, but the trip to London for the Wales and England game is just for the day. Up and over the hill with the dawn; cadge a ride to the station on the only bus travelling that early, the worker's; then the excursion train at seven. Two mackintoshes (his own and his youngest son's bicycle cape); sandwiches enough for a small army; a bottle of orange-juice; a small tin, full of home-rolled cigarettes; two apples, an orange a banana; and in a pocket of his navy-blue suit an old scarlet beret.

Davy Jones is one of 30,000. Most of the rest of us travel by train, corridors full, sitting on newspapers in the corridors, some of us, flagons coming out as the sun warms a little, talking a lot, singing especially loudly if we stop at an English station, arguing so that before we reach Paddington we have each acquired the name, as nickname, of a player dispute has forced us to deify. Many travel by hired bus, two seats booked for the beer. Some, no doubt, by car.

This is scarcely anarchy. The violent despair, the prancing, rollicking delight is for later, for Piccadilly and the incredible midnight train back to where we belong.

Davy Jones knows his way around London. He knows Twickenham, Piccadilly, Paddington. He is at the ground early. In his younger days he had side-stepped and sprinted across the field, decoying the police, while leeks were hung on crossbars, placed in midfield; but he is past that now. He is up to cheering, though, men still young enough to sprint; and is up to singing hymns and Rugby songs. Davy Jones is a different man; his face is bright red; his blue scar brighter; his beret is on his head at last. He is an anonymous soldier in an expeditionary force that will not surrender until the last gasp.

But yesterday Davy Jones did not have a ticket; belonging to no club he couldn't even ballot for a ticket. Only 10,000 tickets were sent to Wales for this game for which tickets had not been needed before. So Davy Jones should have had a morning in bed, taken a walk, called at his club where others ticketless would be staring at the murals of old Wales, had his dinner and settled down in a silent house for the radio-commentary. Should have. But Davy Jones was on the train, was at the gates of Twickenham, hoping, listening to the noise, the band, the singing and, in the end, at a barber's shop beyond the ground, the radio-commentary.

The Observer

Scarlets and Wallabies

By lunch-time the banners welcoming in Welsh, the Wallabies Rugby team to Llanelli or *Sospan* were already damp. From Carmarthen Bay the rain swept across a town *en fête* in its fashion, blackening the grey slate roofs, gathering in pools on patches of industrial waste land.

In the crowded paths and the buses down for the great day from mining villages like Tumble and Cross Hands and from the Towy Valley's market towns, man, woman and child wore, short of divers' helmets, every known defence against rain.

Only those desperately unlucky with manager or ticket were at work. All children had a day's holiday. ("Who will be callous enough," demanded the Councillor, "to oppose this amendment?") Shops were closed, and if you wanted to buy a hat or cap or even a plastic shopping bag you couldn't, and had to make do, as I did, with a handkerchief knotted at its edges and *The Times* like a roof over it. "We want our heads read," said a man wearing a mackintosh, leather jerkin, donkey jacket and sou'wester, laughing at his joke as we walked with the crowd across railway lines and liquid mud to the field, and stood – too late for the concrete terrace – on a bank of ashes and with 20,000 others sang hymns of lament and praise in the wind and rain.

Welshmen believe to be true of Llanelli all that Englishmen believe of Wales. "Rugby is our religion," cried a man in the pub, "and its anthem is *Sospan Fach*" [small saucepan, Llanelli's tinplate symbol]. In this town (pop.: 33,000) the great player is wise man and public hero: the one talent is the most honoured. Wales wears a red jersey and so does Llanelli. Other teams may demonstrate equally the claslessness of Welsh society, but only in Llanelli is Welsh the language of Rugby football. The lively town seems to revolve around the club.

All of which would explain why 20,000 people should tightly pack Stradey Park – only 5,000 under cover – to see the

Scarlets play the Wallabies, even if the powerful, historical relationship between the two teams has been tapped out on the tribal drums and site down by the elders in the tablets.

*　　　*　　　*

Every *Sospan* child in its cradle learns that Llanelli were the first team to beat (8-3) the first Australian touring side in 1908; and croons himself to sleep with a verse that was added to *Sospan Fach*: "Who beat the Wallabies? The good old *Sospan Fach*." He – and she, if it comes to that – also knows that the 1947 match was a rough-house when Australia won 6-4 and had their vice-captain sent from the field.

The evocative facts have been incantated for months around town. So that first one way and another, the size of the crowd and the politeness with which Australia were welcomed on the field last Tuesday were explicable. Over the loud-speakers a voice, barely audible in the half gale, announced the presence at the match of three men who played for Llanelli in the 1908 game. Those who heard applauded the old heroes. The voice delivered a message of welcome in Welsh to the Wallabies. Welsh and British national anthems were sung with enthusiasm; the rain stopped falling; and the big match, scarlet and green jerseys creating brilliant patterns on the bright turf, began.

Llanelli, who are having a marvellous season, never looked like winning. In the first half with the wind behind them they scored a characteristically clever try but that was all. When the rain poured down their faces in the second half their forwards grew too tired to raise a trot and the Wallabies, firstly with a penalty goal, then a brilliant, wildly applauded try, then a neat try, won a surprising victory using, a neighbour explained, the tactics Llanelli had used in 1908.

For the last 20 minutes the crowd was funereal. The low hills half-circling the ground disappeared in the dusk. The black steelworks stacks behind the new opulent grandstand merged with the sky. Everything was very quiet, except for the wind and the sound of the rain on my sodden *Times*.

Sad and wet, the crowd moved away, some leaping a turbulent stream for a short cut, others wading it in gumboats, some, like myself, landing in it. There had been little for myth to feed on, only amazement that the Australians had been so strong. But moralists will be delighted that play was so polite. To echo a surprised reporter in 1908: "There was an absence of foul language."

The Observer

All Black and Scarlet

This was what we had come for, the myth-in-action, the men in scarlet and the men in black, prancing from under the stands on to the field of Welsh praise, now standing at attention for *our* National Anthem, our noise too great to be heard except when the wind swirls suddenly back from the wide, high stands, the sound of a passionate affirmation that at the back of every Welsh mind lives a blind patriotism, uncaged only for rugby internationals, for the only battles Wales has fought alone for centuries.

The "excursion" from Swansea had been full; flagons were bandied about. We all knew what we were talking about. We named the team which had beaten the Newsy-landers in 1905, and were told by the asthmatical old man in the corner, who said he had seen the game, as every old man says he saw the game, how Dr. Morgan had scored the only try. We couldn't name the team which was beaten in 1924, but we could name the winning 1935 team. Hadn't we all heard the B.B.C. broadcast last night? The excerpt from the recordings of the game? The pontiffs pontificating; the centre threequarters earnest and nearly word-perfect at their scripts? We recited the great names – Bancroft of the very old days, Nicholls, Gabe, Owen of the golden days, Wooller, Davey, Tanner, Willie Davies, Cliff Jones. They are names of the light and air of rugby; not, oddly, of the vicious in-fighting, the massive heave and crack of bone in the scrummage. A fan, about fourteen years old, produced a print of an old photograph. It was the 1905 Welsh team, solemn men, all looking much older than they must have been at the time. We passed it round the compartment, we discussed prospects. We all thought it a pity in a way that the Newsy-landers had lost to Cardiff, and a shame in a way that they couldn't beat Swansea. We wanted it as it had been in 1905 when only Wales beat New Zealand. We wanted to curl up in the historic precedent. We all thought the Welsh backs would be better than the enemy's. We shook our heads over the forwards. "Oh," said the fourteen-year-old, "Oh, I hope it'll be a memorable game."

Before the game began, the crowd swayed behind me and I fought against the swell. I missed the kick-off. My first clear and honest memory of the 1953 game is of a line-out in the shadow of a grandstand, the only shadow on the sunlit ground. Two years ago I stood in almost the same place and was crushed against a crush-barrier. It was the day Wales lost to South Africa, and an old man standing a yard in front of me had been taken ill, overwhelmed by the heat and the stench, and had been lifted up by the crowd and passed, overhead, to the touch-line, hand to hand, being sick all the way.

The hallucination, no matter how hard you fight it, is total; if we didn't want it to be, we wouldn't be here. These men are heroes. That tall, athletic young man is a student; that short, black-haired, wild-eyed, vital man is a salesman, his partner a company director; the burly, incredibly energetic man is a boiler-maker; the well-built, suprised-looking man now placing the ball on the ground near a white line is a school-teacher; that slim, young man who is going to kick the ball in a moment is a doctor; that tall, older-looking man over there, with a streak of grey in his hair, is a Justice of the Peace. A middle-class bunch? One of the ways of becoming middle-class in Wales is to play for a big rugby club. There are certainly few manual workers in the team but there are many sons of manual workers, the Grammar school boys. There are also sons of the bourgeoisie. (Look on the programme for the men with three initials.) The crowd look, as an Englishman once told me, like a soccer crowd. Not here the tweedy, bescarved, sun-burned hearties, the pretty, healthy girls – they are Stand-people, not Field-people. Here are the blue-suited or brown-suited men, off the peg, who know what it's all about, this game, and didn't learn it at a Public school. A characteristic Welsh ground has steelworks at one end and a ribbed, over-hanging mountain the other; the banks are coal-tips and the stands are made of zinc; the spectators are as ready to boo as to cheer. Playing the game doesn't mean exactly the same thing.

Something has gone wrong. The Welsh lead disappears. The Newsy-landers are ahead and we have nothing to shout, a lot to be quiet about, a quiet that can be heard all over Cardiff. New Zealand camp, as they say, on the Welsh line, a brawling, hectic camp, under tents of massive men, with one sentry more than any other, the Welsh fly-half, Cliff Morgan, running and kicking and tackling, the smallest man, one of the most intense and talented rugby players ever seen. Griffiths, the young centre-threequarter, leaves the field, injured. The quiet is pro-found. The players' shouts echo back from the stands and the massed heads that have turned to stone. But New Zealand seem unable to score and gradually we all realise that this refusal by our side to allow a score is, in its way, heroic and memorable. Griffiths comes back on to the field and immed-iately runs, confidently, elegantly, through the New Zealand defence and rouses us all. Wales score. Ten minutes to play and the scores level. Where I am becomes a jostling, mauling, howling place. I am kicked behind the knee. People are throwing other people's hats in the air. The crowd sways and fights bitterly against the sway. The Welsh team have gone wild, perhaps because we have gone wild. The noise must impel them like a great gale. Cliff Morgan avoids Clarke again. The Newsy-landers are tired. He kicks towards the corner-flag. Elsom of New Zealand catches it but Rowlands tackles him. Oh, Rowlands! Thomas picks up the ball. He's in touch. No. Yes. He's not. Oh, what's he up to, kicking across the field like that. There's no one there. But there is – Ken Jones, Olympic sprinter. He's caught the ball. He's run around the full-back. He's going to score. He scores and we've won. Five minutes to play, and we've won, and Jones has become immortal with a try.

The New Statesman and Nation, 2nd January 1954

Heroes

Outside the Royal a young man, understandably unnerved by the exhausting afternoon, puked into the gutter while his friends pranced around him in the style of the Welsh three-quarter line, but chanting: 'Willy can't take it, Willy can't take it'. Along the road a pub manager was informing a group of grapplers: 'You can knock each other's teeth out, tear off each other's arms and legs, but not on my premises after stop-tap'. At which a gang of hustlers hustled them off the premises and they resumed their grappling amiably on the pavement. Rain was now falling. In the cocktail bars girls who had been crossing and re-crossing their legs, and then their eyes, had to face up to promises. In the bars where draught beer was sold, people who had never seen each other before, and those who had, barely articulated arrangements for the next time. 'Great game. Marvellous', we all agreed.

From the Welsh point of view the game with England is always the occasion of the year, a fact which, in itself, explains why: that sense of defeat, after seven centuries, still flourishes. Old scores may be worked off and, last Saturday, were. What made the Welsh victory so satisfying was that the English were quite trampled into the sod by a Welsh side all the pundits had been despondent about. More than that, we were short of a forward all through the second half. Peryf ap Cedifor, a 12th-century poet, although writing at a time when the eight-man pack of forwards had not been envisaged, put it rather well (roughly translating): 'We were seven men, faultless, indestructible, in attack irresistible; seven men, unshakeable, who would get stuck-in till the last trump; seven men, like the heroes of the past, who would not let them pass'.

Before the match the jokers had been active, helped this year by the fact that the selectors of the Welsh team had been overcome by gas at the Newport club during their deliberations. (One must remember that selecting the rugby team is the nearest Wales gets to self-government, so that the process attracts the degree of criticism and gossip associated with Cabinet-making in England). Otherwise inexplicable nominations for the Welsh side were being referred to, inaccurately, as the CO_2 men.

Not that all the current jokes had to do with football. There were non-parochial asides about having a gamekeeper's kit for Christmas. But the match, by its passion, its unexpected exhibition of skill, its closing minutes of almost intolerable tension, raised the occasion above this level of vulgar comedy.

Afterwards, trembling a little with singing and pleasure and the fear that, in those last few minutes, the awful luck of the English would pull them through to a victory they did not deserve, pressed in the crowd, we made our way to the nearest bar, open at half-past-four for the occasion. In the street a man still sold Welsh favours. 'Missed your shift, mate?' Two men sold steel-grey balloons in the shape of Zeppelins. A gang ahead of Zeppelins. A gang ahead of us bought one. 'What we'll do, see, Davy, is make a hole in it and fill it with beer. Be nice for the bus back'. (Speaking as a man who was once arrested, but very briefly held, in such a situation, I could see their night unfolding. There would be a bit of a punch-up, and the driver would stop out of fright, and a policeman would be handy, and eventually all would be well, after speeches on all sides.)

'What a difference from those boring Boers', said a friend in the first bar, referring, on the one hand, to the high quality of the match we had just seen, and on the other to the presence, undefeated, in this country of the South African rugby team. I said that I wouldn't know. How far, I put it to him, slipping into gear, is your boredom with the Boers due to their desire to win at all costs, and how far due to your guilt feeling that you've watched them in spite of your liberal principles? 'I was kidnapped', said another friend, 'when the South Africans played Wales, I was taken to London. When I returned the next day, Cardiff was under water. I was driven home in a motor launch through the streets of the capital and took the salute in the prow. There were pictures on television'. Since this was a friend who had once left us at closing-time and gone for a stroll near Llanberis and had later been seized by the Mountain Rescue people while staring at the dawn from the summit of Snowdon, we believed him.

'Watch this', said another friend. (All the world is present at the match with England.) We followed an ex-international of our acquaintance into another bar. In a corner was a quorum of an education committee, the men all in heavy spectacles, the women in large hats. We listened. 'Headship' was the key word; our acquaintance shook hands all round: those years of side-stepping and tackling had not been in vain.

In the cocktail bar the evidence for notaries of social change mounted steadily. 'How much?' asked a tinplate-worker, ordering his round. '£2 11s 6d', said the girl. He paid with a five-pound note and carried his Benedictines, Drambuies, brandies and whiskies to a corner crowded with friends and, which is the crucial social change, their wives. At the bar a man asked what was the point of living in London if you hadn't seen the girl with the snake perform at Raymond's Revuebar, a performance which he had witnessed during the Motor Show.

We soon shook him off and went across the road to where hymns were being sung with spirit, if little acquaintance with the words. 'People don't know the hymns they used to know', we said. 'When no one knows the hymns, how will we be different from the English?'

Morosely we then analysed this situation, forgetting the evidence of the afternoon at the Arms Park, until the beer ran out. We moved out into the street again, a gang who had been behaving in this way, on international day, as long as we could remember, and began planning the trip to Paris for the match with France. 'If we catch a special bus to a field near Folkestone, there'll be a plane, believe me, that will take us to within 60 miles of Paris', said our kidnapped friend, 'for a mere eight quid'.

Two years ago, on an overnight excursion to the Paris match, he had been slipped a mickey in a Mountain bar, robbed of his wristwatch, money and passport, spent the night drinking with the chief of police, raised the Embassy on a Sunday morning, and arrived back in Wales on Wednesday after we all had assumed his demonic talent for the bizarre had at last found him out. This time he hopes, we hope, to see the match.

New Statesman, 27th January 1961

Dying Demonology

'Punch, Jesus, punch!' shouted the Mexican in the aisle seat at Earls Court. In a pool of light in the centre of the stadium the Mexican Jesus Saucedo was doing badly against a thin Scot, few in the crowd paying much attention, except the Mexican spectator, who really cared. Suddenly there was a roar of joy, a sound more savage than the roar for a goal, the pleasure angrier, almost bitter. Jesus was down. His leg would twitch occasionally, otherwise he was still. A man looking like a doctor came into the ring and then St John's Ambulance men with a stretcher. They carried him through the crowd who cheered in what's known as a sportsmanlike way. He was in a coma and, for all we knew, near death. My neighbours, discussing the situation in Welsh, observed that the Mexican had been behaving peculiarly during the fight: he had twice walked to the wrong corner at the end of the round. The pageantry of the world title-fight that followed immediately afterwards seemed tawdry and distasteful.

Recorded trumpets blew a fanfare. Two searchlights in the roof broke the darkness, searching for the challenger, Howard Winstone, and finding him in a scarlet robe surrounded by men in white carrying flags, one the Welsh Ddraig Goch, the other the Union Jack. The banners drifted in the smoke while national anthems were sung, the Welsh, naturally, with most the 18,000 crowd had come up from Wales in the hope that Winstone, the Merthyr feather-weight, would be the first Welshman ever to win a world title.

I wouldn't care to defend boxing against the usual charges: that it is crooked, that betting men and gangsters move in the shadows of the game, fixing and threatening; that men die in the ring, damage their brains, stumble through the rest of their lives. A few weeks ago I talked to an old boxer, once adulated, who now confused the decades in which he fought, burst into tears from time to time, and needed to hold his drink with both hands. Neither would I care to peddle the line that it's a useful substitute for brawling in life, that a polite society needs its public punchers to sublimate and expiate its violence. (See Mailer on Clay *versus* Liston for a brilliant analysis of this.) I don't much go either for the thesis that pro-boxing is an extension of the Theatre of Cruelty, offering Artaud-like insights into those truths of hatred and passion which respectability conceals. If I shared that view, I suppose I would have been delighted to discover one evening two years ago, when Howard Winstone and Brian Curvis, two Welsh British champions, were on the same bill at Wembley, that my ringside seat was covered with the blood of two heavyweights who had just finished a preliminary bout. Here was 'reality', involvement; hypocritically, no doubt, since boxing is bound to be bloody, it made the occasion revolting. Yet here I was again, and there was a Mexican being carried away on a stretcher. The defence I would offer is that it is hard to escape from the demonology of a particular kind of industrial society, and hard for anyone brought up in a British coalfield to see boxing quite in the fashion it appears to more genteel regions.

Boxing offered miners riches beyond the avarice of shop-keepers; nothing else did, not even professional football. Good boxers became famous. When I was a small boy, we would see champions walking around the streets. An uncle of mine used to run a 'boxing academy' – he wasn't, we gathered, well enough to work down the mine. We would gather on Saturday mornings on the first floor of disused colliery workings, probably illegally, and wave our feeble fists at one another while he recalled the skills of Driscoll and Wilde. Beneath the ring were the cold waters which had flooded the pit years before and drowned a few miners. Old champions then, and later, endlessly recounted or invented anecdotes. One day a few leading pugilists – or so the story went – organised a small crowd that threw a mob of policemen into the River Towy at Llandeilo during the General Strike. They all pleaded guilty at the Assizes but the jury found them not guilty, at which the judge fell down foaming in an epileptic fit. There was more admiration for the elegant boxer than the big puncher, and a romanticism about bygone stylists. Was it not passing brave to be the champ and ride in triumph through Tonypandy?

Nationalist pride in Wales has always been inextricably involved with poverty; it's easier to see now that poverty promotes fighters, and that the United States has the best because it still has the hungriest. The crowd at Earl's Court last week seemed, in a way that's hard to specify, seedier than one remembered. Society is being cured of boxing as it is being cured of poverty and its supporters come to have the air of men enslaved to some lewd anti-social taste: apologetic, conscious of being near the fringe of society rather than, as in the first 40 years of the century in British industrial communities, near the heart of it. This is why Howard Winstone had been a bonus for the dying sport. He has a sensible manager, Eddie Thomas, once a British champion himself. He trains and lives simply in Merthyr. He has saved his money, having made £60,000 in the past six years, and plans to open a motel in the Brecon Beacons. More than that, he boxes in an old 'classical' style, and makes the sport look like an exercise in high skill. Against the world champion Saldivar at Earls Court he needed to fight defensively since he was less strong – this wasn't clear until about the ninth round at which point Winstone still seemed to be holding his own – but he fought that kind of fight at extraordinary speed with the footwork of a dancing master. He lent to a rough and dubious profession an athletic grace. So long as there was grace, it has been possible to enjoy boxing's hilarious rascality.

No British fighter or manager quite matches up of course, to a pair like the American middleweight of the century's first decade, Stanley Ketchel and his handler Wilson Mizner. Said Mizner of Ketchel's famous fight with Langford in 1910: 'Why, it was written like a play. We had it surge to and fro like a melodrama. First, Ketchel in dire distress, then Langford, then Ketchel, and so on. It's the old, old plot.' Ketchel disliked punching people he regarded as nice and had to be persuaded they were unpleasant. At a New York brothel he was discovered weeping in front of a picture called *Lost in the Storm*, 'showing a sheep lost in a blizzard.' Runyon wrote: 'Ketchel prejudiced the judgement of everyone who ever associated with him. They can see no other fighter'. He was murdered at the age of 24.

I wouldn't like to suggest the British boxers of one's acquaintance live lives so baroque. They have become earnest, introspective about tactics and motives; but I remember the trainer of one British champion for a week before a bout sleeping like a dog outside the champ's bedroom door to keep this boy's wife from 'draining his juices' as he put it; and another one keeping dogs at a door to stop a pugilist sneaking out, not for gin, but for icecream. Feckless, gambling wildly, gaily disrespectful of themselves and the future, pugs and their handlers were for company and great men for funerals, when they would weep unashamedly. The trick doesn't work any more. Nothing is so distasteful as a dead romance. Jesus Saucedo lies in a semi-coma at the Atkinson-Morley hospital: 'his condition is unchanged.' He may live. Boxing may not.

New Statesman, 17th September 1965

Hymns and Arias

For yet another rugby match of the century we arrive in a sunlit Paris in a novel and memorable spiritual condition. Naturally, we are familiar with, and kindly about, the glib misrepresentation of the Welsh character, about the envious barbs to do with eloquence and lechery, hypocrisy, arrogance and drink, absenteeism in the steelworks and over-industry in the media. So it may seem hard to argue to the hostile that here is a mass of patroits expensively pitching up to support the boys in an unexpected and moving state of grace, a state that may forever redefine the Welsh character.

From Aristotle to Camus shrewd thinkers have anticipated the peculiar poignancy of our present condition, although they may possibly have had political rather than sporting matters in mind.

Essentially, it is a matter of true heroism. To make a journey here as the Welsh team and their supporters have done, awash in the brilliant triumphs of a decade of elegant success, expecting defeat, brave in the face of it, must speak of a noble condition. (Yes, I know it's on the fixture list).

Aristotle was hot on the need for the fall to be a great one. The hero needed to be elevated. Who can question that? Camus, unlike Aristotle, but like the Welsh, a member of a colonial (in his case Algerian) people, more shrewdly saw the rare courage of behaving in the expectation of success, while convinced of the probability of failure.

And so, with these grave matters on my mind, strolling past the Opera House, brooding on the relationship between the Grand Opera and Welsh and French rugby and so on, who should I see emerging from their rehearsals of the new *Don Giovanni* here but three friends. Margaret Price and Stuart Burrows are true Welsh people; Kiri Kanawa wishes to be and is regarded as being honorary Welsh. Moreover, they had been harassed by orchestra and singers and stage hands about the match. They were clearly upset about it. So what does one do?

The dilemmas that confront us on these occasions are

147

serious. I had promised to drive some 15 miles out of Paris to watch our HTV rugby team play their annual match with ORTF, the French television service. Meurig Thomas had been explicit with the details of how to find the distant field; it was near a television aerial. It crossed my mind that we also would lose, and two defeats in one day is enlarging cheerful melancholy to the point of masochism. We don't usually win against ORTF, except once we had a great success when, by some administrative oversight, our team was composed of members of our audience rather than the staff.

My firm view is that the quality of the programme is in inverse proportion to the quality of the rugby, but I said it quickly and in French to the ORTF man at the party.

Shiftily, therefore, fired by this concept of the Welsh being in a state of spiritual grace, I mooched off to lunch with the great opera singers to propose a plan. There were a few jokes, since they are amusing people. My contribution was W. C. Fields's 'You should never eat lunch on an empty stomach.' Kiri thought that sounded lewd, for reasons she couldn't explain. Mr Burrows offered the thought that he had once scored two tries at Cardiff Arms Park, playing for Cilfynydd, and I'm sure there are not many Mozart tenors who can say that. Margaret had just flown in from Vienna, Kiri from Philadelphia, Stuart from the Met: jet-lag is in the interest of the journalist.

And therefore, indifferent to the arrival all over Paris of some 10,000 of one's fellow-countrymen, which is yet another index of Britain's industrial collapse, the plan was proposed. There would be this opera, set in Paris.

It would probably have to be more in the style of Verdi than Mozart, who is the marvellous specialty of my companions. The Welsh team, of course, would be the heroes, the French team the villains. Stuart Burrows would not commit himself whether he wished to sing J. P. R., Gareth, Gerald or Phil Bennett. Supporters would accompany them, I thought, after the overture; vainglorious, yet being restrained by the team from too chauvinistic a barrage.

148

The problem immediately became clear. Where was the role of woman in all this? I tried rather shyly to plant an aria which had occurred to me, which as a Shakespearean variation begins: 'An expense of spirit in a waste of shame' is still the best way of passing the time. This was not well received since it is held that Welsh rugby supporters do not behave like that.

But how would the opera end? There really could be a most complicated and charming conclusion. Consider our friends in a state of novel spiritual grace, arriving as champions, in the expectation of defeat and then winning. As far as I know the Greeks had no word for so insufferable a piece of arrogance and even the Welsh language would be hard pressed to find one. I can think of a French word for it. But, as it happened, melancholy won and we may have heard the end of a lovely song.

The Observer, Sunday 6th February 1977

Sad news about the Welsh

That Golf is not a game had always been my opinion. Having played it for the first time that remains my view. But, chancing my incorrect arm, how was I to guess that it has become a Welsh game – one, quietly like so much else in Welsh life, shattering the past and so transforming long-accepted social and perhaps political attitudes. Fellow-citizens, I tell you, strange things are happening. Where shall I start? There was irritation in the roads around the St. Pierre course at Chepstow last week when hot shots like Ballasteros, Woosnam and Langer were at play and I was held-up in traffic-jams. That was not important. More to the point was the discovery raising the subject with friends, at serious news about rugby clubs in South Wales, about which more later. A revelation also was playing a round myself.

Humankind is clearly divided into those who like hitting a

moving ball and those who like hitting a static ball. Similarly, the division makes clear, there are those who like playing a game or match against other human beings, and those who like playing a match against themselves. Most of us belong in the first category I think: golfers among the rest. I had always assumed that Welsh people, given their political history, would choose the amiably combative exercise against themselves. Obviously there would be exceptions: we can think of a few Welsh narcissists, always playing by themselves. Historically, though, Welsh sport has involved a team against a team. Our heroes and heroines have been thought of as playing for Wales, or involved in a match. Therefore when I came to my first round of golf I was firm in my view. Always, although abandoning some forms, due to the infirmities of time and mode of life, I had been a rugby, cricket, tennis, table tennis and snooker player. Only the last three are now possible, and only then through the cunning devices of experience to dismay the dashing young.

That in my golf round I should be matched with a glamorous woman is a different chance, properly equalised by her being some sort of champion. Had I been a male chauvinist kind of fellow. I would have been dismayed at her hitting the ball from the tee out of sight straight down the course. Since I am not and, indeed in other ways, stupid – no wonder some males pretend to be feminists in political fields – I spent the afternoon under instruction. It was no good. When we reached territory that demanded a seven iron and reached the green and putting was required I wasn't bad at all. She had to hit the ball for me to be near enough for a seven-iron. It was no good my trying to hit the ball as if this was cricket. The arm, you dope, has to be differently held. There is, I was told, the exercise. The fresh air is good for you. At which, I'm afraid, being accustomed to walking the country, and suffering too much fresh air at home I hired a buggy. Golf is not a game.

This, for any student of politics and literature, is a stunning piece of news. Lloyd George was determined golfer. I was even present myself at a Harold Wilson putting practice in

Downing Street. P. G. Wodehouse's work has hilarious golfing tales. Among my friends, a most applauded Welsh bard finds the game a sole means of escape-although I'm told he swears a lot while playing. A composer I'm working with wears fake Scots tartan to dismay opponents and believes golf the only route to a simple battle with nature and the elements. (His wife has just discovered a device to rescue abandoned golf balls from the lake at the Rolls course in Monmouth). Golf teaches man his imperfections, men golfers say. The women who play golf tell me it makes them feel serene. Work that out. Could be I just know some strange people, except that all people are strange.

Many aesthetic points may be raised by this confirmation of the nature of golf. More relevant than an understanding of its tortured and tormenting role as a personal struggle is the class and political revelation offered by its growing popularity in Wales. Once upon a time, I used to think, golf was what free-masons, brewers, aspiring schoolteachers, barristers, bank managers, university professors and that sort of people did. Builders, of course, and town clerks; solicitors, no doubt. But not the rest of us. Now, I'm told, there are rugby clubs in Wales where more of the members play golf than play rugby. What does this mean? I find it difficult to believe that they find the game satisfactory as a game: golf is for those who do not understand games. Can it therefore be the case that those who once enjoyed the comradeship of the team, now search for satisfaction in being solitary? There is no harm in that, except that it is different from the past. Can it be that golf is an activity that defines the bourgeois? That it carries a class memory, one not to be abjured but embraced? If so, then this really is a mark of social and political change. For myself, I'm sticking to tennis, table-tennis and snooker as long as the puff lasts, and yet find it sad that Wales should be a golf-playing nation.

Western Mail, 20th May 1987

From Side-steps
A Rugby Diary 1984-85

This proved to be the most touching and sentimental day I have known for a long, long time. Morriston, the suburb of Swansea in which I spent most of my youth, were playing Tumble, a team from the anthracite coalfield further to the west, beyond Llanelli. For Tumble it was an important match since, if they could score a try or two against Morriston, then they would be guaranteed the West Wales Division A League Championship and thus would become the best team in a hard school. They were coached by Clive and Alan John, brothers of Barry. Clive was at the match. For Morriston it was a less serious matter since, after a brief spell in the senior division, they were about to be relegated. Later in the day the celebrated Morriston Orpheus Choir (*Côr Meibion Treforus*) were giving their fiftieth anniversary concert in the Tabernacle Chapel, the cathedral of that most democratic of Welsh nonconformist sects, the Congregationalist or *Annibynwyr*. It was a big day and, for me, moving since I had both played for the Morriston club and sung in the choir. The connection between both remains as close as ever.

What a transformation, though, in the prosperity of the rugby club. When I had played as a schoolboy between 1945 and 1947 we would meet at the Prince Inn and change either at the Graig Infants School or in the Tabernacle vestry, and climb the hill to the Lan where the field had a slope of one in four. After the match we would wash in two five-foot zinc galvanised baths, the water warmed, I now gather, by a committee man who never saw the team play. I also now learn that there was a regulation of the Welsh Rugby Union and the education authorities that schoolboys were not allowed to play for the school in the morning and the local club in the afternoon. If that rule was known, I never remember it mentioned. Certainly it was never followed. I dare say nowadays the observance is more honoured than the breach.

My memories of playing for Morriston have become confused in time with those of playing for the Swansea Grammar School, which is not surprising since we had fixtures in the same towns and villages. One distinction between the two teams has a sociological importance which I gather is still relevant. Playing for the Grammar School against Ystylefera, say, or Ammanford, we could expect a rough ride because we were the Swansea Jacks, the big town slickers. At the age of fifteen I was carted off to the Amman Valley hospital with concussion because I'd been kicked in the head for coming from Swansea, only to find my attacker joining me before the end of the game, despatched thither by my friend who was the open-side wing forward. What a way to behave! Matches between our school and Gowerton School were even cancelled because of rough play. At least that was our view: theirs is that we were not worth a fixture. In turn, when we played Cardiff High School, we would treat them as city slickers. Another distinction is that the school would often win matches: Morriston seldom did.

The main reason for this is that the team was not much good but contained within that generalisation – and here fellow-players of the time may have a different recollection – there were certain habits not conducive to success. The fifteen was usually composed of young men, often schoolboys, behind the scrum and of older men, steel and tin workers and coalminers, among the forwards. Often they would come off shift to play. In that time Morriston was a centre of heavy industry, the Swansea Valley in which it lay loud and smoking with furnaces at the Upper Forest and Worcester and Dyffryn, and with many small collieries. The steel workers and colliers considered two or three pints of beer at the Prince proper preparation for a game of rugby.

Often we would play the first half of a match down the slope, when our forwards would be in fighting form, full of beer, steam and fire. The backs, myself at full-back then, would have a fine time. The second half the pack would be exhausted and our opponents would rush at us young backs and trample all over us and the game, yet again, would be lost; and those of us of a philosophic nature would reflect that there was one of life's lessons to be learned here if only we could put our finger on it.

Therefore, when I drove along Chemical Road to meet David Jones, the club secretary, at a ground new to me, the buds of the past were already in flower. I arrived at a large club house as the Tumble team bus drew up. There were proper dressing rooms. There were three playing fields. How different, I said to David Jones, from the days when we played among the cowpats on the hillside. Here was flat ground on the bed of the valley. He pointed out that, in fact, there had been an unfortunate accident. One of the playing pitches was not in use that day since subsidence from an old colliery had created a hole in the ground. Just as well no one was playing at the time, we agreed.

The Morriston club house is perhaps unusual in that a large window overlooks the first team pitch. The window is in the bar. The bar is by some local regulation allowed to be open during the hour and a half the match is played. This enables spectators to keep out of the weather if, as this day, the rain is heavy. Before the match began we had time to consider the unusual history of the club which gives it a rare distinction in Wales: its fortunes match industrial change.

In the season 1893/94 Morriston played Cardiff, Llanelli, Swansea, Neath, Aberavon, London Welsh, Treorky (*sic*) and took a winter tour to Devonport Albion and Torquay Athletic. It was one of the best of first-class clubs, winning most of its matches. This was because it was one of the main industrial centres in Britain, its coal, copper and other metallurgical industries being made more productive by imported German processes. After the first world war a decline began, matched in the fortunes of the club, and local boys went to play for Swansea instead: there were five Morriston men in the Swansea side which beat the New Zealand All Blacks in 1935. The nadir was reached in the years in which I played. But recovery was soon to come.

The revival was pioneered by a handful of enthusiasts like Robert Gwynne and Leighton Davies. A Treasurer was appointed to rescue the accounting from the backs of envelopes, and an interest-free loan of £750 from the WRU purchased the new ground, on which the match with Tumble had just begun. The pattern was clear: Morriston were spoiling around the scrum, Tumble were trying to move the ball among faster backs. The Morriston tactics, as we watched through the huge bar window, looked effective. I gathered, as we chatted, that the club's turnover every year was £100,000, mostly through the bar. £1,400 was spent annually on players' insurance. A set of jerseys costs £300. The club officials compared their experience with a club like Swansea Uplands on the more salubrious side of town. Morriston was a working-class club; the Uplands middle-class. Lately the latter had held a champagne party and raised £2,000, just like that. Here on the east side it was not so easy. Laundry was more than a £100 a month, did I know?

Paying a little more attention to the play, we saw tumble score two penalty goals and then after half time score two more. They could not, though, for all their side-stepping, barging, variation of tactics, escape the tackling of the Morriston back row and centre three-quarters. That try they so much wanted to score could not be scored, and as their committee men came from the field into the bar, they were anxious to know how their rivals for the Championship, Ystradgynlais, had done. We didn't know, but one of the Morriston men offered to try and find out. He made a phone call and brought the bad news: Ystradgynlais had scored two tries. Therefore in their next match Tumble really had to score a few. [They were to, and won the title.]

Before the players came into the club house for their sausage and chips, a subject was raised almost in passing, which delighted me, although it should not have surprised me. Morriston Rugby Club have a choir good enough to join that London Welsh extravaganza at the Royal Albert Hall of one thousand Welsh voices. They would be singing there once more in 1986. And did I know that the Chairman of the Orpheus Choir the previous year had been a former Morriston player, Geoffrey Richards?

As the players arrived a dramatic and encouraging event occurred. The club steward announced that he had just heard that Cardiff had beaten Pontypool 24–3 in the semi-final of the Welsh Cup. Everyone cheered. This acclamation demands analysis. Normally in any part of West Wales any triumph by Cardiff is bad news. Nobody west of Bridgend cares for Cardiff. Therefore when a Cardiff victory is applauded in a Morriston club house, the significance transcends parochialism in a manner difficult for the stranger to comprehend. Here were anti-Cardiff citizens, football players, hard men some of them, some dancers, joined in a judgement about the nature of rugby football. They disliked Pontypool rugby *so* much that they would prefer Cardiff to win. Their instinctive delight at Pontypool's defeat was therefore an aesthetic statement about the nature of the game they played. They were the artists as critic.

Barry John earlier in the season had said that he regrded the morose, remorseless play of the Pontypool side as a 'cancer' in Welsh rugby. His brother Clive, the Tumble coach, who was with us, concurred. There is, as ever, an irony here, since in popular understanding West Wales rugby is as rough as it comes: that understanding is incomplete. Within the toughness of West Wales, whether in Seven Sisters, Tumble, Morriston, Kidwelly, Cefneithin, Llandovery, Gowerton, or wherever, there is an instinctive understanding of the balance of the game. Whatever may be necessary among the forwards must not inhibit the skill of half-back or three-quarter. If there has to be darkness, then equally there has to be light; a harmony that is a part of nature, as we all know, and therefore part of rugby. In this analysis, Pontypool is all darkness; and that cannot be right: and how can it be fun?

We resumed our conversation about the rugby club choir. A remarkable parallel emerged between the problems of men playing rugby for Wales and those singing in the Orpheus

Choir whose concert I was about to go and hear. The choir like the Welsh team is amateur; the men are in work and have families. But between now and September they are singing in London, in Brittany, at Chartres, making a television programme, going to Poole, then Chichester and Birmingham. Their rehearsals are as demanding as squad training. It takes a great deal of time and work. And so good singers sometimes opt out of the Orpheus and prefer to sing with the rugby club choir. Among the rugby club choir seventy per cent were Welsh-speaking, as in my childhood in Morriston: among the rugby players only twenty per cent.

I discovered that the present Chairman of the Orpheus Choir was Huw Madoc-Jones, a fellow-member of the RAF Officers Training Corps course at Spitalgate in Lincolnshire early in 1950. If you can manage to live long enough the circles of experience do grow small. I was thus enabled to offer the curious tale of how I came to play rugby with International players. Being no good at firing rifles or Bren guns or flying aeroplanes I realised that the only way I could win a commission was by serious thought. My first step was to seize the editorship of the course magazine and write a flattering portrait – indeed deserved – of the course commander. Within the rugby team there was a severe dispute between two Scottish Internationals and three Welsh players as to who should captain the team. I was proposed as a compromise. Since we played teams who had no players of a comparable standard, we always won. As Captain I was given the credit: I also kicked the goals. I did little else at outside-half but give the Dalgleishes the ball. Therefore, I recounted, I became an officer in the RAF. Later this evening Hugh Madoc-Jones thought my account may have some truth in it.

At which some of us set off for Tabernacle with its grand spire and Welsh baroque interior. When young I used to find it not at all confusing that on a Saturday afternoon we would change in the vestry to go and play up the hill and then spend the evening in the chapel with the Orpheus Choir listening perhaps to Kathleen Ferrier and Heddle Nash sing like angels.

I was wearing now the Morriston Rugby Club tie with which I had been presented. It bears the emblems of the town's Castle Graig and St John's Church which, in the days I went there with my mother, conducted its services in Welsh. It was now that the day truly became awash in sentiment in a style that may be foreign to rugby clubs elsewhere but is not peculiar in Wales.

When the concert began and I saw in the Orpheus Choir members of the rugby club, that direct and untroubled connection in a Welsh society acquired a strength that was memorable. My mother had been a friend of the first conductor of the Morriston Orpheus, Ivor Sims, who had made it in the 'forties one of the world's great choirs. I dare say that was one reason why I was permitted to be a second tenor in its still-celebrated recording of 'Y Delyn Aur' and 'Myfanwy'. that was in 1947. The choir had sung at my grandfather's funeral.

The soloists this evening were Dennis O'Neill, who came back for the occasion from the Metropolitan Opera in New York and another local star, Eiddwyn Harry. Both, as did the choir, sang their hearts out. We applauded until we almost broke our wrists and were not at all embarrassed by our tear. I doubt if there were many in the audience unmoved by the knowledge that a choir begun by Ivor Sims half a century before should be still so eloquent in its harmonies and sophisticated in its techniques. that the rugby club should have been so transformed in the meantime may not have been on their minds that dazzling evening: it was on mine.

23-31st March 1985

IV

MISCELLANY

A Parish Pump
in a Dry Dock

Arrivals and departures at the Heaven include Viking and Irish pirates, kings, men about to be kings and Roundheads. Milford was founded in the 18th century by American Quakers needing a whaling base. The Quakers stayed and built a town notably symmetrical in design. Latterly smaller fish have been caught and the town is now the fourth in importance of the British fishing ports. There is a scheme in hand to make the town important in other ways, to capitalise on one of the world's most magnificent natural harbours, which, except in time of war, has been most oddly neglected.

The scheme which was announced in January by the new directors of the Milford Dock Company — when they took over after the shares had risen sharply — is simple. It involves building into the Haven three docks, 800 ft by 320 ft, one of them dry, capable of accommodating ships of up to 45,000 tons. The docks will be built in the style of the Mulberry Harbour and will cost two million pounds. There are other minor improvements already being carried out within the docks but this is the most important scheme. Its aim is equally simple. The Directors have recognised that the new trend in the oil trade is to build tankers of high tonnage, often of 45,000 tons. There are no docks available in this country for servicing and overhauling these tankers — for these services they have to go to Holland or Japan. They also recognise that the size of these ships presents problems of unloading to other ports in the United Kingdom. They hope, in fact, that the tankers will come to Milford for repairs and, once they are in the habit of doing so, that they will unload there as well. The oil can then be pumped by overland pipe-line to refineries in the United Kingdom.

There are advantages peculiar to Milford which help the scheme. The Milford Dock Company has the unusual right to the water of the Haven to the five-fathom line, a statutory right granted in the 19th century. To consolidate this right the Company is introducing a Bill into Parliament this session. Building out to sea is cheaper than building inland, so that all in all it looks like an extremely enterprising move. It also looks liek a scheme one would think the inhabitants of the town and the County of Pembrokeshire would rejoice at. But such isn't the case at all.

Disquiet has many sources in the town. There is the instinctive disbelief of the small man in the presence of big schemes — a healthy enough reaction. Here the disbelief is conditioned by a history of failure in the Pembrokeshire ports. Once upon a time Fishguard was to be the main Atlantic port; railway lines were laid direct from London; a great hotel was built. But the sea was too rough for passengers to disembark from liners, so the great ships went elsewhere. The hotel stood empty and neglected until it had a glorious if eccentric hour when John Huston's 'Moby Dick' company took it over this summer. There is the fear of the trawlermen, which reassurances won't dissipate, that the Dock Company — the landlord — will concentrate on the new enterprises at the expense of the fishing fleet. The fishing industry is in a condition bad enough to make this extra worry assume exaggerated proportions. There is a suspicion among people who care about matters of that kind that the Dock Company is becoming too paternalistic, is too much the Commanding Officer. The ogres of Company shops, Company engineeering works, the Company newspaper, the Company town are being bruited about by articulate Jonahs. The Company's Resident Director, Lt. General Durnford, is not exactly loved in the district. He is a dynamic and resourceful character with, for some people, too strong residual army traits — not a popular image in a country where the Service Departments occupy a great deal of territory, much of it of remarkable beauty.

Criticism of the Company is most lucidly articulated in the Haverfordwest *Western Telegraph and Cymric Times*. But before going into the complexities of a provincial newspaper controversy it is important to realise how strikingly devoted the people of Pembrokeshire are to their local Press. The population of the county is 90,000. Normally one could assume that this indicated some thirty thousand householders. But Pembrokeshire has an unusually high proportion of young people who, one may assume, are not taken up with parochial affairs. Shall we say these are 5,000 households? Assuming this we must bear in mind that there are a great many Service families in the county who, again are not likely to be held to the fireside by the pressure of local information. Twenty-five thousand household then. But the *Western Telegraph* alone sells 20,000 copies. Its close rival the *West Wales Guardian* — also circulating throughout the county — sells some 13,000. There are three other weekly newspapers, one in Narbeth, another in Fishguard and, which is important to the narrative, one in Milford. These three have purely local sales, but jointly their circulation amounts to over 10,000. Over 43,000 local newspapers to 25,000 households is a state of affairs revealing intense interest. There is a factor which partly explains the situation: the principal newspapers publish on different days of the week. It remains, though, a remarkable testimony to the strength of the society, all the more since the newspapers are seriously concerned with local affairs, report at length, and comment in the proper place with intelligence and vigour.

The main contest is between the heavyweight *Telegraph* (price 4d, circulation 20,000) and the flyweight *Dyfed News* (price 3d, circulation 1,600). The *Telegraph* is critical of the Dock Company; the *Dyfed News* is owned by the Dock Company and was founded as recently as August this year. This *Telegraph* came out at the bell on September 30 with a leading article entitled 'Flotsam on an Ebb Tide?' 'What are the real prospects,' it asked, 'of the much-heralded schemes of Milford Haven as a tanker base?' It alleged that 'from the first it was apparent that the flow of capital to support such an undertaking was extremely slow and not at the rate to promote the idea that there was unreserved confidence in the success of the venture.' It went on to quote the annual report of Bailey's, the Newport ship-builders, which contained the argument 'Prospects in the ship-repairing industry are less bright than a year ago.'

This was a shrewd blow because Bailey's have recently entered into an agreement with the Milford Dock Company and are, indeed, the managers of the Company's subsidiary, the Milford Dry Dock Company. The *Dyfed News* counter-punched at this and quoted at length Mr. H. A. J. Silley, President of the Institute of Marine Engineers, who maintained that the country greatly needed dry docks. *Touché*. Or, if you like, a left to the stomach after blocking the left lead – or partly blocking it, anyway.

The *Telegraph* followed up with an unsigned verse in which a reference was made to the General and his *Dyfed News*: the General, while hoping to be a 'press baron,' had simply created a 'barren press'. The *Dyfed News* came back with an anonymous poem of its own:

> The General has Milford at heart
> Has no wish to tear it apart.
> Some mistake his intentions
> His many inventions
> And wish he would quickly depart.

The poem goes on to ask for fair play and finishes up with the confidence that the General will laugh longest because he will laugh last.

Ideally, in these controversies, it seems to me, more points (as in boxing) should be awarded for good blows landed in attack than for those in defence. But the situation is not ideal because the editor of *Dyfed News* doesn't want to be in the ring at all. He believes — he is a war-time R.A.F. Group Captain and former test-pilot — if not in exactly turning the other cheek, at least in closing one's eyes, at times. He has, though, the edge on the editor of the *Telegraph* because he *knows* what is going on while his opponent has to torment himself and his readers with deductions from crumbs.

When I was in Milford events took an unexpected turn; the attack opened up on another front. It was the question of land, its sale or compulsory appropriation, than which there is nothing more stimulating these days to a newspaper editor. Let's call it the 'Point Street Affair.'

Alongside the existing dock wall in Milford is a street of old houses officially classed as slum dwellings. This is Point Street. I rode along it with the editor of the *Dyfed News* when he was taking me, in a fine Atlantic drizzle, to view the sea where the docks would be sunk. The houses did not look desirable. At the end of the street, some twenty yards from the dock gates, was a tobacconist's which depended for its custom on dock workers. The Urban District Council wanted to buy all Point Street. The tobacconist did not want to sell. And here one meets another of the Company's minor schemes which has soured local opinion. One of its subsidiaries has acquired a local cafeteria and established it within the docks. It is a cosy café, brightly painted; above the counter is the Company flag, dark blue for the Navy (one of the directors is a Commander), red for the Army (Lt. General Durnford) and light blue for the R.A.F. (yes, another senior officer). Its presence is severe competition for the small trader at the gate who did not want to sell his shop.

His central role in the Point Street Affair was clear. Certain elements in the county would not have been unhappy if the drama could have reached a second act, if not a dénouement; if the U.D.C. had been forced to purchase compulsorily. But the tobacconist was offered a good price and an alternative site around the corner. He sold. The U.D.C. offered the land to the Dock Company. The offer was accepted.

The following day the *Telegraph* made this comment:

165

The voluntary sale of the property removes what might have been an interesting constitutional point. Could the Council, had they acquired the property by compulsory means have passed it on to a previously selected private undertaking without offering it to others who might have been interested. This action of the Council in committing themselves to a sale to the Dock Company smacks of privilege and undue preference.

Hard words. Five days later the *Dyfed News* came back with the headline: 'Work On New Dock To Begin Next Year.' The acquisition of Point Street by the Company, it said, was the beginning of the scheme. It only remained now for the formalities to be gone through — Act of Parliament, issue of contracts, etc. — and Milford Haven would gain its heritage. And where was the money coming from? The *Dyfed News* answered the *Telegraph* with the words the General used to me: 'It is not the liability of the Board of Directors of a Limited Company to make public announcements concerning the Company's financial policies, and no statement can be anticipated.'

The gulls squabble over the fishing boats, the fish trains pull out for the markets; in the brilliant blue of the Haven a white ship is immaculate in the sun. Everyone is waiting for June, 1955 and the concrete to be lowered into the sea, waiting with infinite variations of confidence, with a hope that will allow itself to appear for fear for a smack in the eye.

The New Statesman and Nation, November 13, 1954

Evans, Thomas and Lewis

Belonging to a small country which one can't be sure is a nation may, as recent contributions to THE TWENTIETH CENTURY show, create private torment. How much more complicated it all becomes when one can't even be sure one belongs to the country at all, a situation in which the Welshman with no knowledge or a forgotten knowlege of the Welsh language may painfully find himself. Obviously, on one level anyone who cares to do so may call himself Welsh, and leave it at that. A lot of people do this though it is often difficult to discover where their Welshness lies. Sometimes, 'Oh, but I'm Welsh, you see' is used as an excuse for an otherwise insupportable argument or otherwise unjustifiable poem or symphony, a permissible romantic gesture. This kind of Welshman is never troubled about the value of his claim to nationality. He thinks he is Welsh, therefore he is Welsh. In this way the Scot seems to have a happier time of it. The historical fact of their country's more recent unifying with England permits him a sense of an independent national history a Welshman needs to search for into an alien medievalism. He only needs to think he is Scottish to be Scottish. He hasn't around him a large body of people speaking the national language, enjoying a culture and literature utterly distinct from the English even down to the letters of the alphabet.

The general linguistic and cultural position in Wales nowadays is widely misunderstood outside – where anything is known. I have met English people who believe no one speaks Welsh. In Ireland recently everyone I spoke to about this believed that everybody in Wales spoke Welsh. In fact, rather

167

less than a third of the people in Wales speak their national language and there are only 44,000 monoglot Welsh. Bilingual Welsh people are under continual pressure to speak their Welsh less and less; the places where the monoglot Welsh live suffer depopulation for economic reasons and increasingly meet English influence in their business life. Welsh publishers, those that remain, find their markets contracting and writers hard to come by, especially good writers. Last year two novels were published in the Welsh language and while a volume of verse will sell 1,000 copies – which compares strikingly with sales of English verse remembering that the Welsh-reading public is one-fiftieth of the English – the sales are mostly to ministers of religion whose wages won't permit this kind of patronage much longer. All in all the situation is the familiar one of the distinctive culture swamped by the vast, oceanic English language and its attendant mass-values.

If then, the language situation is deteriorating so rapidly why should it raise doubts about nationality? Of course, the man who is born in Welsh Wales, which is most of the North and West, hasn't any of these doubts; they are the preserve of the man born in the industrial South, in the anglicized towns along the coast and up-valley, the man whose parents are, perhaps, Welsh-speaking, but who, himself, for social, economic, even 'cultural' reasons, has not been taught the language or has permitted his knowledge to die. The man who has been brought up in Welsh Wales will always be conscious of his nationality. Should he leave his home district as so often, if ambitious, he must, he will carry it with him like a torch, with a missionary zeal. Finding himself in the industrial south he will with the Welsh politeness sometimes mistaken for servility, speak English when addressed in English, thinking how nice it would be if the English would take the trouble to learn Welsh when in Wales, but recognizing the impossibility of such a revolution in manners. It is the presence of these men from Welsh Wales in the anglicized towns, with their Eisteddfodau, their literature, their chapels, their B.B.C. programmes, that stimulates the doubts of the 'Anglo-Welsh', as the phrase goes or, rather, *some* of the 'Anglo-Welsh'. There are others among these 'Anglo-Welsh' who, for various reasons, detest the 'Welsh-Welsh', and who claim to be just as Welsh as them.

Outside Wales these distinctions in kind of Welshman are little known, mainly because the portrait of the Welshman presented, especially in England, has been drawn by people writing for an English audience. Welsh literature, that is, verse and prose written in Welsh, about Wales, is rarely translated. More popular is 'Anglo-Welsh' writing, at present represented ideally by Dylan Thomas and his *Under Milk Wood*. This, for many people, is Wales. This is how the Welsh behave. I don't know if these people ever wonder if life *Under Milk Wood* is conducted in the Welsh language. In fact it might well be. There are many small seaside villages in Wales where the natives speak Welsh to each other and English only to visitors like Dylan Thomas, who cannot speak Welsh. In such villages, as in most small, seaside villages anywhere, there would certainly be the old man with nothing to do but sit around, dream and observe, the drunkard, the loose woman, the houseproud, the husband who hates his wife, the husband who loves his wife, the postman who knows everybody's business, children with singing-games, the lovers, the lechers and the gossips, so that, as far as it goes, *Under Mild Wood* is accurate. In some ways it even reveals the nature of the 'Anglo-Welshman', the man with some acquaintance of the Welsh culture, brought up speaking English only; here is the peculiar fluency, the loving eye for the eccentric, the fantastic, the whimsical which one finds at the fringe of the Welsh culture, on the borders between it and the English. And it would be absurd to criticize Dylan Thomas and *Under Milk Wood* because its view of the life of the village is not a Welsh view. Why should it be? Perhaps it would have been a more revealing portrait if as well as being richly comic it possessed dramatic action or if the compassion were not a little too indiscriminate. But these again are not exactly anthropological inexactitudes.

169

The reaction to *Under Milk Wood* in Wales is a rough guide to its value as a portrait. There was no public outcry. No *parchs* protested, no councillors attacked the B.B.C. This was probably because Dylan Thomas does not seem to have been concerned with the Welshness of his characters, only their humours. Most of the things Welsh in it, while they may be new to the English, have been heard very often before, have come straight out of stock. It gives no secrets away either because Thomas knew no secrets or, if he knew, wasn't interested in them. His few public utterances about Wales indicate tha he wasn't particularly interested either in the language or nationalism. Not for him the cultural roots the Nationalist Party or the Ministry of Education (Welsh Office) has to offer and which a number of intellectuals in Wales are burying themselves with these days. He didn't have a lot of time for questions like: The predicament of small cultures; what price survival? Some nationalists find it difficult to forgive him. To quote a nationalist poet: 'He wasn't Welsh.'

Evans, writing about West Wales, was having his say in a family quarrel; Thomas was reporting for the English-speaking world. Evans's concern was a moral concern; Thomas had no fixed base. Neither of them was in any doubt about their nationality or language, although they stood at the extreme of certainties. It is in between the doubters stand, the people with memories of Evans's world, but with the habit of looking at things as Thomas looked at them – to place both writers in positions they don't exactly occupy. People who can speak a little Welsh and don't know whether they should, out of a sense of social duty, brush up on it; whether they should more closely identify themselves with the Welsh 'way of life'; or whether it all matters anyway. I am dealing with these people because it seems to me that the various schemes, officially through the schools, unofficially through small, voluntary organizations, designed to teach Welsh depend on the sympathetic 'Anglo-Welshman' for their success; and because I come more or less in this category myself.

To the firm in faith the twinges of doubt, the nagging conscience, the disquieting guilt seem contemptible. If one is Welsh one should speak Welsh *or* if one doesn't speak Welsh then learning it is a pointless, even at best sentimental gesture. The arguments against bothering to improve one's Welsh or even learn the language are complex and confused. There is the hostility against what is thought to be the Establishment, a sinister hierarchy of Nonconformist ministers, civil servants – especially those at the Ministry of Education – B.B.C. producers and executives, Welsh departments at the university, all of whom are supposed to be united in a society of mutual advancement, plotting all the time for the establishment of a Welsh state and the universal teaching of Welsh. Conversation with Nationalists would disabuse people of this notion; they would be only too grateful for such an Establishment. There is the hostility against the Welsh in its identification with the morality of the Nonconformist chapel, against Caradog Evans's Wales. A minister of religion said a hundred years ago: 'The Welsh language is a bulwark against the corruption of our faith and a barrier against the inroads of vice, immorality and crime.' Very often, in the public mind, vice, immorality and crime mean Sunday cinemas, Sunday drinking and other pleasures and amenities. When the chapels oppose these things it isn't difficult to identify their position with the Welsh language and culture. The National Eisteddfod becomes identified with the dictatorship of the old morality. Isn't it dominated, in its administrators and its bards, by Nonconformist ministers? The decline of religion relates to the decline of the language. (Also, of course, contemporary means of entertainment, mass-circulation newspapers, radio, the cinema, television have relieved the chapel of one of its vital functions. The recreations in vestry and schoolroom are no longer necessary.)

The realists question the value of teaching Welsh to children. What's done is done and cannot be undone. Why put back the clock? Or, less intolerantly, what purpose will it serve? How will Welsh be any different from French as a second language? Hasn't bi-lingualism neuroses all its own? How can anyone hope to resist the English monolith? And while it may be very pleasant to introduce children to Welsh literature, how many are going to care about this?

These arguments seem to the Welsh-speaking man to dodge the issue: This is Wales, a nation with a living tongue; the language must be kept alive by all means. It is time Wales asserted herself, became more than a proving ground for War Office weapons, a place where reservoirs and power plants may conveniently be built to leave the English coutry-side undisturbed. (It by no means follows that a Welsh-speaking man is a political Nationalist. There are many who would leave Wales like bullets from a gun if Nationalism triumphed.) The apparent inexorability of the final English triumph must be tested all along the line. Without her language Wales will become indistinguishable from England and European civilization would suffer. England, especially, would be impoverished. There is, too, the argument that small cultures are vital; that a man needs a firm sense of nationality, needs roots for the richest development of personality.

It is the intricate relationship of the Welsh language with religion which can so disturb the Welshman in No Man's Land. Neglecting his language is like neglecting his religious faith and the two neglects may coalesce so that it becomes easy if absurd to confuse them. Embracing the language again often means embracing the traditional life associated with it. It may be argued that so self-conscious a gesture must be a little suspect, but it has been made and in two directions because there are two traditional Welsh 'ways of life', one Nonconformist, one Catholic. A number of distinguished young Welshmen have 'gone over', as it were, to Nonconformity and the Welsh language, the most notable being Mr Emyr Humphreys. There are others who have followed the example of Mr Saunders Lewis, the most eminent Welsh poet, playwright and critic and become Catholic converts.

Mr Lewis is a writer almost unknown in England because he has written in Welsh. In most of his plays he recreates the pre-Reformation Wales; his criticism and political polemics are designed to restore in Wales a knowledge of the true nature of the national spirit. It doesn't follow that everyone who enjoys the superb Welsh literature of the thirteenth and fourteenth centuries would like to see the economic circumstances which surrounded their writing repeated. What is common is a desire to recreate the rural communities which have been the ground out of which Welsh literature and culture has grown. For many people this a matter of returning to where they were born. For others it is a matter of starting all over again. In both cases it means turning one's back on urbanism.

This movement has scarcely begun, is hardly more than an idea. Its attractions are obvious to a kind of intellectual. Unfortunately for the Welsh language, the country children are still moving away from home, into the towns of South Wales and into England, and many will be unable to return. The number of people who feel the need to return to the country will never quite replace them; and, many who would like to return will be unable to; and many who would half-like to will never make up their minds.

All this bother may seem to be unnecessary. Perhaps the simple and honest solution, once the question arises in the mind, is to learn as much Welsh as possible, speak it when-ever the chance presents itself and leave it at that. The gesture has been made. One's nationality is firmly established. The trouble is that once that step is taken, that decision made, one becomes involved in other aspects of national expression. Language can become a cause. What begins as: 'It's a pity the language is dying out. I must do something about it,' continues as: 'It's time something was done about the language dying out. We must fight this

English culture.' But it's too late for the 'Anglo-Welshman' to do that. The English culture has mostly made him and continues to be his primary interest. He is member of a very small lost battalion. His guilt, his involuntary act of treason don't measure up to much perhaps. In their way, though, they exemplify the unpleasantness of being trapped between cultures.

The Twentieth Century, October 1956

Tinplate Valley

From time to time I go along to one of the villages in West Wales or to a town such as Llanelli (*Tinopolis*) and watch men demolish a tinplate works. These works always stand on a river bank, looking like big, black sheds. Often there are fields or green hills across the river.

Also watching the stacks falling will be men who have worked there a lifetime and who, until a few weeks before, were practising the exhausting, dangerous and, for the observer, dramatic skills which the old-fashioned 'pack-mill' method of making tinplate demanded for over 200 years.

Their skill is no longer wanted; more efficient and economic methods of production have made it unnecessary. And an authoritative study*, just published, makes it clear that in all economic reason these works should have disappeared long ago. Tinplate (or *fer blanc* or *Weissblech*, where it began) has an absorbing history, partly because towards the end of the nineteenth century its manufacture became permanently and hugely concentrated in South Wales: even, to localise, West Wales. There it fell into the hands of Welshmen, who fashioned it after their own nature. Mr. Minchinton is clearly impatient with the manner in which they developed or failed to develop this important industry.

In boom-time all was well. As the American market

expanded in the nineteenth century – until the black year of 1891, when the McKinley Tariff kept out British plate – works sprang up all over West Wales. Villages were built around them. Welshmen came down from the hills and made tinplate in much the same spirit as they gathered the harvest, and sometimes just as seasonally. Groups of local men subscribed a few pounds each to a new factory: a Pontardulais company formed in 1883 had nineteen shareholders, among them 'seven grocers, two builders, a gentleman and a hotel proprietor.'

Owners and workmen were sometimes brothers in fact. Not that labour troubles didn't consequently exist; apart from arguments over wages, there were some men who weren't altogether satisfied when a seigneurial hamper arrived to compensate for a lost eye or leg.

Joint consultation and welfare schemes arrived early, but even in the time of boom two sinister characteristics marked the owners: they were suspicious of their local rivals and they were not especially interested in money. Their empire was the parish. They were interested in power, but only over their own village.

Megalomanes occurred, writing about themselves as if they were Carnegie, collecting their private papers devotedly and willing them to libraries where they gather dust. But there was no Welsh Carnegie. Wasn't the Bible against the making of large fortunes? When the slump came, and especially after the First World War, these characteristics were to have serious consequences. The Americans, for whom emigrant Welshmen had built an efficient tinplate industry, learned the virtue of combination: they experimented, they scrapped old methods and old works; in the twenties they built strip-mills and cold reduction plants. In Wales, writes Mr. Minchinton, 'the existence of a large number of small, mutually suspicious firms was the barrier to improvement.' Owners and union leaders and workmen resisted attempts at modernisation until there was no choice.

This resistance it is easy to represent as folly; but it is very endearing not to want to change something one knows and likes. The men who have left the old works for the new grieve over the old. Conditions and pay are better: what they miss is friendliness and humanity. Mr. Minchinton, whose history is economic rather than social, has covered the ground admirably. His book appears at an appropriate time both because the old-fashioned works are now vanishing and because, in South Wales, the politicians are once again becoming active at the news of a new plant's coming. As ever, the sociological claims of the villages in the west are being urged over the economic advantages of the east. Economics and the tinplate industry never got on well together.

The British Tinplate Industry: A History. By Walter Minchinton. Oxford University Press. 35s.

The Observer, 1957

Off to the Smoke

We threw the last darts, this summer, and went out of the old drovers' pub at Llangadog and shook hands all round. Pity was regarded as the proper emotion. Naturally there were other sentiments expressed, like good luck, but not with much force, country people being great realists and recognising that no amount of luck could make a move to London anything but a severe blow. I felt sorry for myself with everyone feeling so sorry for me. 'It is a far worse life that you go to, boy, than you have ever known,' said one joker. 'Dickens' said his friend.

We lay in the back of the open car and considered the moon on the drive back to Swansea over the Black Mountain. At the summit we stood and looked back over Carmarthenshire and its thousand small fields, and then ahead over the coalfield and towards the sea and breathed the sweetest air there is and drove on through the mining villages singing old Welsh songs.

On the day we drove away from Swansea for the last time – now persuaded that we were travelling to a remote jungle in which few survived, not just a city 190 miles up the road – a friend, a one-time European boxing champion, stopped us and took it upon himself to tell us that when economic disaster had forced him to work in London, he used to go home every month and needed to get blind drunk every time he got on the train for Paddington, otherwise he would never get on it. We offered our thanks for this cheerful message. Not at all, he said, shaking his head sadly. If he'd been a religious sort of man, no doubt he'd have crossed himself.

It is necessary to understand, for all this not to seem incomprehensibly maudlin, that people born in Swansea which, on the face of it, is just an average-sized town of mixed industry, a port for a coalfield with a polluted river, with monstrous slag heaps and ruined factories in its shallow valley, with sandy beaches, a rocky coastline – that they make a cult of the place. Even in Wales where most people made a cult of their birthplace, 'Swansea boys' irritate others to distraction by their romantic attitudes to the town. When the time comes for anyone to pack his traps and move away there's a sense of bereavement – his not the town's. Edward Thomas noted this half a century ago and remarked that Swansea was like a village with a population of a 100,000.

In Swansea we lived in a house with a view of the bay, which reaches for 20 miles in the shape of a horseshoe. W. S. Landor – it is this kind of thing which irritates people unbearably – compared it with the Bay of Naples. To the west we could see Gower and, at the right time of day, remarkable sunsets; to the south was the town on a narrow strip of a land between the hill and the sea. To the east was the docks, the ships anchored among the derricks, the start of the industrial side where I used to live and which, with its belching chimneys and wasteland, was as impressive as the other view. Short of the Summer Isles from Achiltibuie, or the Maam Turk mountains, or set-pieces like Snowdonia from across the Menai, it always seemed to me a remarkable spectacle this bay. But, of course, this image at the doorstep wasn't the half of it: the attachment is to the football ground, the pubs in the dock, the town, Gower, that you lived with the people you'd been born among, who were never short of something to say. In the evening the only sounds we could hear were ship's hooters or owls in the park.

The flat I live in now trembles when the underground trains roar by; traffic changes gear in the street below: dirt gathers on the windows. The view again is certainly remarkable. To the north, I take it, is Hampstead: those rolling hills to the south are, or so I'm told, the Sussex downs. To the east lies the great metropolis, and on the horizon St Paul's Cathedral and the Houses of Parliament. Jet planes roar directly over our heads, to New York, I suppose, or Rio or some other glittering capital city.

But because I don't like the taste of smog in my mouth while I'm being crushed by the battling mob on the tube, I wouldn't like to be thought of as denying the metropolitan dream. I'm sure it is here in a city still firmly on the Paris-New York-Moscow axis that great wits flash after dark, that glittering prizes are won and lost and lovely women stoop most often to folly. Young men and women, no doubt, still stride with the seven-league boots of ambition past the historic stones and along the streets that famous men have trod, now and again being jostled off the pavement or fending umbrellas out of their faces. I wouldn't like to be thought of as impervious to the charms of the Thames at dusk, except when the grit is blowing the wrong way from the power staion, or the trees in autumn. In fact, I have trees outside my office window and barristers walking about dressed in a very traditional mode, and I can see church spires.

But think, I had cried, excusing my departure, of the concerts I can go to, the operas I can hear, even, if things get very dull, the plays to be seen. I was granted a point there, except that I was to think of the money you need to live in London, of how unfriendly the people are, not like us. Consider too how far you have to travel to a rugby match, not that there's any point in going to an English match, the play being so poor and gentlemanly. You need to wash more often

178

in London, too. And think of the snare of falling into London habits of thinking – the intelligence and motives of metropolitan critics of anything being held in very low regard outside the metropolis. I will think, I said. I will watch that washing business with close care. And so I stand, dusting the smog from the window, and look out over the great city and the brilliant lights and think of the momentous events that march here, gently brainwashing myself, and think of the concerts, of the heart of empire, of the million houses across the wen and bear in mind the times of the trains from Paddington.

New Statesman, 28th November 1959

Dark Deeds at Ebbw Vale

At the Richard Thomas and Baldwins steelworks here they have a pilot furnace in which the new LD process for infusing oxygen into a steel charge is being tried. The object is to produce as much steel in an hour as would normally take ten, but at present its main public effect is periodically to envelop the lower end of the town in a huge cloud of orange smoke. People you are talking to suddenly vanish.

Out of this orange mist their voices complete sentences like: 'In the dictionary it says carpet-baggers come from the north. But here they come from the east and the bloody west as well'. But even this comes to seem a relatively commonplace experience in the struggle to find a successor to Aneurin Bevan as Labour MP for the towns of Ebbw Vale, Tredegar and Rhymney. 'If it wasn't so serious', one of the candidates put it to me, exaggerating out of the bitterness of his feeling, 'this would be the wildest farce in the history of Welsh politics'.

Aneurin Bevan's dominance of the constituency for the past 30 years is partly responsible for the present chaos. 'We have been in a political deep-freeze, and now we are boiling all over the place', as one potential voter said. But it would be a mistake to think that the cloak-and-dagger techniques, which have preserved excellently in the deep-freeze, possess, like farce, only an internal logic. Rumours may be spread that a certain candidate likes his glass. Grubby notes may be intercepted and plots uncovered and scotched by swift telephone calls. Certain candidates may roam the streets in search of key votes like teachers in search of a headship (an old Welsh custom). There may even be some truth in the generally-held view that the first short-list (which excluded Michael Foot and the miners' Alderman Whatley) was composed as it was because some women on the local executive were flattered at being spoken to nicely by some of the candidates. But the cloaks and daggers aren't worn for their own sakes. Each candidate more or less represents arguments capable of respectable recitation.

Thus Michael Foot, as well as being the nominee, presumably for political reasons, of branches of the steelmen, the Transport and General Workers Union and the Trades Council, represents certain non-political arguments. Ebbw Vale, says one group, wants a famous man again, so that when Ebbw Vale people find themselves in other parts of Britain, people will know about them because their MP is always in the news. As the candidates go into the straight he is the favourite, his only liabilities being that he isn't a local man and, curiously enough, that he has the support of the Bevan family.

The second favourite, unexpectedly, is not Ron Evans, the local party secretary and a first-hand melter at the steelworks, but Gordon Parry, a Pembrokeshire schoolteacher whose father was a bold miner who became a minister of religion. The great argument in his favour is not simply the local connection, but that, being young, he can be one of a new generation of Labour MPs untouched by the divisions within the national party. Many local politicos also fancy him as a good MP because not famous and so, by some strange logic, able to bring new industries, to Tredegar, which, in fact, doesn't need them. If this doesn't move you, then the

180

alternative argument is that he may become famous. Mr Parry has the edge on Mr Evans because he is the better orator.

Heading the rest of the field in the local book is the ex-member for Baron's Court, Mr Tom Williams, a barrister who is local in the sense that he was born in Aberdare a few miles away and whose father was a collier. But, like the other two candidates at short odds, he has not himself ever worked in heavy industry. Why should these men be thought of by practically everyone as most likely to win a seat famous for its coalmines and steelworks while Mr Evans, the steelworkers' nominee, and Alderman Whatley, the NUM's man, are regarded as outsiders?

The simple explanation is that the British Iron and Steel and Kindred Trades Association, the NUM, and the T&GW are now roughly of equal strength in the constituency. Once upon a time the miners dominated local politics, in the same way as their industry was the sole prop of the local economy: the Tredegar lodges were among the most powerful in Wales. Came the strip mill and the post-war 'doll's eye' factories – a sheepishly risible generic term for light industry – and now no single union controls affairs. Buttressing this general change is the particular feeling in this week-end's little election-to-decide-the-by-election that neither BISAKTA nor the NUM has chosen an outstanding candidate; while the T&GW (who have many members in the steel-works) have not nominated a candidate as such. On the first ballot on Saturday evening, votes will probably be cast as mandated (although even this is not certain). Thereafter it will be a 'broken field' formation. Much as the steelworkers and coalminers may regret that there will be no one to reflect in the Commons their peculiar tough, comic and romantic vision in their own charming accent, they will have to pick themselves a professional man.

Not that it follows that one of the favourites will win, as hardened horse-backers in the pubs masochistically remind one. Look at the executive short-list, they say, from which Whatley and Foot were excluded. But that analogy doesn't quite hold: on the executive there are few trade unionists, and anyway on that famous occasion there were 25 people each with five votes and the sixth man (Foot) had only six votes less than the first man, so scattered and planless was the voting, so surprisingly absent were any Machiavellian designs which, the result had students believing, ensnared Ebbw Vale.

On Saturday there will be 200 people voting. It's reckoned that the favourite will start with a quarter of these. The question then is whether 50 votes are enough to create the psychological effect of success in a situation where the usual political pressures will not be operating. So many people have been told by so many people to vote for so many different candidates that they will be left at the mercy of a weird amalgam of emotions – flattery, illusions of grandeur, patriotic Welsh ardour, longings for times past, genuine leftism and disgruntlement.

Ah, yes, they'll still tell you in the ugly valley where Ebbw Vale makes the district's living, and in the pleasant old town of Tredegar where a candidate's relatives are discussed with even more enthusiasm than his ideas, but watch the favourites cut each other's throats and the outsider steal through on the rails.

Practically everyone is enjoying the contest and looking forward to Saturday night like an old-time fair, with hints of a wake. Aneurin Bevan's inheritance was obviously of an impossible status for any man easily to step into, so that the current confusion, so similar to a popular kind of Welsh drama about disputed wills, was almost inevitable. But this may be said in its favour: at least it shows that politics can have the stuff of life about them.

The Spectator, 24th September 1960

Pride in the melting shop

All this was designed as rhetoric in praise of Wales. Not the country of white sand, green hills and the Bible-black west which we all know and love, but the abrasive industrial south. Yet already to my dismay I see the argument reach out and acquire the rhythm of a peculiarly romantic Welsh cycle.

This phenomenon is not new. It has always begun with a generous gaiety and invariably declines into melancholy: enthusiasm concludes as a case of the sulks. Thus Celts in their medieval wars would win the first battle, fighting with zest, inventiveness and, one reads, a genuine pleasure. They would then grow bored. All right, they'd say, that's it. We've had war, now let's try something new, boyo. The enemy meanwhile, lacking such refinement, incapable of the aesthetic insights of the Old People, would boorishly march again, and scatter the handsome and red-haired Welsh as they lounged, reciting verse and practising atonal harmonies, in their decorated tents. Or something like that.

The tradition survives and a cultural overdrive governs the mind. We've had praise, let's try something new.

I had meant specifically to hymn the marvellous qualities of Welsh industrial workers, which is done seldom enough. Last week I revisited the Abbey Steelworks at Margam where I worked in the melting shop from 1952 to 1954. The scene was as spectacular and stunning as ever.

In the two years I worked there, dull though my job was, I can't remember ever being bored or even for a moment losing a sense of wonder, heat and uproar notwithstanding. Furnaces are larger now and different and produce a crimson cloud of smoke that from the sea appears to lie like pink dew on the mountain grass; nature, it looks, is imitating the impressionists. That is new but in the melting shop the faces are the same, and there is no reason why they shouldn't be, since the work is just about the best paid in industrial Britain.

It isn't simply arrogance, though to experience a slight

shock at seeing everyone you worked with once working still in the old surroundings. It's a kind of inverted Berkeleyism as if the bishop had said that if people can't touch you then they don't exist. But see people again in a familiar setting and it's briefly hard to recall what you've been doing since. What did become of all those years?

It's not the same any more, was the general view. Life is earnest. Fettling may proceed, the scrap bogies rattle, the charger perform his duties as phallically as ever, 'but the laughing's gone, see'. I find that impossible to believe. The hilarity of the shop floor or, in this case, furnace stage is seldom understood by people who have never known the mild hysteria of shift work in heavy industry. Elaborate poker-faced jokes were commonplace, played usually on the pompous among the managers or on visiting journalists.

Even then we thought we were mourning for a dead Wales, that land of the razor sharp and eloquent autodidact. Gloomily we prognosticated — a favourite word — that this vast new works, the largest in Europe, would destroy the gusto which had characterised the small now vanished Welsh steelworks. Had destroyed it already even, we said. We were wrong. At which point, oddly enough, falls the shadow; the cycle swings down into depression. The special quality of Welsh melancholy is that there is no situation or idea, no matter how pleasurable, which it cannot manoeuvre to its own sad ends.

You'd think, on the face of it, that the new vigour of provincial and regional life would be a subject inimical to the dying fall. Confidence has at last returned to the once depressed parts of the land — which is as true of the North of England as South Wales. Therefore rejoice and, of course one does. The dismay it is possible to extract from so admirable a state of affairs is quite personal. No reflection is intended on anyone or any society.

The dismay is this. My contribution to the night-shift debates on the superiority of the provincial over the metropolitan culture. The case is familiar. Never would we go to London and sink up to our ears in the Great Wen. The magnetised capital, I used to go on, impoverished Britain. Only strong communities in Wales, Scotland and the North could hold off an American kind of urban alienation. I believed it then and still believe it, but at that time I also lived it. Now, revisiting the scene of the debate, I realised that it would take more than lay immediately to hand to persuade me to abandon the metropolitan life, its films, its opera, its parks, its spurious but beguiling excitements.

Did this mean, I asked in a dispirited fashion as we drove around the steelworks dock, ore carriers unloading from Sweden, that my belief had not been genuine in the first place but merely an optimistic view of the life one is forced to live at any given time? It's a shade humiliating to discover that arguments dearly held are no more than Pavlovian responses.

The lesson is to leave your past alone. Yet nations are held to be healthy when they concern themselves with their history. The difference is that a country can learn from its past because its future is in the hands of new people. The flaw in the study of one's own past is that a man has to conduct his own future. And if that isn't a melancholy Welsh thought, name one.

The Sunday Times, 20th February 1966

An angry memory of grief

Anger will be a better memorial than pity for the Merthyr children suffocated by half a million tons of wet, waste coal. The test of sympathy should not be contributions towards wreaths for a funeral which, like the tragedy itself, is intolerable to think about, but for the more difficult and important and compassionate exercise of making sure it will never happen again.

Other people's disasters lie easy on the memory. Television bears witness. But however moving, like '24 Hours' on Friday night, the images flicker away; the vision of horror is erased.

To remember demands a fury that anything so appalling should be allowed to happen in a civilised country, a fury which will persist through the boredom of finding political means, through voting public funds, through paying money, to dam its repetition. It may be that this disaster, because it touches parents more nearly, will produce a response more enduring than that which usually follows mass accidents in mining villages. When it is the men, in this case the children's parents, who die together in a sudden explosion of nature, society also feels pity. But the colliers's way of life is alien. People far from the coalfield find it hard to imagine life underground. Equally they can scarcely be expected to comprehend the omnipresent awareness of danger and its consequent camaraderie that gives coal valleys their tense and exhilarating air. Either way, disaster can be shrugged-off as something requiring a brief sadness but which belongs to a separate world. When the dead are the children of miners it may be different.

It's impossible to believe that anyone in Britain with children could have failed to look at their sons and daughters in a special way in the last few hours. They went off to school in the morning, laughing or grizzling, but they came home again. There isn't a room in the house littered with destroyed toy cars, small shoes, gaudy pictures, that will never again be occupied.

The menace of accidents is always in a parent's mind and is hard to bear, but that is more tolerable than the idea of a child gaily settling down in his classroom with his friends and being killed in a swamp of black mud, so that his parents wait through a night hoping without hope that magic might have preserved him. To feel that way is not selfish but is, I think, an understanding of the universality of this particular tragedy.

All coal tips, of course, are not dangerous: some are. In any mining community they are taken for granted. The conical mounds become part of the natural landscape. Grass grows. There was one slag heap in the Swansea Valley, known as Twympyn Six, where we found flowers transported by ore-carriers from Chile. On tin trays we used to slide down them.

Further up the valley people would complain that the tips were moving-in on them, which was serious, except that no one bothered very much. They were, after all, part of the Welsh geological structure. Only greedy, cynical or ignorant men would ever have dumped waste coal near houses or schools in a land where rain is heavy, but that was always the habit of the coalowners. The villages were built for colliery workers, the houses and schools handy for the pit. It was cheaper to heap the coaldust there as well rather than sacrifice profit by carrying it further up the valley or the mountain. The coalowners departed the richer and left the slagheaps as monuments to their enterprise.

Because the tips were there and didn't often seem to offer menace, however disfiguring they might be, and because they grew part of the landscape of the Welsh experience, the tradition outlived the coalowners. Planning rules have since limited their size. Otherwise they have not been taken very seriously even when, as in this devastating instance, complaints of danger have been made. 'There's blood on that coal', miners are given to saying in their darker moments: the remark has a new, undreamed-of poignancy. Expiating it will be a long process. For the Coal Board to examine, to conduct research into, those tips which even remotely could threaten a community will be an expensive business. The effects of rain, of mountain streams, of smouldering in slagheaps, can be discovered but takes time and money. Would people be willing to pay more for their coal?

That would only be a beginning. Britain, compared with the Ruhr or the American Appalachians, has been intolerably slow in clearing-up the refuse of the first industrial Welsh coal and iron valleys which are made hideous and occasionally dangerous by old workings as well as tips. The North and the Midlands also have them. Anyone who has made a serious effort to demolish or remove eyesores had faced difficulties — often problems of ownership. A greater problem has been indifference both by local authorities and central government. When a valley has been worked for a century and is chained to a dying industry it's the easiest thing in the world to forget about how it looks. It's even possible to forget its traps for children. I can remember occasional accidents when, on our way to school, we used to play in disused collieries and quarries. There would be a local row: it would quickly be forgotten.

This week's stunning tragedy could easily pass from the mind and Merthyr come to seem a long way away again. And, of course, it's scarcely any consolation to the bereaved to try to rescue from their misery the chance that their fellow-country-men might be saved a similar agony. But the only small meaning that can be given to the pointlessness and waste of this terrible Friday is that it creates a determination to demolish the mess of industrial Britain. That, too, will cost money, and require an angry memory of grief. Nowhere in the world are children more adored than in Welsh mining villages. There isn't any place where the death of a child creates a more enduring emptiness. That is just one of the miserable ironies of Aberfan. Another is that a past which was bitter enough, should sweep down and obliterate the future.

The Sunday Times, 23rd October 1966

How I lost Europe

The shoot out was at high noon in Carmarthen, Merlin's town, for the Labour nomination for the Mid and West Wales constituency: six of us to appear out of the 28 who had entered for a contest that had proved to be a sporting event combining the chance of the Grand National with the tactics of stud poker. The meeting should have been on 3rd February but had been postponed because it had been pointed out to the Labour party executive that Wales' rugby team were playing Ireland at Cardiff on that day and that many of the 120 delegates might have put country before party. And so, although it was the case that Wales were playing France in Paris on the 17th, it had to be then, or never. All but ten of the delegates to the selection conference arrived. I almost did not.

The night before, I had stayed at the Royal Ivy Bush in the town where my copy of the party policy for Europe was waiting for me. It is not easy to recall an experience so poignant as discovering that I was a serious candidate for an election I cared about when I agreed with scarcely a word of my party's policy: indeed found its spirit repugnant. Never before had I grasped the force of that anecdote of the American wit, gold-prospector, playwright and boxing manager Wilson Mizner, when he recounted his time handling Stan Ketchel before a world title fight. Hours before the bout Mizner had gone to the champ's room to ensure he was resting. He found him drunk in the company of two blondes, 'And what did you say, Wilson?' 'What could I say', replied Mizner, 'except: 'Stan, move over'.'

Dismay and a heightening sense of the ridiculous, reading the document, increased when I watched on television a film I had just written about the question of devolution for Wales. It was not simply the normal vanity of seeing how awful I looked, but how much really was it helping my cause to observe myself cheerfully saying that when Augustine met the Celtic bishops there were acusations of skulduggery, and rumours of bouts of fisticuffs, and so the tone of Welsh politics had already been set in the sixth century. And there was I reciting a verse I'd been unfairly accused of writing, describing the constituency in the twelfth century:

Brecknock is full of treason and there is war in Ystrad Towy
In Ewias is found hatred and starvation,
In Glynbwlch are mangling and sharp words;
In Talgarth robbery and shame, bribery and lawyers.

Puzzled at what I should do the next day, since there was no way I could argue for moving out of Europe, which the document so heavily was hinting at, I spent an hour reflecting on how great the gulf is between writing about politics and running for something. Stendhal is good on the matter, but he never ran. Milovan Djilas whom I've had the luck to talk to a few times on the subject, is, of course, fascinating: he was a bit contemptuous of my saying to him that I hadn't run for Westminster because I shared Camus's view that if you're not prepared to order people killed, you should never seek power. But, then, Mitteleuropa, not to mention the Balkans, have a different historical experience, you might say.

There was no way, of course, in which I could have won. Three weeks only before nominations were closing I decided to try. Partly my motive was to see if it was possible for someone who was pro-Europe to win a Labour seat. And there was the sentimental feeling that it would be a pleasure to represent the people I grew up among and still believe to be the most serious, charming and entertaining people in Europe. Also it was one of the loveliest, and largest of constituencies, reaching from near Monmouth, where I live, down to Swansea Bay, down to St David's Head in Pembrokeshire, north to where the Wye and Severn rise in Plynlimmon, across almost to Oswestry: a little Europe in itself, as I would say in my speeches, with all the problems that predicates.

So I wrote a letter saying who I was and where I came from and why Europe was important, and that I'd played rugby and given concerts as a boy soprano; and a trade union friend with an office had it roneoed and we sent off 700 copies to all the delegates in the eight constituencies. Work out the cost of the stamps. Eschewing gangs or the well-heeled did not make running cheap: neither did it help being in work. And that was before, as *Milk Wood's* poet of the constituency put it long ago, 'the weather turned around'. Snow, ice, car crash and work became, in the end, it seems, more hazardous than one's view of the European Monetary System, the history of wars between Germany and France, the British government's errors in negotiation, the character of European socialism; and there were more hazards yet, which were to do with myself.

The first ward meeting I went to in Swansea I never spoke

at. It was raining. Peers, professors, ex-MPs were collected in the corridor of a schoolroom. My opening remarks were prepared. I was going to remind the audience that I'd been at the opening morning of the cinema down the street in 1939, and did they remember Buck Jones? That around the corner was the house of the choir conductor who used to give me piano lessons and that when I arrived at nine on a Saturday morning he used to shout downstairs from bed: 'Go and get my chips'. I would go and buy his chips and, while I played, he would lie in bed eating them, occasionally snarling: 'Forte. Forte'. Before it was my turn to address the delegates, there was a power cut. I was nominated.

Not being stupid, I took the pleasure of lunch in Swansea with the West Wales boss of the Transport and General Workers Union, Dai Davies, the wittiest and most ebullient of trade union leaders. After an enthusiastic description of his heart attack, Dai offered advice. 'Don't', he said, 'believe them. If they say they are going against you, don't believe them'. 'In which case, Dai', I responded, 'why should I believe anything you say to me?' 'Exactly', he said. 'And one thing I would say, John', said Dai, 'try and lay off your views on the Common Market. It's not popular around here.' 'But I've got to say something'. 'Play it down'.

The Swansea East and Swansea West constituencies invited me to address them. After the East meeting a few candidates with myself sat in the bar, waiting to hear how we had done. One was Gwynoro Jones, who had been MP for Carmarthen and who was a member of the local party. 'The reason', he said, 'they are taking so long deciding, is that they are thinking of not nominating three candidates for Carmarthen, but just putting up one: and that is me'. A delegate from the meeting announced to us that three were nominated, and that Gwynoro Jones was not among them. There was a row. Within days the local underground newspaper, *Alarm*, carried a story that there had been a bout of fisticuffs between Mr Jones and Alun Lloyd, a powerful figure in the organisation.

The following night, in Swansea West, I also won and so

was now in a position of some strength, according to my friends in Swansea. I might have already 30 votes out of the 120 at the final selection conference. Alun Lloyd, however, had already pointed out to me some weakness in my general approach to the question of being elected. 'Look', he said, 'you've met these people like Willy Brandt so why don't you advertise yourself more. The others are all selling themselves like mad'. So there I was, with my home town on my side – although anti-Europe – and my letting them down. Having won the two Swansea nominations, I now began to learn of the dirty tricks rivals were up to, having told my friends I wanted no part of any tricks at all.

One rhetorical passage I used to offer in speeches, following the boys' advice to advertise myself, did please me. There I was, I would say, one of you, rubbing pens at the *New Statesmen* with Martin, Crossman, Wilson, Castle, Freeman. And, in the late Sixties falling out with the editor, Paul Johnson. We quarrelled because when he was away and I was editing the magazine, I wrote the front page saying that Europe was a good thing. I, my speech would continue, am here: Paul Johnson is supporting Margaret Thatcher. Think on that.

The two favourites for that seat, all along, had been Mr Jones and Ann Clwyd, a journalist colleague of mine. As it turned out, Mr Jones did not reach the short list, although he had more nominations than any of us. He appeared on television attacking the party for this curious state of affairs. Ann, therefore, was bound to win, although I gather some of my supporters spread the word that she was a carpetbagger, no less, since she was standing in every Welsh seat going. I thought that she would win for no reason other than that the party had treated her cruelly in not nominating her for the Westminster seats she deserved over the years. As my wife observed: the Labour Party don't care about Europe, therefore they will see to it that they can exorcise their guilt about their male chauvinism by giving Ann a seat that does not matter.

I was fascinated to learn of the attacks on myself. The proper one was that I had, unlike everyone else involved, never stood for election before. More improper I thought the rest of the chat. I was held to be a smoker of opium. Clearly a fellow befuddled by the pipe would not be a hot shot for Strasbourg. Where would his intellect be as he stormed in on Roy Jenkins in Brussels, raging for grants for industrial development in Llanelli? I suppose I should never have written an account of how in Saigon and in Cambodia a few minor journalistic coups had come my way by being in Marshall Ky's and Prince Sihanouk's company, and sharing a pipe.

And so I went and made my speech and said how sad I thought it that the party I had supported all my life should take such a narrow view. I believe I even made a defence of the butter mountain by describing the experience of famished Europe during the great wars between France and Germany. But once the questions began, I knew I had no chance. A fierce man from Llanelli in the front row asked me how I could sign a document which was the party document when I clearly did not support it. 'Perhaps', I said, 'the party should not have its documents written by public school and Oxbridge people'. It was the last laugh.

I do not share Chico Marx's view, (he spoke as a gambling man) that it is better to have lost and lost than never to have lost at all. My love of my home country is deep. I also believe there is a possibility in Europe of creating a society better than we have and that it could be a socialist Europe. And while I will continue to soldier on in the Labour Party, I regret profoundly that the mean spirits within it encourage good people in wrong notions. Socialism is about hope: the Labour Party's view of Europe is about despair. Experience, wrote Wilde, is what people call their mistakes. This experience of mind was a delight.

Spectator, 2nd June 1979

The quiet unemployed

On 27th September, *The Times* offered a page of advice to those about to be made redundant from their work. Officially, the unemployment figures stand at over two million, unofficially at nearer three. Next year the official figure will been three million, the unofficial four. In Wales the figure is as high as in 1939, when war was declared; in the North East the position is worse. A Right to Work march from South Wales to the Tory Conference at Brighton is being cold-shouldered by the Labour Party and the TUC – as was the Thirties' Jarrow March – on account of its Trotskyist origins. The Tory government ordains that next month it will reduce the dole by five percent below the rate of inflation and, in two years time, abolish the earnings-related supplement for those thrown out of work.

There are two curiosities about the present state of affairs. The first is that those on the dole are quiet, and the second that metropolitan society appears indifferent to the fact of unemployment in the country. Obviously the two are related. Equally obviously it is understandable that those in work and, even more so, those in power should be indifferent to those out of work. They never meet them. Many of the unemployed belong to that 25 percent of the electorate which does not vote. Until recently it was the custom of the English bourgeoisie to suppose that those without work were work-shy. As Scrooge asked, were there no workhouses and prisons for such riff-raff? Shiftiness now surrounds such attitudes. In the palaces of government there is an extra diffidence that springs from the vague feeling that the Thatcher-Howe-Joseph policies are merely an extension of those pursued by the Callaghan-Healey-Benn cabinet.

There are many reasons why the unemployed should now be quiet, although one should remember that even in the Thirties not much attention was paid in the South East to the devastation in the coal-fields in the West and in the North. The formidable images of the documentary films did not bear fruit until the 1945 General Election. Now there are redundancy payments. More women work than did. Whole communities are not being destroyed as in the past. When, as at Merthyr Tydfil, unemployment stood as 80 percent the tragedy was of such proportions as to seem almost an act of God: surely a Fifth Horseman was at work. But then there was a possibility of migration since there was nothing to lose except happiness remembered. Now, unemployment does not create comrades, it isolates. In one street there may be, indeed there are, families in which here a man, there a woman, here an adolescent is out of work. But in terms of community or political action, there is no sense of a Marxist proletariat, but rather a set of Leibniz's monads; and two million monads do not march. Since trade unions are institutions created for the benefit of the employed, there is little they can do.

Contributing to this question is the belief that the crisis is a short-term affair. The monetarist 'shake-out' will end, world production will increase and back will come full employment of the old kind, oiled along by the North Sea Bubble. The images endure of great plants silent while the masses congregate, waiting for demand once more to rise, for the switch to be pulled, and for all to strive happy ever after. But what if this is not the case; that we are instead genuinely involved in a reappraisal of the character and extent of what we have meant by work since the 18th century?

Take the Welsh steel industry, itself the inheritor of the iron trade, the foundation of our society. For two centuries each new generation has expected to inherit its grandfather's or father's job, whether in the melting shop, the coke ovens, the finishing plant, or at the tinplate works down the road. My family worked so for many generations; I even did myself for a while. Now this heroic cycle appears to have hit the wall. Young men from Porthcawl through Port Talbot, Neath, to the villages north of Swansea, see their inheritance snatched from them. Lately I have met men in tears, not only because they have lost their jobs, but because they have been separated from friends of decades in the plant. Perhaps, we say sternly, such sadness is the inevitable concomitant of the character of world production, of the Korean producer being cheaper and the Indian worker better suited to the under-capitalised mass-product. The consequences for Welsh children are more serious than mere melancholy.

Their parents have been applauded for taking their redundancy money so readily, unlike those frightful French who have rioted and suffered casualties while arguing that the children's jobs were more important than mere money. The Welsh steelworkers, received opinion has it, have been contributing to the success of 'Thatcherism' and to swelling the membership of her Samuel Smiles Club of cheerful self-helping entrepreneurs. Some will, and some will not. Some are going to watch the cricket in the Caribbean. But much as I admire the ingenuity of moonlighters, there is a limit to what even that market will bear.

Among the difficulties young people will face is the surprising hold of the idea that to be without work is to be a failure. In my youth the puritan ethic, as it will be forever known, was strong, but it was mitigated by the general misery of unemployment. Even so, I can recall the unease that we felt when my father was out of work, not to mention the financial problems. Glibly, it was thought that the advance of radical thinking in the Sixties had got rid of this association of unemployment with failure. But it seems it did not. Now young women also feel that they must work.

Formidable prognoses have been made of the consequences of unemployment for young people. The CBI and the Labour Party have both expresed concern that there could be 'social unrest', something more serious than football hooliganism. (Oddly enough, the last outburst of football hooliganism in Wales occurred in the 1890s when a United States tariff created unemployment in the Welsh steel and tinplate industries.) My view is that something worse than unrest will occur, which is nothing. As unemployment mounts, the clever or the privileged will flourish, as ever. The country will move steadily towards becoming a high-wage economy; wealth will accumulate. But some people will decay. These people will remain unorganised, sporadically heard from and ignored, a lost generation.

Spectator, 4th October 1980

V

JOHN MORGAN'S WALES
1985–1987

1985

The sweet taste of failure

The Daffodils are late this year in the woods on Offa's Dyke for St David's Day. But what is that flower there struggling among the snowdrops to be born? Surely it cannot be that plant so much loved by a few, thought poisonous by many – to wit, Devolution.

There are similar manifestations in the North. At Coleg Harlech this weekend Mr John Osmond introduces his edition of essays – *The National Question Again* – in a conference among formidable company.

All political parties are represented, along with distinguished academics. It will be interesting to learn if the grounds of argument have changed since St David's Day to six years ago when the desire to remain within Britain was so overwhelmingly displayed in the ballot-box.

And, of course, HTV's entertaining series of programmes on Welsh history has been sharpening the wits. One of those wits – a senior television executive – tells me that his son asked him, "Are we watching *The Two Ronnies* tonight, Dad, or the *Two Dragons?*" How children humble us.

What happened in the last Devolution debate is, to coin a phrase, misguided history. It may be that people were right – it may be that they were misguided because they were misinformed.

Certainly reporting it for television I met some odd remarks among the more sensible responses. Into which first category fell the observations of Welsh-speaking men in Gwaen-cae-Gurwen that they fancied staying with the English in case Government money ran out. This still puzzles me.

And then there was the fact of the Labour government arguing for, when entrenched party supporters in the council power-bases were against.

There was the fear of the Welsh language mysteriously exerting some Bolshevik-like control over jobs. And hanging over all was the fact that, while Welsh people outside Wales would have voted for separation, however limited, English people in Wales who actually had votes would not.

All of which preamble leads to an argument that troubles me. I would have liked to have offered it at Coleg Harlech this weekend had I been free to go – the self-employed writer is always at the mercy of the market, alas.

The background of my trouble is this – in the late Forties I was lucky enough to be a student of Professor Glanmor Williams at University College, Swansea.

The agility of his scholarship as an historian was matched by his skill as a wicket-keeper – not that he was much troubled by my off-spin bowling since batsmen knocked me about the field.

In the 38 years that have passed Professor Glanmor has begat a tribe of Welsh historians. He still stands head and shoulders above them, but many have done brilliant work. His achievement has not, though, just been quality of his work, but that work's function as the propaganda of the deed. That deed has been to make Wales aware of its past.

Whether it was his aim or not, many of us took his intention to be that the national and cultural awareness would have a political consequence. In a sense, any aim was irrelevant – scholarship has its own poetry. Nevertheless he did raise the temperature of political awareness. When I was at the Swansea Grammar School we had one slim volume of Welsh history to study; now children have scores.

Professor Glanmor's influence therefore has been powerful. He was a governor of the BBC. There have been changes made. The teaching of Welsh in schools and, indeed, on the BBC has been transformed. There is S4C. Road signs propose

Wales is not England. But, for all that, Devolution went down the sink, and might again.

So can it be that the flowering of Welsh historical studies is not producing the effects some of us wished. And, if so, why not?

On a crude political level it could be because the English in Wales are not being beguiled. It could even be that they are alienated by the harvesting of the past. The historian will properly reply that he is indifferent to the consequences of his scholarship at the ballot-box. The case is, however, that we are not all historians. There needs to be a practical interest in the future.

I used to believe that learning about the past would make the future more generous; that the more we knew about where we came from and what our people had been through, then the better we could move forward.

In most countries that has been the way things have gone, although we always have to bear in mind the Swiss proverb – unhappy the land whose history is interesting to read.

What seems to be happening in Wales is that the study of history is becoming a victim of traditional traits. We know how much sweeter the songs over battles lost are the accounts of battles won.

Don't they look pretty those snapshots of old holidays; and weren't we so young then? Historicism is in danger of becoming an evasion. Success is harder to live with than failure; failure is more cosy; let's fail, boys, like in the old days.

There have been some recent, dashing signals of a change. At our Writer's Union of Wales conference the Plaid Cymru MP Dafydd Elis Thomas offered the phrase, "English is a Welsh language," but then wandered off in pursuit of an intellectually defunct and electorally unpersuasive Marxism, as I understand him. Yet a way was being pointed out.

Therefore do we conclude that, for all Professor Glanmor's great achievement, historicism in Wales may defeat the future? It could be that the rigorous, difficult intellectual task of the thinking classes in Wales is to learn forget the past. Warbling the descant of the old songs is a permanent pleasure, but it is not enough.

Western Mail, 26th February 1985

Does the miner's tale contain a moral?

What possible connection can there be between the distinguished Welsh tenor Robert Tear singing Schumann's songs for the Merlin Society at Monmouth the other evening and the ending of the miners' strike? I think there is one which, if surprising, is ferocious in its melancholy.

Mr Tear is a singer not yet as celebrated in his home country as he is in London, Paris and the United States. He gave us a recital as fine as any I have heard, a tour de force, travelling through a dazzling range. But nothing he sang was more moving than his performance of Schumann's love songs, *Liederkreis*.

Driving home down the Wye valley, my first efforts at humming a tune were directed feebly at the *Modnacht* (Moonlight) since it was such a night and the poet, with unabashed romanticism, was singing of the bright stars, heaven kissing the earth and the soul spreading its wings to fly home.

Next I tried a song about loss and death and realised that here I was driving down this lovely valley after so memorable a musical experience while only a few miles away to the West were the parallel valleys where there had been the long anguish of the miners' strike, a strike which had been lost and which itself had been a cry from the heart.

The strike, I know, can be interpreted as merely a political event. Here were determined men trying to change the nature of power in Britain by the use of industrial action; confronting Parliament in a populist or Communist cause. Or it might be, here were men trying to argue for the perpetuation of jobs for generations at public expense, arresting the sweep of progress.

Or perhaps it was that here was a Tory government maintaining law in the face of anarchy, or whatever. The whole year-long agony is commonly referred to as a "tragedy." But – and this is what the Schumann song about death prompts me to ask – what is the nature of that tragedy?

I accept that some metropolitan commentators will find the use of that word as melodramatic. Some will simply have seen the affair as the exploitation by ambitious men on both sides of an argument about closing a pit here, a pit there, a few jobs lost: so what? People can migrate. In history men and women always have. This is true. Most of us are migrants from some-where or the other. I am a migrant from a family of colliers, uncles and cousins in the anthracite field.

It was easy for me and many like me. I enjoyed a fine education in Swansea and the Fifties was a creative time and jobs abounded for most. But even then relatives in West Wales pits found it hard when the slants were closed. So how much more difficult now.

Those brisk commercial minds who conduct matters nowadays can have no comprehension of what is happening, never having lived in coalfields; nor of what the strike, I think, represented. If they cared to they might learn a little by walking those paths now so helpfully arranged through the new forests of Glamorgan, as I have been doing these past few years.

The vistas are often splendid, sometimes wondrous, the air a pleasure and the exercise itself suitable for the unfit: a picnic helps. Often you park the car near a village – Glyncorrwg, say – or find yourself driving through the old steam coalfield. The towns, the houses are visibly depreciating as a civilisation which flourished briefly looks to be collapsing.

There is an irony in the manner in which the trees have grown on what once were slagheaps while the villages themselves whose industry produced the slag are in turn falling into desuetude.

Local politicans are familiar with this wretched state of affairs. Something, they say, must be done. They argue with genuine feeling that "surely in this day and age we cannot see people rot!" But what is so special about this day and age? The phrase proposes that contemporary compassion embraces an economic system; that our epoch is very different from that period in the 18th century when Goldsmith wrote of wealth accumulating while men decay. What evidence do we have any more that we live in a superior society?

It is in the context of this belief that we live in a seedy time that the miners' strike can be seen as a tragedy. It was an attempt to ask directly, for all the uproar of the campaign, a direct question: are these places in the South Wales valleys to die or not? Are talks of efforts of bringing help of one kind or another masks worn to disguise a truth, the truth being that nothing can be done?

It may be there is a little doctoring to be done here, a little there, but behind these manoeuvres lurks a foreboding which no one dare articulate. It has happened before in history and can happen again. The earth is rich in abandoned villages, even towns. Why not therefore the Rhondda and the upper reaches of other valleys?

The tenor Robert Tear whose recital provoked these reflections was born in Barry, Davies of Llandinam's port, from which Rhondda coal rode to fuel the world. In one Schumann work Mr Tear sang, in one of the greatest of lieder, of the anguish of man: "My mother and father have long been dead. How soon will the day come when I shall rest with the forest above me?"

It's poignancy is universal. We all come to such a fate in the nature of things. The tragedy within the miners' strike is that it raised the question of whether it is equally in the nature of things that a part of a nation should suffer so. I have a fear that because the miners lost, the answer is probably yes. The moon that shone on the Wye Valley that night was not the same moon that shone on the Rhondda.

Western Mail, 13th March 1985

Words of worship and the language of belief

Each year as Easter nears, we confront, with varying degrees of piety the wondrous cross on which the Prince of Glory died.

This year a curious speculation has come to mind, whether for reasons of middle-age advancing or another, I'm not sure: How much has the behaviour of earlier generations and mine been governed not by the faith of Christianity but by the language of the Welsh church and a chapel upbringing.

Perhaps the speculation is due to someone asking why I choose to live my life at best in an operatic, at worst in a self-dramatising manner. I replied that many Welsh did, surely, and for the same reason. To consider these grave matters in terms of one's childhood is a dangerous course, with snares everywhere. However, I have to admit to being, when young, one of the most cheerful and indefatigable occupiers of pews and choir stalls that I have ever come across.

On Sunday morning and evening I would go to Church in Wales services in Treboeth, Swansea, and sing in the choir; and trot off in the afternoon to Sunday School in Welsh at Horeb, Morriston. At Horeb I learned *The Messiah.* In 1941 this religiosity, if such it was, had practical consequences when the large family to which I belonged went broke. I was made head choirboy at the Swansea Parish Church where, with weddings, I could earn at the age of 11 ten shillings (50p) a week when the average working wage was 50 shillings (£2.50). It was a help.

Therefore my experience was perhaps not typical. What was typical though was the sense of wonder and delight in the language we were using in the old Bible and Book of Common Prayer. How could words of such power not persuade one that life was to be an exciting and dramatic matter, rich in colour and passion? Existence should be conducted in terms Ecclesiastes would understand. (Although I suspect now in considering his abrupt change of tone, that Ecclesiastes must have been drinking at the time.)

I am not suggesting that the content of these great works was not important. It remains so. If we consider the service for next Sunday, it carries its message in its account of Judas. No one who has been betrayed by great friends or by colleagues can fail to understand it. In our less religious age the treacherous – of both sexes – do not quite imitate Judas, who hanged himself and, in the famous phrase, was buried in a "field called the field of blood unto this day." Nowadays, the betrayer tends to prosper, at least for a while.

Would we have behaved differently if this language, these concepts, had not been the stuff of our nurturing? Perhaps lived quieter lives? And there is for the Welsh a further element in the argument. A school of psychological study in Switzerland maintains that a life conducted in a language other than one's first itself produces a quasi-neurotic quality which enhances more than it troubles. To exchange Welsh for English in childhood was once a common experience.

That 17th century language is passing away. But rather than face the distressing case of the versions of the Bible and Prayer Book now current. I'd prefer to shy away and consider the threadbare terminology which has suceeded that old language of church and chapel in political and social life. Would we have been different human beings if we had been brought up on words like "prioritise," "supportive," "constraints." And then there is "caring" (as in "caring profession" rather than in "I have stopped caring about the Welsh rugby team"). "Commitment" is an especially interesting example since it aspires to some seriousness.

I recall being in Berkeley, California, in 1966 during the uproar there when this word came into use among the New Left. One meaning was, I took it, pledging oneself to the cause. Another, more hilarious, was young male seducers committing themselves to young women. ("I'm committed to you, baby.") When I would suggest that the word meant something different to me, as for example, in my youth when sick relatives were "committed" to the mental hospital, there was puzzlement. Worse: I would quote the Service at the Burial of the Dead . . . "We therefore commit his body to the ground: earth to earth, ashes to ashes, dust to dust." And even worse when I offered the view, carrying, I thought, an appropriate Californian simile, that women's liberation, then burgeoning at Berkeley, offered a Klondyke to Casanovas. My American radical friends, although generous, with fine teeth, were, like so many of ours, weak in a sense of humour. Inevitably, the lingo crossed the Atlantic in a semantic cloud. "Commitment," among other terms was soon heard in London with, in sexual terms, similar consequences.

It might be objected that a word of that daft kind is understood by those who use it and consequently is fine. I believe it is not: a port-manteau has many compartments and how can you tell what lies in them all? The devotional may think it improper of me to use Easter, the most holy of tragedies and triumphs, as a basis for these reflections. My excuse is that its resonances echo powerfully down the most unexpected caverns. In one of those caverns we sit, a small, happy band of anchorites, trying in our humble way to defend a different faith: the vigour and truth of language. I wonder how we are going to do?

Western Mail, 26th March 1985

My 14-hour trip to find a good lunch

Was this, we asked ourselves a few days ago, being a small crowd of travelling men and women at a large table in a collapsing farmhouse above a bend in the River Lot in the South of France – was this the furthest we had ever travelled for lunch? The journey had taken 14 hours by train, a couple of planes and car, from Cardiff the afternoon before, leaving rain for heavier rain, cold weather for colder.

Someone proposed Chicago to San Franciso as further, but was regarded as frivolous since that flight was short. Another made a claim for a trip from Swansea to Edinburgh in the old days. My boast of a car ride from Warsaw to Munich was disqualified on a technicality which I cannot now recall for a reason – its name is prune brandy – which will become clear.

Our trip had an earnest journalistic purpose – this was no idle feast. We had heard that this little-known region of France held up a mirror to industrial West Wales. And so it proved. The contours were those of the Swansea, Towy and Teifi valleys, the green of the hills comparable, the rivers and streams as alive.

In West Wales, industrial settlements like Gwaun-Cae-Gurwen and, further towards the sea, Drefach Velindre on the Teifi are found in lovely country. So here a steel town like Rodez. Here, too, collieries have been closed and many workers have moved away. Second homes may be bought for £12,000. We were going to watch a game of rugby between teams composed of working-class players, as if it were Morriston versus Tumble. The resemblances were to be as striking as our guide, John Welsh, a former Llanelli player now a film-maker in France, had promised my co-workers Gerald Davies and Don Llewelyn from HTV.

The difference was that good rugby players are invariably found jobs in France. But the object of these reflections is not football and its socio-economic role, but the food we ate in the old farmhouse and what it has to say about the tourist industry in Wales. The walls of the room were rough. The fireplace was a cavern. Sides of bacon hung over the wood fire. Our long table was old, as were those at which peasants sat and, after a while, shouted messages. During the war rugby players had come here to eat illegally.

We began with onion soup. Smoked pork was followed by a pork terrine. We moved from a local wine called Grappe to one which seemed to me to have a suitable name for the occasion, Buzet. Chickens arrived with a memorable garlic stuffing. The next dish puzzled us – there was fish certainly, but cooked with a cheese and vegetables hard to place. Local cheeses were then eaten and a prune tart.

It was now that the trouble began. The proprietors, both

very old, decided that we were friendly invaders and offered us a home-made prune brandy. Having, a few years ago, been paralysed elsewhere in the Languedoc drinking *framboise,* I should have advised my colleagues against that type of French drink. However, as the lyricist has it:

> *The will is strong*
> *The won't is weak.*

Therefore we neglected the message that home-made prune brandy has two powerful characteristics – the swiftness and certainty with which it hits the target. Pointing this out to our generous friends, they responded that the only answer to the condition was a champagne unusually curative. At which, local French airs were sung and some Welsh. Full of confidence, I offered a version of *Sospan Fach* I've been working on which attempts to convince that it is written on a 10th century atonal scale. Not many know that. The peasants offered us cigars at this performance perhaps hoping for a fit of coughing.

Two facts are important about this interesting meal. The first is that we had discovered earlier that the rugby match we were filming was not until the following day. The second is that the cost per head for all that food and drink was £5.50. How could this be? Where in Wales or, indeed Britain, could such a feast be possible at even three times the price? We are all in the Common Market. Diligent, if incoherent, inquiry revealed that all the food we had eaten had been produced on the family farm and made at home. The wine was local. The truth, I suspect, is that the profit was negligible. If that is the case, as I have often suspected, being given to spending a lot of time in restaurants, for reasons of work and pleasure, we may conclude that the reason that prices are so high in Wales is that it is the proprietors more than the customers who are greedy. This is, on the whole, just as well since the proprietors are more likely to be satisfied than the customers. How pleasant it would be to think that somewhere above the Towy or the Teifi there were farmers like those above the Lot River who could so provide; and how improbable. More likely is that soon there will be no such people in France. What happy chance, then, to have travelled quite so far for lunch.

Western Mail, 23rd April 1985.

Farmers, friends and villains

As the lambs gambol and the sheep shout and the sap rises, there is no better time to be brave, even reckless and face that question we are all too shifty about in Wales: What is to be done about the farmers? We are craven because so many of us come from the land and because the countryside is held to be the repository not only of the language but some mysterious truth learned in the soil. Both are dubious propositions.

I write as someone living between farms for whom this one day had offered three distinct insights. A friend in Gwent rings to say that a farmer has planted trees that will grow tall in a field across the road which will block a lovely view. Asking the farmer why he had done it, he was told that there was no reason why there should be a fine view of that sort. My friend was a writer, wasn't he, not a farmer. Near me there is a pig factory, a huge building in an area designated as an area of beauty. We made a bit of a fuss about it being built. There was no point in bothering since farmers may do as they please. Planning permission, the necessary procedures which inhibit the rest of us, do not apply to farmers. This day, by happy chance, I noticed a small gang of little pigs had escaped from the factory and were at a gate. I gave it a small kick, just a very small one, and it was nothing to do with me, honest, and away they ran. There is uproar.

Another difficulty arose after some animal liberators, or clowns, had released mink from a place nearby. Some of the mink arrived at a stream, a tributary of the Wye, which runs under my house. From my place they went up-stream to a trout farm next door where they killed a few score fish. Mink are odd; they kill the trout and then don't bother much with eating their victim. Psychopaths rather than carnivores. My farmer neighbour, indeed friend, became so enraged that he bought bullets that could have stopped a rhinocerous. The afternoon has been loud with the sound of mink being blasted. I thought a small calibre shot would have been quite enough. I was taken to learn that the heavy bullets were made by Nobel, he of the Peace Prize.

I describe all this because I wouldn't wish a serious matter of the subsidising of farmers to seem to come from some urban hick. I recognise that Welsh farmers have not profited, as have the Eastern English and the City, from the grain and wheat and rape fiscal techniques. Most have not destroyed hedges, troubled bird-life, drained wet land. I am sure this is because of their good taste rather than the absence of temptation. I know, too, having been down near Newcastle Emlyn a year ago of the trouble caused and the demonstrations launched over changes in the dairy trade. A livelihood has to be fought for. Even so, there is an imbalance in the European economy which touches on Wales through the sentimental passion for protecting the farmer. Investment is inhibited in industry, monetary confusions occur between currencies, there is even a danger of protectionsim. The Welsh farmer is the least of all in Europe the villain, but he is part of the problem. He may observe the present Government being hard with the Welsh coal industry, soft with him and, being human, not really be concerned about whether we need expensive surplus milk or lamb more than we need expensive coal.

However grandly, or objectively, the arguments are presented though, in the end affection can work. I spent a lot of my childhood at Brynhyfryd farm in Llandybie in West Wales. If you regard that territory as a spiritual home it is hard to be cold-hearted about farmers. The truth is, though, that farmers, are unpopular. Even in the countryside they need to stick together for warmth and comfort. Where I live they gather in the same pub and not merely out of camaraderie, but because they know they are not liked. What is, to coin an agricultural phrase, the root of this dislike? First, for the stranger, the disfiguration of the countryside. More important for others who live in the country, I guess, is the matter of farmers not paying rates. If, as is probably true, all politics is about taxation, then the argument against those who work our land is that they are too favoured. When, in a village, everyone knows that a farmer may win a grant to mend his roof because he is not paying rates when those who pay cannot, noble issues like preserving the countryside against working it, fade to nothing.

Those who live in towns may take against farmers for a range of reasons. The problem now is that farmers are becoming isolated in the countryside. Which of them will be the first to propose they pay rates? If it is the case, as certain poets have tried to establish, that there is virtue in the soil, and that an acquaintance with nature may even induce a purity of soul, what a formidable spectacle it would be to see, say the farmers of Dyfed march on Carmarthen town hall demanding to share the rate burden of their fellow citizens. I would like to be there.

Western Mail, 21st May 1985

A plot walled round with silence

By a winding route, as if along a country lane, I think I may have discovered, to borrow from *Hamlet,* something rotten in the state of Wales. I am tentative because the matter needs more resources than I can command, to be sure, whether I am right about the treatment of the deranged in our society. To put it bluntly: are there sick people in gaol hospitals because mental homes won't take them?

My interest had an odd origin. Earlier this year I had

suffered a bad emotional shock, one offered with rare deceit and vulgarity. It led me to having a black-out at the wheel of my car. By good fortune I just missed a lorry and drove through a hedge and was not killed or maimed. Talking about it to neighbours and friends, I discovered that several had suffered so. One couple, a two-car family, had each crashed their cars on the day they had learned that their son had been told that he had a disease that was to be life-long. A London BBC colleague told me that he had had a bad crash the day a woman had shocked him by her behaviour.

Being of a curious disposition, I raised the question with some friends who are doctors. We hear, I said, so much about accidents on the road caused by drink. How many accidents are caused by grief or emotional shock? They were non-committal, even wary on the matter, from which I take it that the answer is many. That evening two young men drove their car into the wall of my house and I sent for the fire brigade, police and ambulance and a doctor. There was blood and glass on the flagstones. The firemen took a long time to save the boys from the crushed car. I thought, as one does, since they were my son's age, and he drives, that it might have been him, and they might die; and then how it might have been me, after my shock, if I hadn't hit a hedge. The young men, although still in an intensive care place, are still alive. Brushing that aside, I pressed on. What would happen to someone who committed an offence, something for which they could be convicted in court, when they were believed to be manic-depressive, or otherwise in a dangerous or unstable state? At which I learned that there may be something rotten in the state of Wales.

The position appears to be this. If someone is in a bad way and sick and is violent in his or her village or town and is arrested and is convicted they go to gaol. He is then held in the gaol hospital. There the facilities for treatment, as you might expect, are not the best. This is through no fault of the staff. They are expected to deal with people for whom they do not have the resources – the recent account of conditions at Holloway gaol demonstrate that. Why, I pressed on, are

215

people so convicted not sent to mental hospitals where they can be cared for, even though convicted? The reason is that there are not enough nurses in hospitals to care for patients who might be violent, who have, in the medical terminology, been 'sectioned'. Therefore they have to go to the prison hospital, unless, of course, they are rich enough to pay to go to one of the expensive English places for the deranged. That is bad enough. Worse is the fact that someone may be sent to the prison hospital without even being convicted. This happens because they are held in court to be unfit to plead. Thus, they have to go to prison because there is no mental hospital that will accept them, one which is a "secure" unit.

The police I gather are unhappy about this state of affairs – I am reporting private conversation. Many people who are nuisances where they live are not arrested because the officers of the law know of the distressing consequences of a conviction.

What we seem to have, therefore, is a conspiracy of silence, mostly well-intentioned, but not healthy. And how strange it is that, as so often, when a subject is raised, everyone seems to know about it, but no one wants to mention it. I think it would be useful if those journalists or television companies who have the resources to discover how general is the problem I came across by unhappy chance, were to describe it to us. The Government might then pay some attention. I might even think my near-miss with the Grim Reaper would not have been without some consequence.

Western Mail, 3rd June 1985

A job I would be really at home in . . .

What are we to make of the prospect of a chair or, at least, a lectureship in tourism at the University of Wales? If entertaining visitors is to be the principal industry, then clearly the need is there. Who, though, is best qualified for such a post? A chef? A sociologist? One of our band of charabanc historical guides? A lapsed politican? Or, to put it crudely, someone like myself? Never, through ingenuity, luck, idleness or bravado having had a job, nor even having applied for one, in my whole life, I think my hour has come. Inexperienced in the formulae of supplication, my tactic is to be bold. I propose that the post should, in university terms, be extramural. In other words, it should be established in my house.

Tourists pass my front door in their hundreds in the summer. Many walk down the Roman, and even older Celtic road from Offa's Dyke and stare as we play a complicated game of cricket on the lawn. For example, if you hit the ball twice into the stream, you are out. If you hit it over the wall among the cows and aren't prepared to go and fetch it, you are out. Here, surely, is a subject for the tourist department's first doctorate thesis, "Accommodate traditional games to the measures and contours of the Welsh countryside."

In considering the appointment of part-time staff or consultants, I would recommend the film director Gareth Wyn Jones, of North Wales, if only on the delicacy of his Avocado Tŷ Gwyn, which is decorated with laverbread and prawns. This matter of the imaginative use of indigenous and foreign material might be the subject of a thesis for the department's first master's degree. I would encourage the students to feel free, even to the point of not bothering them at all. No man, my inaugural address might begin, is not only not an island, he is a tourist. Ask not, I would declaim, for whom the gong rings for dinner – it rings for thee. I would then sing the praises of the Cawdor at Llandeilo – of happy memory – to show familiarity with the best of Welsh hotels.

This vaunting ambition of mine to take a part in scholarly life has been fired by a touching piece of news. Along with many distinguished academics, I am to be honoured as one of a small group of honorary fellows at my old University College at Swansea. None of my fellow-fellows will be offended, I hope, when I report that among all of them it delights me that the one I'll be standing alongside at the Brangwyn Hall in July is Haydn Tanner, the former Wales scrum-half and captain. The last time I spoke to Mr Tanner was at one of those famous matches at St Helen's ground in 1943, when professionals played with amateurs in games of rare quality. I was the boy, in my grammar school jersey – they had hopes in those days that I would be a hot-shot player – who threw the ball back into play. Haydn Tanner once came to the touchline and took the ball from me. "Here's the ball, Mr Tanner," are the only words I have addressed to him.

I would then recommend myself to the interviewing board by pointing out that I possess in my own life that characteristic love-hate compact with tourists which we all share. There is a distaste that they take up space; there is the knowledge that their money is needed. I think that there should be some fund available in the department for the exploitation of guilt among tourists. This is a neglected aspect of the work of encouraging tourist to which the present board might address itself. Since we are so good at guilt ourselves, why not profit from it? Guilt as gilt?

There are, I will carry on, two arguments which are not part of my supplication. I have read in *The Times* that women at Oxford University complain of sexual harassment by dons. It seems that if Hollywood moguls have their casting couches, then so do professors their exam couches. I am not sure if that kind of thing goes on at the University of Wales, although gossip about one or two, I gather does pass the time of an evening. It would not be the style in the department of tourism. How many other candidates would make so firm a commitment? It is, after all, the duty of women to make passes at idle dons. Neither would I argue that the life of the professor looks so easy to those of us who have to struggle in the market place. I would be tactful enough to eschew Bernard Shaw's remark about the exchange of the hurly-burly of the chaise-longue for the comfort of the marriage bed. I would keep quiet about how enviable the life of the don, always to have enjoyed a captive audience, his students, afraid to boo, or walk out, having to note and repeat the absurdities of their tutor, needing to feed his vanity because they wanted their exam marks.

Myself I was fortunate in brilliant teachers in school and at university, but there is another kind of teacher, I gather, more in love with themselves than with subject or students. There will be none of that in the new department of tourism. It cannot be good for the soul to be paid well to hector fellow-citizens, however young. It may be that there is more public sympathy for the present Government's treatment of higher education than there should be because the world of scholarship has not learned how to beguile. So how nice it would be to have at home an extra-mural department of affable students putting up with aphorisms and gossip about travels, not captive because I was the professor. All of which, as an application for a job, makes it just as well that I have never applied for one before. I wouldn't rate my chances high.

Western Mail, 18th June 1985

So who was Draig Glas's Dark Lady?

Welshmen are all liars and, if sportsmen, cheats and drunks. Welsh women are immoral. Our choirs cannot sing; our chapels have never heard of the New Testament; our literature loses everything in translation because there was nothing of merit there in the first place. Can this be true? These revelations are offered in a work I had not known before this week, *The Perfidious Welshman*. It was written by "Draig Glas" (Blue Dragon) and published in 1909. Its style and content raise issues of local, wide-spread, not to say frivolous and grave substance. The author is in a rare temper throughout. For example, he offers the view, almost in passing, that the shorter, darker kind of Welshman is of Mongolian origin. That is, he has "black hair, low forehead, full lips, dark, beady eyes and large, low set ears; without doubt the craftiness, vanity, ignorance and fanaticism of this kind of Welshman – who poses as a Celt – are partly traceable to the same (mongolian) source". Which, while it makes me relieved that I'm nearly 6ft tall, is not otherwise encouraging.

The memory of the Evan Roberts Revival of 1904 rouses "Draig Glas":

> "If you looked in upon one of these congregations you would have seen before the immoveable, speechless Prophet women shrieking on the floor, and pouring out confessions of sins between the intervals of praying, weeping and laughing.
>
> "Men would be wrestling in mad anguish with ghostly enemies, dancing epileptic jigs or throwing themselves down to bite the dust of self-abasement."

At which he (or she?) offers a scholarly footnote about the sharp rise in the number of illegitimate births after the revival. "Draig Glas" then mocks Welsh claims that Prince Madoc, not Columbus, discovered America.

The book, if we put to one side that matter of whether it holds up a mirror to our nature, raises general questions. Would a writer today be permitted to publish so savage an attack on a people? I doubt it. Again, what had we done to him that he should so take against us? And, even more generally, why should hatred be so productive or entertaining if, of course, quite disreputable prose? I find this last peculiarly interesting since a recent experience may square with that of many, if not of our "Draig Glas". This year for the first, and, I hope the last time in my life I have had cause to hate another human being. I gather I've been lucky. The emotion is held to be a deplorable one: I used to think so myself. What has surprised me is how fruitful it may prove. I have never written so busily; never slept so little. Where love makes for lotusland and trouble, hatred concentrates energy. Is this, then, what the moguls of industry are made of? Exhibiting, as ever, the columnist egocentricity, I have begun a little light research. It may seem an enigma that jokes come easily when hatred is the spur.

You may argue that all this is very fine for a writer. Most men and women who suffer enough to feel hatred have to resort to tears alone or to the dangers of arrest for grievous bodily harm or whatever: they cannot have the last word, for what words are worth. Even so, authorities as various as Dr Samuel Johnson and Sigmund Freud assure us that the capacity to joke is a piece of good fortune in emotional, hard times. True, they consider grief rather than hatred,but the two are not, spiritually, unlike: one may be the consequence of the other.

So, what was it that so reached up the nose of "Draig Glas"? *The Perfidious Welshman* contains a powerful diatribe against the Welsh habit of attending funerals. Here the motives of our fellow countrymen are held to be mixed. Certainly the sad event offers to dodge work, but there is that other benefit of trying to ensure a good crowd at your own burial by pitching-up at others. I see no clue there. More to the point is his criticism of Welsh hotels. Eat only, he writes, at those owned by the English. Could it be merely that the polemicist had just had a bad meal? "Draig Glas" praises Church of England clerics at the expense of Welsh chapel ministers. He usually refers to David Lloyd George as George. At this we approach the heart of the matter, perhaps. The author would thus seem to be an Anglican Tory. But a man or a woman?

At which we find the key. In my opinion "Draig Glas" is a man who has been doublecrossed by a Welsh woman; a rare event, perhaps, but not unknown. Consider this passage:

"The most remarkable fact about the damsels of Wales is that although they often have more than the average amount of good looks, by the time they reach a 'marriageable' age they are old women — toothless, anaemic and with a distinct inclination to shrivel.

"It has often been a marvel to me how Taffy, the least couragous and most cautious of men, can bring himself to marry a Welsh girl with such a prospect in view. But it is often a case of Hobson's choice."

Here, surely, there is an unusual solemnity in the prose: an uncharacteristic compliment if offered. And so, as we brood on the identity of "Draig Glas", we must also ask: who was the woman? What did she do, this "good looking damsel" who wouldn't marry him? Did she keep an inn; and was she chapel? Soprano or contralto? Did he meet her at a funeral? It was a long time ago and they are all dead. And yet, "Draig Glas" went away and wrote an hilarious and disgraceful book that is still read. Perhaps someone knows his real name. Who would know the woman's?

Western Mail, 2nd July 1985

Looking back on giving up

"The rain in Wales is mainly in the vales," is not a couplet that can be set to any tune like the exuberant tango of *My Fair Lady's* 'Rain in Spain being mainly on the plain.' Rather, it should be set to the *Dead March* in *Saul*. It is time to take the rain seriously and wonder what it is doing to us. Research contradicts the experts. How can it be the case that this year has not been unusally wet? I read that 1980 was as bad. I remember 1980 and then we didn't every day look at the drizzle, were not woken by a downpour. No doubt statistics will show that while we were all asleep the moon shone from a clear sky. So what?

And if you think already that this prose reads oddly, that it lacks the normal calm grandeur of the column, you are as sharp as you believe yourself to be. This is the first article or whatever written for 40 years without the help of an untipped cigarette. The consultant at the hospital said: Give up smoking. It was my first visit to a hospital as a potential patient, although I had been often to visit parents, wife, friends. Oddly, being the afflicted, I found the experience less troubling. My main aim was to avoid seeming frivolous. Since childhood one of my favourite aphorisms had been a Sir Thomas Browne remark in his *Religio Medici:* "As for this world I count it not an Inn but a Hospital, a place not to live but to die in." Could I resist making the remark to the distinguished surgeon at St Lawrence's in Chepstow. I managed, just.

Before the visit there had been days in the rain when affable amateur doctors around the house had been showing concern and offering fashionable analyses of how it came about that this fungus appeared on the floor of my mouth. My cynical appraisal that if I was going to be hit anywhere it would be bound to be there, since I talk a lot, was not appreciated. One school of thought proposed that its flourishing was due to emotional shock, but then demurred at my bad taste in suggesting, with that incurable, characteristic Swansea whimsical anthropomorphism, that I should name the growth after the person concerned. Smoking won many votes. Those who have never smoked will never understand the anguish, being like eunuchs in a harem. I doubt if my problem is worse than most who have tried to abandon the delight. I have promised to say never again that giving up smoking is killing me – the rain has resumed as I write. A peculiar difficulty, though, but perhaps not so peculiar is that one of my dearest childhood memories in Treboeth in Swansea is of the scent of a packet of the Senior Service my father smoked. Not the fragrance of the cedars of Lebanon, not the perfume of the hanging gardens in Bali, since match the delight. There are real problems in a happy childhood.

There is also a religious point to be made. Vanity was the reason for the growth being discovered. Always having been someone indifferent to my appearance, I was urged to have something done to my teeth, which were in a shabby state. So I went to the dentist to have teeth capped. He noticed that there was something odd. Thus vanity proved not to be, as the Bible has it, a vexation of spirit, but a saviour. Is not faith sacred?

Talking about all this and the rain with some poet friends in

Pencader I discovered, to my surprise, that they found me less demented than I thought. It seems that there has been an unusually high level of marital, emotional or otherwise sexual upheaval among the middle-aged in Wales this year, and that many put it down to the rain. Have there, then, I asked, rhyming among poets, been bizarre disruption, comic conjuntions? Sure thing.

Poets are better poeple to trust than statisticians or academics. In the company was the fine Pencader poet Douglas Houston, who shares my theory about the rain and has allowed me to quote from one of his several poems on the subject:

> Here there are all varieties of rain,
> Some fine as mist, plenty of spattering drops,
> Dense hedges that resent the hidden roads . . .
> No, it does not make me think, this valley,
> Half way down which rain drums like hard boiling,
> On the thin roof of the lean-to kitchen.
> Her green fist in my throat, the rural muse,
> Would have me believe nature is enough.

And since we are on the subject of rain, I said, have you noticed that the Welsh fly has changed its character in the recent wet? That flies have grown plump and idle had been generally noted. Had a new arrogance been detected? I reported that when I picked up my French *Scorpion* mug for an early cup of coffee, two flies were fornicating in it. Normally you would expect flies so engaged to move, or at least realise that they had been observed. These were quite different. What does one do? I read the Scorpio characteristics – this was a present from Avignon – about how we are "Dynamique . . . Reserve et mysterieuz . . . ami loyal . . . rien impossible . . . sensual, mefiant . . . jaloux . . . agit par sympathie . . ." and so on, and in the end could only put it down to the rain that these two flies could not care that they were in my coffee mug cavorting in that fashion.

Therefore should one argue that if my poet friends are correct and the middle-aged Welsh are behaving like the flies, that we have here an unusual social discovery; one due to the rare perception offered by giving-up smoking, some might argue. More serious is the news that the wet season is officially due to begin. Less so that, as you read, I shall be driving down the Wye Valley to Chepstow to the hospital, quite convinced that all is well, and steeling myself not to quote from *Religio Medici*. It will be raining.

Western Mail, 24th September 1985

Why I am lucky to be alive . . .

For those unfamiliar with Welsh or Roman history, Chepstow may seem an odd staging post on the road to Damascus, but so it proved last week for one pilgrim, to wit, myself. St Lawrence's Hospital there witnesses a conversion almost as dramatic, if more secular, than St Paul's. *Timor Mortis Conturbat me* is, no doubt, how that priggish disciple would have put it: me I was just frightened stiff.

What follows is not nice. This column, indeed, like a cigarette packet, carries a health warning. I am reluctant to write it and only do so under heavy pressure from medical advisers who are lucky to be nameless. Why not, for once, they say, perform a public service instead of playing the fool? One man's public conspiracy. All right, all right, I said, in a surly fashion, celebrating my great escape in sunshine on a bank of the Wye. You are, the surgeon had said, one of the luckiest patients I have ever had. Considering that I had spent the previous week in some pain and discomfort since he had stuck a scalpel in my mouth and dug a piece of it out and stitched it up, the eye I cast upon him was cold. As he continued, my blood ran ever colder.

The background was this. All my adult life I have

smoked untipped cigarettes, for most of the past 25 years some 20 a day. For various reasons I had been smoking over 40 a day since mid February. In July I went to the dentist to have teeth capped. In a gap of a fortnight between visits a growth appeared in my mouth, detected at once by the dentist who sent me to my doctor. From there I went first to one consultant at St Lawrence Hospital, who told me to stop smoking at once, who then sent me to one even more expert in the field. All this was on the National Health. Never having been ill in hospital, nor having had any kind of operation and being incapable of taking myself seriously, it was only suddenly noting the wary glances of family and friends that made me realise in the few days before the results of tests and so on were known that there was a fear that I might have cancer.

So what does a middle-aged Welsh writer, one scornful about anti-smoking propoganda, one who had even written to the chairman of British Rail complaining about the increase in non-smoking compartments, what does he do? Chance had it that the days before the news were being spent filming for HTV Wales with colleagues Gerald Davies and Don Llewelyn in the places of my youth.

Was this an omen I would have wondered, had I been taking the matter seriously? So we sang with the choir at the Morriston rugby club. I showed them where I'd lived at Plasy-coed Terrace; where Gwrosydd had lived in Treboeth, and we sang *Calon Lan*. On a lovely morning I marched them on the cliff walk between Langland and Caswell. And not a single smoke. And then, after the match between Treforis and Carmarthen Athletic, drove off, as planned, to a dinner party at Dinas Powys given by Mrs Jeanne Moorsome, to which I was being taken – to borrow the style of a social column – by my hosts Mr and Mrs Euryn Ogwen Williams to meet novelist and director Mr Gareth Jones, and wife, and Polish intellectual Mr Bogdan Szajkowski, and wife, in some project as if I had a future. Which church to go to? I settled for St Jerome's at Llangwm Uchaf, near Usk, where the flowers for the harvest were more abundant than the place can have seen for 700 years, but also because St Jerome has a handy prayer, 'Deal favourably with me according to Thy good pleasure.'

Not that is all that is what the medicos want me to be writing. What they want me to say is this – that I am lucky to be alive. Had it not been for chance I would have been dead next year, probably around about St David's day. The good luck, it seems, as I try and understand the lingo, took several forms.

Had I not been to the dentist and had he not been sharp enough to notice, the growth would have eaten through my mouth into the bone before I had felt any pain, by when the cancer would have been inoperable. Let us suppose, they carry on, the growth had been instead in the wind-pipe or lung, where it would have been unnoticed, then by the time I had felt any pain, it would have been too late to do much about it.

If you have, said the surgeon, even one cigarette a day any more, you will be dead soon. Come on, I said. Three years ago, he said, I had a patient where you are now and said the same. Would you, he said, care to come and see the way in which the patient is dying today? I'll believe you, I said.

The heat of the smoke, I think he said, will make the growth cancerous. Like, I said, breathing on the embers of a fire? May I use that, he said? Feel free.

Therefore my duty is done. The greatest smoker in the West has packed it in after 40 years, man and boy, and those who may not have my amazing luck had best brood, I suppose. What the medicos won't perhaps comprehend, which puzzles me, is quite why I should be keen to continue to dance down the vale of tears.

Western Mail, 9th October 1985

Chance to tell us what Wales wants

The romantic will forever believe, whatever colder spirits maintain, that Welsh politics is about Carmarthen. So how encouraging that the recent Plaid Cymru and the approaching Alliance conferences, not to mention what may happen to Labour in Merlin's hang-out, suggest that at the next general election we are all going to have a high old time which will have the necessary merit of serious import for Wales.

Having been brought up on tales of the scale of bribery and the wild antics of 19th century polling in the town, tales which make Charles Dickens's Eatanswill look a Sunday School class, my occasional involvement in the drama of the latter part of this century has given memorable pleasure.

In the early Fifties I had to appear at a judicial inquiry into allegations that BBC Wales was under Welsh Nationalist influence. My offence had been a passing remark in a report on a Carmarthen election that some voters objected to having to mark an X on a ballot paper because there was no such letter in the Welsh alphabet. The judge, or whatever he was, dismissed me.

In the later Fifties I spent a week travelling around with Lady Megan Lloyd George in her by-election campaign – in those days people left the Liberal for the Labour party. The giants of the party were with her. There was a nice moment in Llanfihangel ar Arth when Lord Elwyn-Jones, then a mere backbench MP and QC, remarked that he had never seen such a beautiful night, at which the local Labour party agent responded that the only reason for that was that Lord Elwyn had never been in Llanfihangel ar Arth before.

And then there was the melodrama of Mr Gwynfor Evans's victory and I even had myself the experience of appearing on the short list in the shoot-out in the town for Labour's seat in the European parliament. There was a moment when Mrs Ann Clwyd Roberts was afraid she was going to lose to me, while I was dismayed that I might win. My speech at the selection conference had begun by my saying that I thought the Labour policy on Europe was a disgrace; a bold gesture.

And now it seems, if the tea-leaves are read correctly, we have ahead as interesting a conflict as the Towy has seen. The nuances of the Plaid conference are, to judge by those I've talked to, open to many interpretations. The general message is that there has been a retreat from the influence of the Marxists. While the party remains socialist in a general sense, it has more returned to its Welshness and, more importantly, to its desire to win seats at Westminster. Carmarthen and Ynys Môn have to be won.

The shadow of the miners' strike hangs over this matter as much else in Wales. Plaid Cymru involved itself in the cause, when it was lost from the beginning, whatever its justice. Many well-heeled middle-class Marxist intellectuals egged the miners on when, had they consciences, they should have known better. They still have their jobs, when miners do not. I am not surprised to be told by people in the mining community at the bitterness felt about their role. In Carmarthen, mining matters, not so does much else. The milk question is thought to have seen the Tories off. Rumours that Dr Roger Thomas may stand as an independent Labour candidate create a disturbance. Therefore it could be that the struggle will be between Plaid Cymru's Mr Hywel Teifi Edwards and the Social Democrats' Mr Gwynoro Jones, each, in his way, a charismatic performer. Politics becomes theatre when protagonists entertain as well as guide.

More important, though, is what the candidates represent. If it is the case that the Plaid has shed its Marxist nonsense, as the Social Democrats have removed themselves from Labour Party ideology of the difficult recent past, then Carmarthen becomes a test of a new view of what the country needs. Politics is about either telling people what they need, or finding out what they need and organising it. Marxists and Fascists, as the century has told us, belong in the first category, democrats in the second. The old radical tradition in Carmarthen has been to express the wants of the people. That famous remark about there being a special providence in the fall of a sparrow has always been interpreted there as an expression of the importance of each human being against all authority.

So, while there are, I know, questions within the Social Democractic party about Gwynoro Jones's policy, as there may be about Hywel Teifi's within the Plaid, what Carmarthen could offer in the period before the general election is a great debate about what it is that people want of government and, more particularly, what they want of Wales. Each party has a chance to redefine need. And what a pleasure it would be to think that the place which has offered so much entertainment in the past – as the next election surely will – could be the forum for a statement about the future, one which common sense demands. Carmarthen as a source of common sense is quite a thought.

Western Mail, 5th November 1985

Valium of the prosperous

Why should it be that, with unemployment so high and with distressing reports about the Welsh condition falling like autumn leaves, the cities of Cardiff and Swansea month-in, month-out, witness a shopping saturnalia? This is the kind of economic question that occupies the South Wales mind more than do the theories and concerns of politicians and academics. I believe that there are several explanations, none of which has to do with the spiritual commercialism of Christmas. A simple answer is that those in work have never had it so good. Rewards in many kinds of trade are now some five per cent above the rate of inflation. The amount of overtime worked is high as employer and worker conspire for reason of laws, convenience or greed, to prefer the technique to taking-on more labour. Moonlighting helps. A city like Cardiff has, too, a crowd in Government, banks, broadcasting, universities, either employed or on index-linked pensions, untouched by the state of the nation and especially that of the Valleys. There is also the – I think – irresponsible habit of the clearing banks of encouraging credit among the middle-class young. Why should the shop, therefore, not be packed?

I doubt, though, if anyone looks to this column for so commonplace a set of answers to a question which puzzles the Welsh citizen. Shopping is the Valium of the prosperous, and for those on Valium, the safest way to avoid an overdose. Before developing this observation, he said, I should declare my own position, which may not be unusual. As a child I was a forced, if cheerful, shopper. This was not just the case of being sent out for Woodbines by my unemployed collier uncles at whose feet I sat hearing about great Welsh boxers. Every Saturday morning I would cycle up the hill in Treboeth in Swansea with a pig's head from the Co-op dramatically tied to the handle-bars of my ten-and-sixpenny second-hand bike, as if, looking back on the experience, I was an early member of a bizarre porcine Hell's Angel sect. When I became a man, with the good fortune of marrying young, I put away childish things and did not shop for 30 years. More recently being alone more, writing, I have become a shopper.

But even now, having the good fortune to be prosperous and reckless with money. I have little helpful to say, except that if Wilde had it that the cynic is a man who knows the price of everything and the value of nothing, then I am the shopper as anti-cynic: I know the value of everything and the price of nothing. Like, I suspect, more than have the courage to say so, I need to be a lonely shopper for the little I want. I am unable to shop with anyone, however, near and dear, without suffering an attack of vertigo. This neurosis, which may be peculiar to the Welsh male, has yet to be defined, as far as I know, although I have a theory. All this I mention to assert that shopping is not a simple matter about buying what you need. We all know that, you say: but wait. In the past it has always been held that women only, when low or cross, have expressed or revenged themselves by extravagant purchase of clothes or scent or otiose kitchen instruments, finding either a pure delight at the counter or an enduring satisfaction in a male chauvinist household in creating domestic financial embarrassment. Children have always rushed to shops as to the dummy. Men, it strikes me, are now going the same way.

I have known a professor of philosophy, now abroad, exhibit his emotional dismay by decorating himself at an expensive tailor. It could be that Do-It-Yourself shops flourish partly not out of some uxorious desire for home improvement, but to satisfy a passionate need to spend. Similarly with after-shave lotions. When visiting a house so equipped with electronic equipment that it could fly to Mars, the first question should be what's wrong here? In Wales, as elsewhere, shopping, like Valium, alcohol or, indeed golf, has become the new opiate of the prosperous classes.

And what if you are not among the thousands, I wonder, tumultuous at the counters, hot-shot discriminators among clothes and costly music centres, yet are on Valium and alcohol? But instead are locked in your terrace in Mid Glamorgan, or in some city back-street while your neighbours make it to the super-store and the boutique? The shopping boom then becomes not some interesting subject for a Fancy Dan columnist. When the stores of Swansea and Cardiff are packed day in day out, it is no longer possible to resume Hogarthian or Dickensian images of the poor pressing their noses against the pane observing the extravagances of the rich. The poor may see their neighbours at the counter. Their neighbours are in work and on overtime. When I was at the Swansea Grammar School I was held to be the poorest boy there, but it never troubled me because I was doing all right. But passing through Cardiff the other day I wondered how I would feel if I had been some young man with no hope from the Rhondda and observed the scene.

Western Mail, 3rd December 1985

232

The gap in the fence on the road to Hell

Sudden revelations occur about the Welsh character, or at least, that of some of us, to which the only honest response must be shame. Mostly, we can avert our eyes from what we are up to. Lies are useful; a shifting of blame handy; an imperishable sense of our own virtue quite indispensable: but then the moment comes. For me the moment came last week. I was at the home in Pentyrch, near Cardiff, among Welsh-speakers even, when my host, who is known as the "Sage of Pentyrch," but who describes himself as a born-again agnostic, exhibited a religious poster.

I had not seen it since childhood. Here was *The Broad and Narrow Way*. All that was good in the world, all that was evil, in colour, the characters and signposts elegantly designed, depicted as clearly as memory had it. Which way had we chosen? I'm sure this poster, this matter doesn't occupy me alone: it figures in Welsh religious and secular life. In the Thirties in Morriston my grandfather owned a copy. He was Rechabite, a shy man among women, a teetotal steelworker, his only reading the *Sunday Companion* with its tales of virtuous romance, along with Biblical reminders. We were great friends. He would take me to football matches and offer illicit cigarettes. Both the famous Morriston choirs sang at his funeral in Llangyfelach.

At that time we were sure we were taking the Narrow Way. Sunday school was depicted in the poster. Sober brethren and sistren, as the phrase went, addressed each other in tidy clothes. Here was Christ crucified; water poured from the rock. The narrow path led to the Holy City, a favourite song at concerts I used to give, having been nudged into being a boy soprano. My grandfather was in the audience at the Patti Pavilion in Swansea. The poster has a hillside hermit offering a lament and much else that is admirable and in which we all believe. How could we have not gone that way when that sign-post in scarlet and black said so firmly that the Broad Way led

233

to Death and Damnation, while ours, the Narrow Way, led to Life and Salvation?

It didn't last. Adulthood chose the Broad Way. And this was no thin primrose path of dalliance, rather an avenue of disgraceful pleasure. The first stop is a tavern and laughter. And then the Ballroom, men and women elegant, no doubt waltzing in their day as we foxtrotted and quickstepped to Sinatra and were livelier with Chuck Berry and the Beatles in our time. The flag of Wordliness flutters on the poster. The Theatre is there. The Gambling House has a suicide dangling from a noose. Another man is climbing into an upper window by ladder. Why? Here I make of myself an exception never having truly gambled, except with my life and work: with money I have only backed winners, like the great Welsh rugby team or the SDP at by-elections, or, for a few months with success, horses with Welsh names running at long odds.

The Broad Way does lead on to what must have been a great evil in the last century – The Sunday Train – and then the flames of Hell with scorched demons ascending. The shrewd will have recognised the mystery in this description, one which may be peculiarly Welsh; to wit, how is it possible physically to have danced up the Broad Way, while remaining spiritually in the Narrow? Hypocrisy is not a sufficient explanation. Neither is protestant pedantry, which it might seem to those who embrace the Churches of Rome or Moscow, where brisk techniques of absolution and an indifference to private conscience make all permissible, he said. So where do we stand, most of us, the averagely sensual man or woman whom this question is vexing at this time of year as it might even more so at Easter?

To my astonishment, examining more closely The Broad and Narrow Way, the poster itself seems to offer an unexpected answer, one it seems almost too vulgar to offer. Contemplating the work with an adult eye I have noticed something which had escaped me as a child and which, certainly, my grandfather never remarked on. There is a gap in the fence halfway-along between the Broad and the Narrow.

How could this be? Naturally, I accused my friend "The Sage of Pentyrch" of deliberately expunging the fence at this point as a joke to dismay his Christian friends. He was so cross at my assault that he sent for fresh copies of the poster to demonstrate that it had not been his doing. Nevertheless, he felt that it was a mere cartographical flaw, of no significance. I responded that only the non-religious could be so materialist in an interpretation. The gap occurs as the delights end and the flames of Hell approach. It is unlikely that those on the Narrow side, as the Holy City is near, would wish to nip through the fence in order to burn in Hell-fire, unless they were masochists of rare spirit. The gap therefore must exist for most of us, enabling us to hope that the days of wine and roses are longer than a poet who had not studied this influential poster can have imagined. I used the word "shame" to open this column and this argument is what I had in mind. On the other hand, it isn't every day you find a stern text proposing that it really is possible to enjoy the best of all possible worlds.

Western Mail, 17th December 1985

1986

The comic side of the Big C

Not that there is anything especially Welsh about cancer, but there is a suffering citizen operated upon in a Welsh hospital among compatriots, which is excuse enough, he said. And what a strange disease it is and how powerful its effect not only on the body and mind, but in its sharpening of perceptions of life, eternity and, to put it more crudely, pain and death. A few have proposed that it's a matter best not written about, to which my response is that no matter is best not written about; and anyway, is it not so that the Welsh whether, in the case of women and cancer of the cervix, or men with the consequence of smoking, suffer more than people elsewhere in Britain? Fear prospers in the dark. I'm sure that scores of thousands of readers who followed this column last year, and have since been hanging by their fingertips to discover what happened to the hero, or baddie, will recall the plot. The memory will be fresh of my boasting of my good luck that my dentist had cleverly observed tumours and of my rejoicing that they were benign. I was wrong. They were malignant. And then there was that analysis of how it came about. It was a combination of excessive smoking, work, lack of sleep, helped on by emotional shock – in my case a needless blow. It seems that grief, divorce, even sudden redundancies can contribute to cancer. The mysteries of the connection between body and soul are formidable.

That the parade of events after the first terror of the news should have struck me as comic is my fault. My wife, and all other women of my acquaintance when learning I was a cancer kid, showed concern, among deeper sentiments, about pyjamas. And there was I thinking they saw me as some hot-shot. Pyjamas matter most. A Welsh trait, I thought, and did recall that in my childhood there was always a drawer in the chest for hospital clothes. Never having been an invalid before, much of the detail of the experience at St Lawrence Hospital in Chepstow may have more to do with surgery than cancer, except that here were men without ears and noses strolling about. I did suggest to a young woman who beguiled me into blowing into a tube to test my lung power that I detected the chance of a new television game that could overwhelm darts and snooker. A red line moved along a graph as one puffed. It struck me – and the idea is here patented – that there was a good pub game, especially if it could be linked with a breath-alyser.

At which I had the fortune to find that my Carmarthen ward companion was Mr David Jenkins, of Lower Row, Dowlais. Mr Jenkins is 90 years old. He has been an inter-mittent cancer-patient at St Lawrence for a quarter of a century. He asked me to promise that I would report our chat. Promises in a cancer ward need to be kept. All you need, as a writer, is luck. Mr Jenkins remembers well hearing Keir Hardie. He attended an Evan Roberts revival meeting. He asked me if I knew of the two famous Dowlais historians Professors Glanmor and Gwyn Williams? He had been born in the same street in the same year as the latter's mother. They were friends.

Glanmor, yes, I said, since he had taught me in Swansea, the other not really, though I met him briefly at a friend's dinner party. Did I know that Glanmor was working-class, while the other, the Marxist, was "crachach" (privileged class) in Dowlais, that his grandfather had voted against Keir Hardie? Nothing especially Dowlais about that, Mr Jenkins, I said. In this very ward a few years ago my friend, the late Philip Toynbee, former Communist President of the Oxford Union, had hoped his working-class fellow sufferers would call him Philip, and was dismayed to learn that he was known as Mr Toynbee. Chat stopped at this point since Harlech TV were showing the classic musical *High Society,* and I suggested to Mr Jenkins that if these were to be our last moments on this earth, I thought it would be sweeter to leave with the memory of Sinatra and Crosby singing *Swell Party* than with the detail of the crachach of anywhere. He concurred.

And then to awake and feel a face the size of a football and above wife to the right and to the left, son and beautiful Irish girl announcing in unison, "We are engaged to be married." At which, sleep. Most of us have the knowledge of the disease in the family. My mother died in dreadful pain of cancer at 61, her father similarly. I observed both without truly understanding. One of my younger brothers had a cancerous lung removed 10 years ago and is still bouncing about. On the other hand, I knew a gifted television writer who went at 38. His, and my, solicitor died of cancer in his early forties. What is fascinating is the nature of the buoyancy of the survivors. For example. I am held to be a bad convalescent by not convalescing. Yet it seems the refusal to accept that the affliction exists may be a means of cure. We shall see. By the chance of having the eruption in the mouth I could torment myself daily by seaching for a fresh display. I choose, even when in pain, not to do so. An idiocy may be a help.

Even so, cancer is the enemy within. Its peculiarity as a disease is its emphasis on the isolation of self. There are famous aphorisms about the nature of the solitary, like Chekhov's remark that you should never marry unless you are prepared to be lonely.

I suspect, although these are early days yet, that what cancer does for the sane is what insanity does for the insane: it demonstrates that your fate is no longer yours to command.

You may work, laugh, chat, make love, watch football, opera or whatever and think that it might well be growing within you and there is nothing much you can do about it.

For those who do not aspire to be saints, a spirituality is acquired willynilly. The question is: should this awareness make for frivolity or gravity? Watch this space.

Western Mail, 10th March 1986

Don't be shy – and live longer

And there was I thinking how nice it would be to write something amusing before setting off to watch the embattled cricket tourists in the Caribbean and cheering on the new Swansea Valley hero, Gregory Thomas. The subject was to be the effort by a Birmingham group to have the City's Scots declared an ethnic minority and so warrant a hand-out. What about the Welsh? And let's suppose the idea was borrowed by Carmarthen. Would the English there qualify for an ethnic community? It is not to be. Just as in Robert Browning's lovely poem *A Toccata of Galuppi's,* the poet's reverie is disturbed as the composer comes in with his "cold music," so do the medicos suggest that I perhaps return to the subject of cancer, just once, just once. So do, to be fair, a number of *Western Mail* readers, not to mention a surprising number of radio and television people who seem to find it strange that the matter should be so openly discussed. I find it strange they find it strange but, then like most who have known good health, medical matters have never before interested me. What nerve has been touched here?

Doctors and surgeons, of course, have a particular argument. They point out that I have a platform. I now also have the experience of cancer. Many have the latter, few the former. Therefore don't I have a duty to help others? All very well, I say, but I have not yet suffered in the manner so many have, and may even be lucky enough to escape for many years. My experience has been mild, if nasty, compared with so many. Forget your modesty, they say, even if it is only to write a little more about fear. At which point, with that dreadful poignancy which middle-age accretes, the news came that a friend of 20 years died of cancer. Only two months ago she and I had been discussing our condition in a cheerful manner. We'd be all right. How swift the decline can be.

A mutual friend and former colleague of mine, a film director now in San Francisco, arrived for the funeral. He had rung the St Lawrence Hospital in Chepstow from Cuba where he had been at the film festival, being of that persuasion, while I had been having my operation. How being a broadcaster does spread the news. Are you afraid, he asked me. I said I was. How can that be, he asked, given what a reckless clown I had been? There are different kinds of fear, Jo I said. He reminded me of an incident I had chosen to put from my mind, still, understandably fresh in his, from a battle in Vietnam in early 1967. It seems that while the shelling and shooting was going on in heavy rain near the northern frontier of South Vietnam, he had asked me how we might best survive. Equally, it seems, I had offered an account of what had happened in the Swansea Blitz. There, I recalled, on a bright, moonlit night, the German bombers had approached the town for three nights in a row. Along the Tawe lay the factories.

Each night the bombs missed them, but destroyed the town and killed the people. Further, it seems I said, had I not myself held Her Majesty's Commission and been in charge of men with guns? So, it seems Jo said, what is the point of all this Welsh chat since people were being killed round and about us? Indeed some of the shell craters resembled, filled with water and mud, those World War I battlefield pictures. The point, Jo, it seems I said, is that the key to warfare is the incompetence of all involved. My analysis is that the safest place in this battle is the most dangerous. Therefore we should sit on the US Marines' ammunition dump. The analysis proved correct. We sat there safely sipping from cans of beer.

To walk into the cancer hospital once a month, as I have to do, given I'm lucky, every month for the next three years, demands more courage than any antics on a battlefield, I assured my friend. Or so it seems at present. Still, I go, and this is the heart of the matter medicos would like understood. There is no need for as much fear as prevails. My own distinguished surgeon – we already have enough dialogue for a one-act play, and I trust it will be a three-acter – explains that if only more people would go and see their doctor sooner, would not be shy, not be afraid of bothering, would grasp that early treatment cures, then the fear of "the scourge" would diminish.

Obviously there are manifestations that cannot be detected until too late, but there are many more that can be. Equally it is silly to suppose that a view of life is not transformed by being hit. There is small chance, too, that, given stress and emotional shock play a part, the human condition will ever put an end to that travail. The argument advanced to me at St Lawrence is not one for perfection, but a simple appeal for less fear, for a shattering of the assumption of inevitable doom. I know that if my mother had not been shy, she need not have died so young. There is much else I learn that is relevant and fascinating about the disease. For example, for some it is a bizarre means of suicide: a deathwish of the cells. For the meantime, however, that is the message: don't be so frightened. Look who's talking, you might say. But, then propaganda doesn't come easy to me. And I'm going to see the Trebanos boy bowl at Viv Richards in Antigua.

Western Mail, March 1986

Beauty with a powerful personality

How many remember a remarkable Welsh film from the early Fifties titled *Three Weird Sisters*, remarkable mainly because it was an eccentric piece of private hilarity sped-on by Dylan Thomas which yet occupied the picture palaces? That so few recall it may mean either there aren't many of us left, or that some memories are more vigorous than others.

The recently concluded and encouragingly successful festival of Welsh films at Chapter, Cardiff, did brood on whether to show it but, I gather, found the print available too poor. They hope to show it next time. My advice is: Book now. It is a hoot.

I raise the matter not only in the interests of enriching the seams of Welsh social history, but because, as will soon become clear, the film bears on the recent sad demise of my old pal, my 19-year-old cat Siani, and her burial. The whimsical, the sentimental, the affectionate, the anthropomorphic, and how they all touch on the comic in the Welsh nature: we are in dense woods here.

The film was a cult movie in Swansea in its time. We would watch it at the Albert Hall cinema day after day. Some of its Dylan Thomas phrases would only need to be repeated for all to fall about laughing. A favourite was a scene in which the actor Elwyn Brooke-Jones, a factotum to the three dotty sisters, driven half-mad by the crumbling household and, no doubt, the script, rushed into a room and said he could stand no more since the place was haunted by "Dwarfs with beards in their noses."

In 1953, when I had the honour, as a young journalist, to spend a day, a month before he died, with my hero Dylan Thomas in Swansea, I spent much of the time wondering if I had the nerve to ask him to recite the line for me. In the Bush Hotel I was too shy. Later in the famous Metropole in Wind Street I decided to steel myself. He had been wondering if we could do well out of *The Observer* for expenses. I was green. I was only 23, but did think that this profile I was writing for them was an important feature in the great London newspaper, so thought we could push the boat out a little.

Declaim it, I asked, in your manner, let's say like, "Death shall have no dominion." "Dwarfs," he intoned, across the empty bar of the Metropole, "with beards in their noses." It was a fine moment. My profile appeared in the *Observer* as his obituary.

Among the many other baroque splendours Dylan Thomas offered in *Three Weird Sisters* brings me nearer the melancholy theme of the day. The late Huw Griffith makes a fierce radical speech from the top of a coal-tip to what one assumes is an enrapt multitude. The rhetoric is fine. At which there is a cut-away shot to his audience. There, alone, sits the orator's milgie, as wretched a dog as even the Rhondda has seen.

From time to time over the past 19 years that scene has come back to me in my perhaps not-so-curious-relationship with our cat. For the past 13 years of her life Siani was a country cat. Writing at home I spent most days alone with her. She was black and beautiful but – and here we go – troubled since her two children, Ianto and Ben, had been killed in our London street when she was two years old. I can see the traps of whimsy before me, which is why I find the Dylan Thomas scene on the coal-tip encouraging. Huw Griffith and the milgie excuse what follows. Certainly I never thought to think thus about a cat. I can recall that when I lived with my grandmother in Morriston in 1943 and she found a new cat, and asked what we should call it, I said, "It is a cat, why don't we call it Cat?" We did.

Siani's personality was powerful. She killed rats until they gave up. Even mink in the stream under the house never frightened her. Dogs kept out of her way. Once I drove off the road in ice and snow driving home to feed her. Neighbours suggested I was being crazy and fed her in hard weather. She was snooty to their cats and commanded their food. So powerful was her personality or weak mine, that steadily she drove me into behaviour my family thought eccentric. For example, her habit of sitting on my lap or shoulder when I was trying to type, in the end drove me to abandoning my comfortable, cushioned grandpa's chair to her, while I sat alongside her on a kitchen chair. "Writing the Great Cat Novel, huh, Siani," I'd snarl. Her voice became a snarl in her last months. Only once, I think, did I try to assert myself and only then because I was fed-up at being woken in the middle of the night by this movement on my chest and opening my eyes to see hers, green, staring into mine, and have her shout for no reason at all.

My response took a complicated form. It was at a time when I had invented an early 19th century Alsation composer named Schwenk and written a script about him and some songs he was supposed to have written. This was for BBC Radio Wales. This idiot Schwenk was a dog-lover, indeed wore a wig of dog-hair. One of the songs I wrote was in the spirit of Rossini's cat duet. In its interests I bought a record of the Rossini and played it to Siani. She was infuriated and went up the lane to live with neighbours for a few days.

When she returned I played her the BBC recording of my "Bow-Wow Duet," which she obviously thought was all right because she moved back in. Clearly, mocking dogs was fine: to have Rossini sending-up cats was bad news.

And so was it not proper to bury her in the corner of the garden where the stream runs from the ford, under snowdrops? If Caradoc Evans could wish to be buried lightly so that he could hear the grasshoppers, why should Siani not heat the water flow to the Wye? Should I have wrapped her in my Welsh red scarf? In human terms she died, I'm told, at the age of 130, yet was never ill. But is it not absurd that when I arrive now at the house and Siani is not there shouting, I am distressed? She was just a cat.

Western Mail, 8th April 1986

A comforting contribution

Why games should so much matter to the Welsh is a serious question for another time. For now, I have a new one, although I went to the West Indies for the cricket. And the heart, of course, bled on that day this month at the Port of Spain, Trinidad, when the Trebanos boy Gregory Thomas was knocked all over the field by the West Indian heroes and finished the match with the feared figures of none for a 100, a century all bowlers have engraved on their memory. Mr Thomas should be reassured by what followed, as should all of us humbler souls who, in our time, have paraded on the cricket fields of Morriston, Carmarthen, Llandeilo, Pontardawe or Gorseinon.

I had cadged a lift from Canadian bankers on a small plane from St Lucia to Trinidad to see that match, as I was to take a bed on a small boat to Antigua with the help of some Welsh sailors for the next Test. In between times I saw St Lucia play the Dominican Republic, sitting among locals in a temperature that also hit a century. My memory of this game is not perfect since my neighbours were all smoking marijuana and blowing in into my face. What, I asked, will you do when these policemen and women stroll this way? At which they opened their umbrellas which I had presumed were meant as protection from the heat or occasional rain. They held them in front of them, as a shield. Had I noticed, they asked, that bright green plant growing in the grass beneath the benches on which we sat? Indeed it was a marijuana plant. How abundantly everything grows in St Lucia.

Gregory Thomas, they told me, without my revealing my origins, is the only man in the English team they admired. He had no chance, they said, breaking-off from calling the Dominican umpire a pig whereas earlier he had been a dog or goat. Fast bowlers can only hunt in pairs: one alone can do nothing. In their eyes Greg Thomas was a victim of the team's selection. Had there been another bowler of his speed and courage, then the Test matches might have taken another course. Perhaps not, but even so, the heart was restored. Thus revived, I returned to my hotel. Since what follows may or, perhaps may not, have some importance for the future of Welsh life, I will try to set down the details carefully for the benefit of social historians.

At the hotel at the side of the swimming pool, gazing out at the ocean beginning to crimson in the setting sun, I ordered the day's cocktail. *Foot-loose* it was named, one ounce rum, grenadine, coconut juice, and a touch of demi-sec. Would tomorrow's I wondered, be *Fancy-free?* I resumed my reading of Stendhal's *De L'Amour* and Talmon's *The Origins of Totalitarian Democracy,* on both of which works I was commiting light plagiary to help write a play, of such was my convalescent task. At which there was an announcement that the Crab Hurdle Race was about to begin.

You see what I mean about the Welsh and games? So what that Stendhal thought that some men saw love as politics, or that any woman who believed a man who said he loved her unless she's known him two years was a fool. Or that Talmon thought the tyrannies of Marxism were already in the mouth of Saint Juste and Babeuf in the 1790s: here was a new sport across the dance-floor under the Caribbean sky.

The race track is a box 6ft long by 3ft wide. There are three bumps, or hurdles, along the track. The crabs are held in tiny cages, or traps. There is a bookmaker who names the runners and adjusts the odds as the cash flows in. He announces – since he will give a commentary on the race – that it is important,as we crowd around, that we do not cast shadows on the runners. Crabs are afraid of shadows. There are seven runners and they are numbered. The bookie, however, gives them names – and all this just before the United States raid on Libya. In this first race, they were Gorbachev, Gaddafi, Thatcher, Castro, Mulroney (there are many Canadians in the hotel), Mitterand and Reagan. So who to place money on? There are not many trivial matters so vexing as placing a bet on an unseen sport, I thought it best to suppose that in crab-racing, as in life, realpolitick obtains, and that therefore Reagan was bound to be a crab with a chance. Since most Canadians present backed their prime minister, while I could not mine, Reagan was at long odds. He won.

Reagan not only won, he was one of just three crabs who made much progress during the race. Three did not move at all, but sat asleep in their shells and traps. Gorbachev and Thatcher moved forward for a while and then moved sideways, bumped and moved backwards, turned around and moved towards the finishing post sideways, by which time Reagan had crawled over the three hurdles and I was collecting my winnings. Mulroney and Gaddafi and Castro were still asleep.

So sensational an event offered many instant reflections. The first was that this was the apotheosis of the nonsense of gambling. Only an idiot, someone wishing to shine a light into the heart of human folly, would lay a pound on a crab. This was gambling raised to the heights of anarchy. Dostoevsky should have known of crab racing. My next reflection was more vulgar. Since I have a stream in my garden and a fish farmer next door, I wondered if by patenting this sport, he and myself might guard against hard times by breeding racing crabs and introducing so theatrical an event into Welsh pub life. At which I learned that these are land crabs, bred in rock and sand. Still.

My third reflection was more dangerous. Given the experience we all have with our compatriots in public and private life, I began to wonder if the behaviour of these crabs didn't somehow suggest him, or her, or them, that sideway shuffle, that unexpected retreat, but thought better of it. Yet it may be a sport suited to us. Instead, let us think, when the Crab Hurdle Race takes hold in Wales of what names they should be given. Name a Crab for Wales (*Enwi Cranc Dros Cymru*). I suppose, as popular taste will have it, they will be, say, Boyce, Kane, Elinor, Nick Edwards, Kinnock, Bassey, Jonathan Davies; or, in different circles, Wynford, Sir Geraint, Dafydd Iwan, Elerydd, Gwynfor, Dafydd Ellis, Gerald. Only time will tell. Certainly it is a comfort for this patriot, burning in the sun, far from home, to feel that he is making a contribution to the life of a nation gifted enough to have the noun *cranc* for crab. No other language is so perceptive.

Western Mail, 22nd April 1986

A thought . . . do our tourist visitors patronise us

There really is no escape from Wales. You might think that as safe a bolt-hole as any would be to stroll out of the heat in the capital city, Castries, of the island of St Lucia in the West Indies, to hear the Prime Minister deliver his Budget speech in his National Assembly, where all was air conditioned. If you think that, you are wrong. Before the truth hit me there was a diversion. Yet even this turned out to be relevant to what follows, if you will stay with me along a meandering holiday route. The Prime Minister was preceded into the parliament by a young woman in elegant legal robes, its senior officer, no less. Two fellow tourists were with me, one a woman, a hard-line, very intelligent English feminist, the other a French lawyer. The feminist excitably expressed her delight that so important a post was occupied by a woman, moreover, a black one. The lawyer offered a male chauvinist view and said how beautiful she was, how he fancied her. Sharing both attitudes I wondered how to avert a nasty public row.

By chance I had been playing for a few days with an operatic idea in which an arbitrator solves a dispute by finding a form of words which infuriates equally both contestants so that they turn on the arbitrator and live happily ever after. Here was my opportunity. And so I said that I'd been reading Sheila Hodge's new biography of Lorenzo da Ponte, the librettist for Mozart's masterpiece *Don Giovanni*. Were da Ponte writing now, I remarked affably, he would have made Don Giovanni a feminist, thus ensuring his success at seduction in our troubled times. No man, said the feminist, can, by semantic and sexual definition, be a feminist. The lawyer sneered vulgarly. Seeing my gambit had failed, I said: The Prime Minister is wearing a University of Wales tie, at which both turned on me even more strongly. When the television lights were switched on and the tie's colours were defined, it was clear that I was right.

Mr John Compton, the PM of St Lucia, had been at Aberystwyth. His speech had passages of eloquence, of a rural and nautical imagery, that might have owed as much to Aber as to the Creole patois of St Lucia. It also sounded like a pre-election speech, awash with bananas and honey and tax-cuts. Mr Compton was proud of what his government had done and much of that was the revival of tourism after the period in office of his left-wing opponents. Since few of them seem to have been relected to the Assembly, they let fly instead in their newspaper. Will any Welsh Assembly or Senate Prime Minister, I wonder, ever read that he has "the most hopeless, inefficient and corrupt bunch of Ministers which has ever darkened the corridors of power?" Or, from the pen of the columnist in the *Crusaders,* "It must be pointed out that Mr Compton's Administration has plundered the national wealth, destroyed national and local initiatives and has turned our young people into drug addicts, rapists, thieves and lunatics." And, as this fellow-columnist's admiring eye turns from the concerned gravity of that, "it must be pointed out," what does he find but a feature omnipresent in the Caribbean press, but not yet known here : CANCER CORNER. In this edition the entry reads *How Does Cancer Spread?* "Cancer cells invade neighbouring tissues and spread to distant parts of the body by way of the blood stream to lymph vessels. The spread of cancer is called metastasis."

All this I had been reading aloud in a planter's house some five thousand feet up in a rain forest, just to try and avert a fresh row between the elegant feminist and the lawyer male chauvinist. We had driven over paths of mud in a truck. On each side coconuts, guavas, bananas, avocados, nutmeg, rare sour oranges, cinnamon and so many other spices grew. A recent movie *Water,* had been filmed there. It was a lovely place. The new row was a serious one. It raises a question which is the point of all this. It even presents a thought about tourism in Wales which had never occurred to me before – not that, I'm sure, it matters as much here as there.

The feminist had been distressed at the poverty of the hamlets we had passed on the difficult drive to the planter's house. The male chauvinist had thought them picturesque. There were we, living on this island in luxury – though it was true that we had paid for a holiday out of work in our own country – while the native people were destitute. Placed in the odd role of being a Solomon or Daniel, all I could say was that this was a problem to which there is no solution. There are worse places than St Lucia where, at least, the fruit is abundant. It's not quite, I said, I tell you, like stepping out of an hotel in Calcutta and seeing corpses float down the street because heavy unexpected rain had swept people out of their hovels at the side of roads collapsing through contractors' and ministerial corruption over sand and cement. That was in 1971.

Calming down, I offered a parable from an experience in St Lucia the previous week. I had been a guest on a boat hired by a Canadian family to go deep-sea fishing in the Caribbean. The boat was named Make. How that macho Ernest Hemingway, who fished these waters, would have liked that.

I spun-in a barracuda. One of the McKeracher family, my hosts, hauled-in a big fish, a wahoo. Alexander, who owned the boat – he told me he had sold windows in St Lucia in the Sixties for a Cardiff firm – said that the wahoo was inedible. Another fish we caught, a rainbow runner, we took back to the hotel and ate. The next day, talking to some locals, I learned that the wahoo is a fish to eat. Alexander would have found a good price for a 40 pounder.

The message of my parable was mainly to change the subject, but along with that went the thought that there is a distinction between and interest in people and how they live, and some ideological concern for them as "humanity." There is a danger that easy compassion becomes patronising.

At which it struck me that while we may think in Wales,

249

too, that we depend too much on tourists, do visitors come and look on us natives as did these tourists on St Lucia? Are there those, well-heeled from abroad, who drive down from Aberaeron, through Pencader, perhaps take-in Twm Sion Catti and head south for Laugharne, who engage in debates comparable to those in the rain forest of St Lucia? Those lucky enough to live in Llanfihangel-yr-Arth, Drefach Velindre – as does one brother of mine – Fishguard or Llanstephan, might brood this season that those people quarrelling in that large car as they pass through, are disputing quite how much compassion they should show towards us. How travel does broaden the mind.

Western Mail, 6th May 1986

This Welsh musical wheel must continue to go round

Not that the chance comes as often as it might, but how much more pleasure it gives to sing the praises of what's fine in Wales, than take an easy-swinging axe to what's not-so-hot. And how much more so when the object of delight is brand-new, a freshly-minted experiment, but one leaping full-grown from the bud. I write, in this garden of mixed metaphors, of the Welsh Chamber Orchestra (Cerddorfa Siambr Cymru). Throughout the month of May this small band of pioneers has been wandering the Principality, led by its conductor Mr Anthony Hose. From Swansea to Newtown to Cardiff to Newport to Aberystwyth to Mold, enthusiastic audiences have cheered them. Of some four thousand fellow-citizens in the crowds, nearly half have taken the trouble to write promising support. This, I gather, is a remarkable statistic.

The performance I caught was at the Leisure Centre, Newport. The hall is not ideal for a chamber music concert, being too large, but was generously offered. On the other hand, its acoustics seem magically improved - or there may well be a practical explanation – since last year's Inaugural Concert when Dennis O'Neill and Suzanne Murphy filled the place. Before the first note was played I was troubled by an uneasiness which is common, or should be, in a country where so many men, women and children put themselves on show at eisteddfodau and elsewhere. In this case it was two-fold. First, several key figures in the orchestra's founding and in this show, were close friends. Secondly, I had brought along a trio of well-heeled characters whom I hoped might help financially in the orchestra's future. But what if it were to prove an amateur night-out, one of those times when only a lying smile and a quick farewell is possible when the last bar is played? It wouldn't be the first time.

I know that uneasiness is not universal in Wales. For some it is enough that something is Welsh for it to be good; for another that it's a member of a family on the platform for critical standards to be given the kibosh. Those of us who think such an attitude smacks too much of sentimentality, even of nepotism, are seldom thanked, but there it is. There is a further difficulty for someone proposing to write about a performance or, come to that, review anything in print. Having lived on both sides of that creative gulch, I know the feeling of having old enemies creep out for a small revenge in the public prints. And just as Swinburne held that literary critics were "lice on the locks of literature," so, a colleague warned me before the Newport concert, coining a phrase, no doubt there were those who regarded music critics as "maggots in the meat of music."

And as if that weren't enough – you may now be gathering quite how edgy I felt – the people involved in the Welsh Chamber Orchestra were some with whom I'd been involved in probably the deepest test of friendship known to man. Sir Geraint Evans, Anthony Hose, Norman Kay and myself had been together for weeks creating a new opera for television. To survive such a desperate and hysterical experience beats battle. It's been known for those so engaged never to speak to each other again. And so how the spirits rose in Newport to see walking on to the stage the orchestra's leader Mr Trevor Williams. How often we'd seen him lead the BBC Symphony Orchestra at the Festival Hall in its great days. He wouldn't be wasting his time here. And so it went. From the first bars of Mozart's Divertimento in D Major K136 – an inspired choice for a launch – for the rest of the evening it was brilliant exuberance, whether Sir Geraint narrating Prokofiev's *Peter and the Wolf* or the enchanting display by Caryl Thomas in a work unknown to me, Dittersdorf's Concerto for Harp and Orchestra. And by "enchanting" I don't mean just Miss Thomas's playing of a piece designed for a virtuoso display, but that she wore a dress apparently made of golden tinfoil to match the colour of her harp so that she looked like one of those angels in a rococo church in Central Europe where the music came from.

So that all was much more than well and everyone was smiling and saying that although this was the fourth performance of the programme, and they were just off to Aberystwyth, they had still rehearsed three hours that day. Sir Geraint went ahead – he is the Chamber Orchestra's patron – the rest of us stayed for a party. At which I suggested to Anthony Hose and his wife, Moira, a beautiful soprano from Maesteg, that this might well be the first chamber orchestra of serious class in the history of Wales that had been independently funded. The Welsh National Opera and the BBC Welsh Symphony Orchestra are helped by the Arts Council: this new birth was not.

They were uncertain about this claim. I can remember, I said, how posh we felt at concerts in Swansea and Morriston when the Morgan Lloyd band would play,but that we couldn't often afford them. That was nice, but different. What we have here is a Welsh Chamber Orchestra of the quality of those which visited Wales, invited from England and the rest of Europe or from the United States.

Anthony Hose, impressed by the enthusiasm he had received for his idea around Wales, saw one of the orchestra's main functions as bringing music to towns and large villages starved of concerts of quality. Mr Hose's record since he left the Welsh National Opera is remarkable. He has created and made a success of the Buxton Festival. Then there is Aix-en-Provence. Last weekend he was in charge at Beaumaris. And then a couple of weeks ago he was in Munich helping that greatest of sopranos Margaret Price – whom he's accompanied at so many lieder recitals – prepare to record Richard Strauss's *Four Last Songs*. All this is done from his house looking down at Aberdare where I've had many a fine night. I was even present when he and Moira received the restored grand piano he had rescued, stained with beer-rings and fag-end burns, from a miners' club.

What, then, of all the pleasures of that musical evening was, apart from the playing, the most memorable? It was, after talking to this all-Welsh orchestra – true, mainly, at the moment down from London, until the money comes when they can be full-time here - and after being impressed by the mix of middle-aged and young, no remark more than one by the leader Trevor Williams. Looking around at his enthusiastic band, he told me, "This reminds me why I became a musician in the first place." It's now up to the rest of us to put our shoulder to this Welsh musical wheel.

Western Mail, 3rd June 1986

Radical prisoner's brush with bureaucrats

The condition of Welsh men and women slammed in the cooler of crimes trivial and serious is not what it should be. It is not a subject that can be expected to stir much sympathy. I know. From time to time we say, hearing of a case, that there but for the grace of God go we, but don't really mean it because we are different, are less desperate, conduct our lives by moral precepts or whatever. The bird imprisoned in a cage quite rightly, as Blake had it, puts all Heaven in a rage; but human beings are not birds: some are even nasty bits of work.

What happened was that I knew that last week I'd be driving through the Vale of Evesham on the way to Birmingham to take in the Welsh National Opera's stunning production of Verdi's *Otello* and had heard that the radical Welshman Dafydd Ladd was serving his sentence in the top security prison Long Larten which lay en route. It was a chance to pass on the good wishes of some mutual friends. The visit was arranged.

*   *   *

Long Larten was a surprise. It looks, with the hundreds of cars parked before it belonging to the prison staff, like a government trading estate, except that there are scores of floodlights on high poles. My surprise was greater perhaps than it should have been since my only previous experience of prisons had been as a brief inhabitant of three in Eastern Europe, with a narrow escape in South Africa.

The first was in Yugoslavia, which was cheerful; the second in Sofia which was nasty since some gipsies hoping to ingratiate themselves with the authorities cut me about a bit: the third sinister in Gdansk in Poland after the uprising where a gun was held to my head and I had a nasty crack when I remarked – thinking no one spoke English – that the names of honour on the wall of the gaol condemned the lives of the great torturers. My crime each time was filming illegally.

Passing over the natural sentiments that here was I walking out of the sun of a glorious June afternoon in so lovely a valley carrying a mound of strawberries bought cheap at the roadside to see someone who had been locked up for four years and would be for another two, I found myself, when heavy doors had been unlocked, in a room where coffee and cakes were on sale among Britain's most grave criminals, enemies of the person, or as in Dafydd Ladd's case, of the State.

He had pleaded guilty in the notorious Cardiff "Conspiracy Trial" in 1983, when many of his co-defendants pleaded not guilty and were acquitted. He looks very well and talks so. We chatted for a while about his past since in his youth he had been inspired in his attitudes by the anti-Vietnam and anti-Apartheid movements which I had sympathy for, since I'd reported on both and been banned from both countries as a result. However, I was and remain against violence in politics here.

Dafydd Ladd now thinks he was right in his causes, wrong in his tactics. He is sent copies of Welsh journals like *Planet* and Plaid Cymru's *Radical Wales:* he finds the former insufficiently radical, the latter too much dominated by "trendy Lefties!" The chit-chat one side, though, what soon became clear was the absurdity of the prison bureaucracy. This creates a general difficulty for Welsh prisoners and a particular one in Dafydd Ladd's case. For the Welsh, the absence of enough prisons in Wales is a problem. Cardiff and Swansea are antique and inadequate. This means that prisoners are sent to England, which makes such little visiting as is allowed difficult for those, which is often the case, without motor cars. There is no prison in Wales for women and while I believe the feminist case for there being no need for women to be in prison at all to be intellectually dubious, even so a fresh unfairness is created.

One answer to this state of affairs has been offered by Mr Ioan Richard, a Plaid councillor in the Swansea Valley. He tells me that he has a plan whereby the gaols in Swansea and Cardiff might be sold off and the money used to build a prison elsewhere in South Wales. Certainly both occupy valuable sites, attractive to hoteliers; and are both,by all accounts, dismal places. Dafydd Ladd told me that in Cardiff he shared a cell with two others: at Long Larten he has a cell – 6½ft by 6½ft – to himself. Dowlais, or some other place of high unemployment, might be a suitable site: certainly, to judge from the cars outside Long Larten, prisons are a well-paid labour-intensive profession.

Dafydd Ladd suffers, of course, the difficulty of distance in visits from family – but here again there is a peculiarity. He is in prison for serious criminals, yet is allowed two visits a month. Cardiff, for the less serious, permits one a month. He has another concern which may seem peculiar but I suspect is not. Since he has been in gaol he has been taking examinations qualifying him to be a translator when he is released. This is a shrewd decision since translators can work at home or among friends and the task obviates being asked by employers where he has spent the past six years. Presently he is about to qualify in German. He then plans to brush up his Welsh, but this may be difficult in English prisons. (There is a Welsh teacher in Cardiff gaol but, alas, the popularity of the all-male classes seems due to the fact that the teacher is a woman).

*   *   *

However, just as Dafydd Ladd is coming to the climax of his German course, one which requires oral work with a German teacher, the prison authorities are moving him to a gaol where no German teacher is available. Ironically, he is being moved to a less-secure gaol, almost as a reward for being such a good prisoner. Friends have tried to help him with the Home Office – one MP Mr Dafydd Wigley has been notably kind – but nothing has come of it. There are scores of less serious nonsenses, like being allowed tape-decks in this gaol, record players in another, alarm watches in one, not another, making for expense when, if prisoners have one thing more than another in common, it is that their families have no money. As Dafydd Ladd pointed out, it is the imprisonment, the deprivation of liberty that is supposed to be the punishment, and is: all else is not necessary. What will happen, I guess, is that things will grow more difficult, too many being put in prison without need, the law's laziness and public indifference grow. Or so I thought driving away, eating in the sunshine the strawberries I wasn't allowed to leave at the gaol.

Western Mail, 1st July 1986

The Gorsedd of Bards: Just Freemasonry in wellies?

If the matter has already been raised in some unreported speech or in some Welsh journal which has escaped the eye, my apologies to whomsoever. I refer, of course, to the relevance for the National Eisteddfod of the question of the pernicious effects on the psyche of prize-winning competitions. If it is bad to have children striving for the line in an egg-and-spoon race, as one headteacher has it, and that team games must be discouraged in the interests of equality, where does this leave the singers, reciters, the choirs, the Bards themselves, at Fishguard next week? The recent antics of the dotty Left over this tricky issue are no more unpleasant than the response of the ugly Right, as it raises the sleeve, in the old phrase, of the "devil-take-the-hindmost."

None of us is unconcerned, but, as ever, I guess, our view depends on experience. Mine is that I enjoy competition in games, am even held to be ferocious at tennis and table tennis, croquet and snooker, yet don't mind losing. Further, I've noticed that consequently I lack false ambition in work or ruthlessness in what, so help us, Americans call "inter-personal relationships." People who have not played competitive games seem to reserve their savage conniving for these important aspects of life. What would happen, though, at the National Eisteddfod if there were no more to be prizes? What if the Blue Riband for soloists were to be the Red Riband and everyone, as in Alice in Wonderland, were to have prizes, or in ideological purity, no one won? The analogy is not quite perfect since, after all, adults are not forced to compete. Neither, you might argue, are children, given you knew nothing about Welsh-speaking parents or schools. But, oh, how we remember.

And by remembering we enter into an understanding of Welsh life which may aid the dotty Left cause. At the age of nine the Swansea lot I belonged to, lost at the National to the

Cardiff Snowflakes Choir. Obviously, we were superior. Our teacher-conductor told us that Cardiff had won because the Eisteddfod was being held there and that the adjudicators had been fixed to give a home-town decision. Had there been no prizes, this innocent child would never have had to suffer such an introduction to Welsh politics. Yet, would Welsh politics change if there were no prizes for children? Was it not as well to learn early? If this grave issue is raised at Fishguard, it will not be the only one. Television, I'm told, is presenting a debate between the Archdruid and the twice-crowned Bard Rhydwen Williams. In the 'Fifties, I was powerfully influenced by Rhydwen in my reporting of the Eisteddfod. In that period, as the Archdruid Cynan in his robust style was transforming the Gorsedd ceremony from its cheerful mess into a display suitable for television's arrival, Rhydwen took a firm and illuminating stand against joining the Gorsedd. This was supposed to be a Gorsedd of Bards: he was a Bard and refused to join. He was guided by the example of probably the finest of all the century's Welsh-language poets Sir T. H. Parry Williams; each, as I recall the chat, thought the Gorsedd ceremony pagan. They, qualified to be members, saw themselves as Christian poets. The Gorsedd was not for them. For whom, then, was it? Times have changed and Rhydwen still refuses. The Gorsedd is now more a Welsh Honours List, men and women elected not, alas, for the quality of their verse or prose, but into a kind of Freemasonry, a Valhalla of the living. Quite a few of my closest friends are members and the subject never comes up and not, I'm sure, just because I remember old jokes about who had "won his wellies." Wynford Vaughan Thomas's resonant couplet about the Eisteddfod Pavilion, where he will be on his home ground next week:

> "*Sacred alike to boxing and to art,*
> *For who in Wales can tell the two apart.*"

will, I hope, no more disturb him than memories a few other pals may have of disrespectful years.

Rhydwen Williams's critique, or any voices from the Left about prizes will not, I gather, be the only rumblings, at Fishguard. There is another small, if sparkling, spring of discontent with the Gorsedd. Some young, sprightly minds think that there is too much respectability about. The more political find the Eisteddfod too dependent on the Welsh Office. Others find it straying too far from that confident, hilarious tradition launched by Iolo Morgannwg's roguery in which present forms subsist. Close students of Welsh affairs will know that earnest, revisionist thinkers have tried to suggest that Iolo Morgannwg's cavortings in inventing the Eisteddfod have some solemn political importance. Among the young this curious analysis appears to have passed away already, and the old interpretation resumed its sway. They would like the old anarchy restored, just a little; mavericks rather than Establishment figures elected, so that origins could be recalled. How many of this year's Gorsedd would dream of running away with the takings, as in 1858? That was a bad thing to do, but it was not pompous. Of course, Wales was a Welsh-speaking nation then.

I was always fond of that old understanding of Iolo Morgannwg. It offered such an affectionate insight into the heart and I am glad if the humorous view is returning among the young. It's not bad a thing for a nation to make a delight of the figment of the poetic imagination, to celebrate and institutionalise an exuberant, daft fancy. This means that the Eisteddfod is not just a place to meet old friends and dodge or, if in good form, meet old enemies with a sharp one-liner, but that it praises poetry and music rather than comparable displays in London or Moscow offer soldiers or missiles on parade. Perhaps we shouldn't be too hard on a Gorsedd dressed up, as the poet had it, in its brief authority.

Western Mail, July 1986

The writer's duty to his art and craft

Be they ever so humble, there are no thoughts like those of home. There, in a place as westerly as you can find was the annual triumph of the Welsh language in the Fishguard mud, while here we had Salzburg the town of salt, and just down the Austrian iron road Hallein (Halen, Welsh for salt). How far we have all travelled from the Danube. And what have we learned? More to the point, what does Austria have to say to Wales about language? In August six years ago I had made a pilgrimage from Salzburg to Hallein, being rather stunned and emotional at having won a prize for an opera libretto in Mozart's birthplace and had found, on arrival, an Urdd Gobaith Cymru choir there on a similar sentimental journey. The past seemed very near. So why shouldn't it be appropriate to discover thoughts of home in a study of language in Central Europe, along that Danube on which the Celts sculpted golden artefacts and made hay. More particularly, I was looking at the work of the century's greatest satirist, the Viennese Karl Kraus, whose works, a half-century after his death, are now available in English. Coincidentally, two charming essays on Kraus have appeared, one by Elias Canetti (*Conscience of the Words*), the other by Erich Heller (*In the Age of Prose*). Dr Heller, in the 'Forties at University College, Swansea was my first sighting of an authentic cosmopolitan intellectual: he went on to fame in Illinois.

Reading all this fascinating stuff, though, my mind was nagged by a speech about language made by another intellectual, one who stayed at home, our excellent novelist Emyr Humphreys. At the Rhyl Eisteddfod last year, Mr Humphreys said that the only legitimate function of the Welsh writer in English was to help the growth of the Welsh language. Let's see, I brooded, on what this means for the immediate political, even economic future of Wales, because it struck me that what we may have here is something that may touch on the lives of all of us.

Wales has no Karl Kraus. He wrote, "In Vienna there are

2,030,834 inhabitants, namely 2,030,833 souls and me." He was ferocious about politicians, policemen, phoney art, bribed journalists, time-serving academics, ideologues, all in the interests in the truth of language and all that sprang from that. He was very funny. His play *The Last Days of Mankind* would last ten nights in the theatre. Like all the best of writers he was governed by that idealistic statement of an earlier thinker, Confucius:

> *"If language is not correct, then what is said it not what is meant; if what is said it not what is meant, then what ought to be done remains undone; if this remains undone, morals and arts will decay; if morals and arts decay, justice will go astray; if justice goes astray, the people will stand about in helpless confusion. Hence language must not be allowed to deteriorate. This matters above everything."*

There is nothing here, I'm sure, that so fastidious a writer as Emyr Humphreys would dispute. The message just might read differently to him and those who support him, some of them recent converts to the Welsh-language faith, than it does to me, and quite a few of us.

My position is even a bit messy since I was brought up in a Welsh speaking industrial family and am a hot-shot in Welsh with five-year-olds, but do not feel guilty, just keen on Welsh surviving. In other words, I think any writer's duty is to his art and craft, to a representation of the worlds as he sees it. He or she may have secondary political or social or cultural interests,but they remain secondary if the cause is as important as the Welsh language. So let's try to suppose what Karl Kraus would say according to Elias Canetti — Kraus was a spell-binding orator – about the present condition of Wales. I suspect he would agree with the view eloquently expressed by Mr Humphreys on BBC Radio 4's *Arts in Wales* programme last week that the century has been "catastrophic" for the Welsh language. Further, he would, as we all do, find ominous the demographic change in West and North Wales in the past two decades. He might have asked why it was the Bretons had done so well in resisting Paris and Carmarthen so badly with London. Kraus would surely find room for mischief of a serious sort in examining some of the understandably extravagant claims of the Welsh language industry, whether in education, publishing or broadcasting. For example, I'm told by Welsh-speakers that many children leave schools where Welsh is the language of tuition and then become adult, sadly enough, in a world where Welsh is not used, and so abandon the faith. What emotional confusion, I wonder, is caused in homes where children speak Welsh and the parents not, or shouldn't one ask? How important is it that simple Welsh is learned by television or radio? How does this differ sometimes from a hobby like weaving or pottery? An objective report on all this would be interesting.

Being, alas, no Karl Kraus, I detect an important political matter in these questions. Devolution is on the cards once more, whether, as the language is twisted, it is called decentralisation or regionalism or whatever. In the last outing in 1979 damage was done by fears, either artificial, artificially induced or even genuine, that a sort of self-governing Wales would fall into the hands of Welsh-speaking fanatics. That famous nepotism, so much exaggerated, although, we know, present here and there, would run wild. In Welsh circles, of course, there were fears of swamping by South Walean party machines. What would be a pity, now that so many engines of propaganda lie in Welsh-speaking mouths, would be for too much vehemence – there are not many ranters – to create hostility. There is a real chance of a change in Welsh governmental structure. The Welsh language will surely prosper through such a change. Or if there is a fear it may not, then people should say so. This must be where I take issue with Emyr Humphreys. In the fascinating three years that lie ahead for Wales it seems to me the duty of the Welsh writer is to write the truth of what we see around us as best we can in the language that so best enables us. If that language be English then so be it. Otherwise, Confucius he say "The people will stand about in helpless confusion."

Western Mail, 12th August 1986.

Could Wales be a fussy Virgo?

What follows is a true tale of Wales. I find it incredible, but find even more unbelievable the fact that everyone I have told it to, finds it quite believable. It deals with witches, one a doll in Welsh costume; with grave afflictions; exercising; spiders; "sunrise" industry; a coincidence of name; mysterious woods; and signs of the Zodiac. Since, in nervously offering it I had thought that perhaps there'd be a suspicion that time's infirmities had led my marbles to fall out of my ear, now that I discover it is taken for gospel, I can only conclude that it is the listener who is zonked. The tale begins with my meeting a man in a pub in the Wye valley. He is a hot-shot in the new technology, setting-up a factory in Wales for gifted technicians. One of his techniques in choosing his staff is analysing their birth-signs in the interests of compatibility. As would anyone, I asked him if, in that case, I was employable, being, as I'd been led to believe, a Scorpio and not liking it. After all, who wants to be known as secretive, mad for power, sexually dynamic? He told me I was wrong. I am, it seems, Libran, which is good news. A Libran values friendship, loves justice and owns a beguiling smile of devastating charm even if secretive in romance. I quite fancy that: it seems more true than Scorpio.

At which, having arranged to travel down this new avenue of Welsh job-creation I had to rush home to let some friends into the house. A young woman was with them: *Gwawr* (dawn) she said. *Machlud* (Sunset) to you, I said. But she was serious: It was her name. She was from Newport in Pembrokeshire and had just arrived from Dubai in the Persian Gulf. In no time she was telling me that she had recently been in Calcutta to consult some sharp astrologer about her future. Gwawr is an Aries, a dynamic kind of leader sort according to the books I have subsequently been studying. She thought my neighbour entrepreneur was perhaps wise in his technique of staff appointments. After all, it's better than tossing a coin between equally-qualified candidates and was not uncommon elsewhere in the world. Here the tale grows macabre. I hadn't realised that the Zodiac entrepreneur was staying at a house in dense woods overlooking the Wye which is known to locals as "Heartbreak House." A friend of mine has recently sold it for £150,000 and moved to Spain.

In the 15th and 16th centuries that lovely part of the Wye had been famous for witches. More recently, due to some tragic deaths, there has been some secret exorcising of neighbouring households to "Heartbreak House." The exorcising has been done by official priests. I have always been sceptical about this gossip of the supernatural at work. However, it seems to be the case that strange things have happened. A while ago, two members of the Welsh intelligentsia lived there, a marriage that broke up with distressing aftermath; similarly with the next foreign artistic occupants of a decade's length. In one case the wife, in the other the husband were gravely ill. Neighbours offer bizarre tales. My friend, who has recently sold it, grew troubled at two signs. The first was when, being fearful of spiders, he was horrified to find a huge spider climb the stairs at him. It turned out to be a child's toy, but no one knew whose child. The second was general alarm when the dog left the dining room and returned with, between its teeth, a rag doll in Welsh woman's costume with a broomstick.

He thought it was time to move on. More recently the house was let to a group of women and some Welsh clown did not help matters by saying he had seen them fly away across the face of a full moon. Naturally enough there is discussion among the *literati* in the valley about who will first write about the place and in which style. There are those who think Daphne du Maurier's *Rebecca* the model; myself I fancy more Thomas Love Peacock, *Headlong Hall* given the Welsh connection, the Zodiac and the artistic pedagogic history. In the meantime, how remarkable compatriots are in studying their birth signs. What a following Mr Russell Grant has in the *Western Mail*. I discover from my editor there (*Aries,* of course) that on Saturdays Mr

Grant must publish the news for those whose birthdays are on the Sunday or there is uproar among readers. How interesting, too, that there the stars are usually pretty correct about family and friends. Surrounded by Taurus, Gemini, Virgo, Capricorn I wonder if they are following instructions from Mr Grant and his colleagues or not. How can he know, for example, that Aquarian women are hard-hearted Hannahs and ingenious with it? That Leo men have dignity and are creative. Those of us who have never studied the Zodiac take years to discover these truths, when we could have known from the start.

Considering all which, if such is true for people, why should it not be true for a nation? When, for example, was Wales born: what is our sign? St David is *Pisces,* sensitive and kind, but also inhibited and impractical. Mr Gwynfor Evans has been, quite rightly, urging on us the celebration of September 17 as Owen Glyndŵr's Day, but that would be *Virgo* which is kind, but domestic and given both to fuss and melancholy? Is that what we want? Perhaps we need someone daft like Iolo Morgannwg to invent a birthdate for Wales as was the Gorsedd dreamed up. In time, it might equally be taken for gospel as, to my surprise, all this Zodiac tale has been. I fancy *Libra* for Wales and not just because it coincides with the serious start of the rugby season.

Western Mail, 7th September 1986.

The Great Divide

One merit of a journey through Wales is that what you set out to discover – or this may be just a weakness of mine – is not at all what you find. What began last week as an earnest political quest, solemnly devoted to arguing a point about means of communication in the matter of nationhood, turned out to be a social comedy about flax and linseed oil. We even began seriously, my companion being my son Aled who is a professional photographer and was taking pictures for a book to be published of these columns collected. Our first staging post was near Pencader in the West, the home of the secretary of our Welsh Union of Writers, Janet Dube; the first item in the minutes of the meeting is a resolution voting we move indoors since the heat was too great in the garden. When before can anything such have been proposed in Carmarthenshire in mid-September?

The target was the Lleyn Peninsula. There we were to stay with my longest-suffering friend and colleague Aled Vaughan. My son is named after him as are both after a lake Aled somewhere up there. Would the road journey, I asked, be any quicker than in the early Fifties when Mr Vaughan and myself used to travel in a large black car recording radio interviews? That was before the tape-recorder time. A union colleague at Pencader, John Osmond, suggested that I was being patronising about roads to the north. Hadn't he himself in the *Western Mail* in the Seventies urged the A470, now-built, to Merthyr as an important step? I was not impressed. I pointed-out that the M4 had been built to bring industry to West Wales; its principal effect seems to have been to take Welsh people East.

Not that poor Merthyr is quite an equivalent case since it has long undergone a more recondite version of Morgan's Law of Welsh Mobility. This law reads "When one Welsh historian shows an interest in your industrial town it is time to pack your bags." And, secondly, "When more than one Welsh historian shows an interest, you have left it too late." Had there been the political will, though, in good time to construct a swift road from, say, Swansea to Caernarfon, what would the demographic consequences have been? Just as the Prussian Von Moltke comprehended the value of railways in the Franco-Prussian War and so changed the face of Europe, would the pressure of England have been diminished if a north-south Welsh road rather than east-west been the priority in the early Sixties? Routes have a political dynamic. At which pleasure intrudes and how fine it is that the road still winds along the coast and through the mountains to the Lleyn. So we put politics one side because there was a particular nervousness in approaching the peninsula, one very urban citizen will comprehend. There were rumours that so sophisticated an old pal as Aled Vaughan had become a farmer.

Twenty years ago Mr Vaughan was the star television director in Wales. He had just made a memorable film about Caradog Evans, another about Tolstoy for the *Monitor* programme, just published a novel. He was a happy man. I rang him one night with the thought we might construct a bid to win the television franchise for Wales and the West. I could see his eyes close wearily even on the telephone: I had been a pest before. I am held to have said that if we won we might so arrange the budget that he could produce films of people falling off Everest rather than Snowdon, while I would write operas. In the end we won prizes with both. He became the creative genius, now retired, of Harlech television. So what was this farming? The chat opened warily. "I have never," I said, "seen a night sky as fine as this above the Lleyn since I was in the Persian Gulf." He replied by saying, "When I went to collect my white robes at the Fishguard Eisteddfod last month to attend the Gorsedd ceremony, I discovered they had run out of robes and so I went fishing instead."

Next day as we walked his acres, past those peculiarly stunted oak trees of the coast, I was quickly reassured that all was well. First, he is writing a 90-minute film to be produced for S4C next year. Even more importantly, as we mooched through a field of flax, or linseed, I knew genius was still alive. Hardly anywhere else in Wales is there such a field of linseed, in Welsh *llin*, from which the words for string and linen are derived. Flax was the common thing in the Common Market. Government agencies are sending a merry band of Welsh farmers to northern France to study the stuff, so help us. My friend was, as ever, to coin a phrase, ahead of the field. "And you," I said, "are going to cut this awful stuff we used to have to pick in our youth at camps in Pembrokeshire?" No, no, somebody else was going to do all that. My heart lifted. I suspect that what the pair of us have in common is that we come from humble origins and so, not being members of the professional Welsh middle-class, are inclined to be patrician.

But if all that was well, it is that the North remains so far from the South. The *Western Mail,* I gather, sells a couple of thousand copies there, the Liverpool *Daily Post* 50,000. For all the work of the BBC and HTV, their news is not our news. This makes for prejudice. Informing my son about all this, I asked him if he had noticed that while we southerners were driving north, all the traffic lights had been red, while as we drove south they were all green. "Green for Gog" I said, explaining that Gogleddwr was the Welsh for northerner, thus Gog. Which created the opening to quote a superb spontaneous remark made by a coloured Cardiff girl in the BBC Club at Llandaff when she was irritated by cleverdicks from Bangor, Better Wog than Gog. We have a long road to travel yet.

Western Mail, 23rd September 1986.

So what is radical?

If at a loss for something better to say this week, whether to fill a gap, break a pause or as some last fling at shaking off the torpor of an evening, try this one: What quality does every political party claim for its programme at the next general election? You have it in one. They are all Radical. Mrs Thatcher is radical; Mr Kinnock is radical and so are Dr Owen and Mr Steel; Plaid Cymru has a journal titled *Radical Wales.* Even your humble columnist does not escape, having been involved in a publishing house named the *Radical Centre for Democratic Studies* based in Monmouth in those early days of the SDP? So what's so funny, you ask? Why shouldn't everyone be radical? All determined in their different ways to bring about "extreme or fundamental change in political, economic or social conditions, institutions or habits of mind?" Quite so, except that the most cursory examination of policies reveals that there is not much in any of them which qualifies for those authentic definitions of the word.

Tinkering might be a more appropriate term for them. What problems, though, such a substitution would create. It's an adjective difficult rousingly to proclaim from a public platform, or pregnantly and sincerely to offer to a television camera. "I promise a tinkering plan for Britain" would bring few audiences to its feet wild with applause. *Tinkering Wales* might not have its Plaid Cymru readers aflame. But as we shall see, this title – for all that the party conference saw to coin a phrase its feminists and extreme Left take a tumble – not yet appropriate. The simplest way of dismissing this fashionable political use of radical is to regard it as linguistic philosophers might, as an example of an hooray word, along with caring and commitment: words designed to raise the spirit and give the mind a rest. That would be too easy. And all who employ it would resist such a dismissal. And who am I to talk? How did I justify an association with the *Radical Centre?* When pressed by rude, scurrilous friends, I'd begin by saying that here was an effort to redefine democratic socialism. Further roused, I'd say that radical here was something novel, a form of dynamic commonsense, a cutting-out of the roots of shibboleth.

Wits would quote, falling into a trap, Aneurin Bevan's famous aphorism about middle-of-the-road politics: If you walk in the middle of the road, the great man would say, you'll be run over. I once, in 1959, I'd reply, had the temerity to say to Aneurin Bevan that far more people were knocked down by stepping off the pavement to a driver's extreme left than ever were in the middle of the road. He laughed his generous laugh, to my relief.

In Wales, of course, the use of radical has traditional weight. How proud we were to be nurtured in a society, rural as well as industrial, that held up the torch to Britain. Radicalism – that is, Left radicalism – was the calcium in the bone, the iron in the blood. We marched with our heroes. Nowadays, though, as we contemplate the dreadful condition of the valleys of the expired industries, the thought will cross the open mind that perhaps, perhaps, there was a flaw somewhere.

So let's be practical and consider a genuine radical policy, one that would meet the dictionary definition and so consider which party might embrace it. Nothing would so transform the British economy as the abolition of income tax relief on house mortgage interest payments. What comparable single act would so shock the system and change society's habits of mind. The present mortgage system is creating a deepening, if concealed, crisis. The reckless extension of credit inflates prices far beyond the rate of inflation. Cash ostensibly for houses is borrowed from irresponsible lenders by irresponsible citizens for the buying of consumer goods, usually from abroad. Billions of pounds which might be available for investment in private and public enterprises to reduce the disgraceful levels of unemployment are involved in purchases and borrowings which create nothing. That this process has many of the characteristics of the South Sea Bubble, or those wild purchases of stock on margin whch contributed to the Wall Street Crash of 1929, is lost sight of simply because a house is built of bricks and mortar, so how can there be a bubble, how can a house crash?

Lesser incidental results are also serious. Houses are priced beyond the reach of young people. Mobility of labour is stymied. Land prices are inflated, so inhibiting new building. A frame of mind is created whereby buying houses diverts the public imagination from investing in manufacturing. Citizens carry a financial burden throughout their working lives, assuming that the prices will always work in their favour. What if they do not? So let's suppose we do have here a truly radical policy, one so revolutionary that even our home-grown revolutionaries and especially those with mortgages and even second homes, might think twice. Can we therefore expect it to be on offer at the general election? There is still time. We can. Plaid Cymru has adopted such a policy and so kept a radical Wales alive. Will the policy though win or lose votes? Which brings me to a more likely explanation of the free current use of radical, none other than the old one: Always

270

assume, when a politican uses a word, that he means the converse. From this we conclude that the prevailing mood must be conservative and traditional, that the political parties sense that what the electorate wants is indeed just a little tinkering here, a little tinkering there, that the election will be won by those looking most likely to tinker well. So what's new, you ask.

Western Mail, 2nd October 1986.

To my Lady Nicotine

Sweet, to borrow and amend a phrase, may be the uses of infirmity. And what follows to decorate so important a text can be taken either as an insight into the origins of a work in a high art form, or simply as an example of Welshmen clowning in a late-night cafe: or, indeed, both. The place was just around the corner from the Birmingham Hippodrome after a wonderful performance last week by the Welsh National Opera of Verdi's *Masked Ball.* There we sat, two hardened veterans of the non-smoking campaign, the one our great tenor Denis O'Neill three years ago a 40-a-day man, and myself until 14 months ago to the very day in the same class, he belonging to the Pontardulais puffing tradition, myself to the scarcely less powerful Morriston. The object of the meeting apart from pleasure, was to resume discussion about an opera libretto I'm writing about giving-up smoking. It is a ludicrous if erotic work entitled *My Lady Nicotine.* Denis has agreed to be the tenor.

Also present was a friend and former colleague of 20 years standing, Monica Foot. She, after a career in journalism and the Labour Party is succeeding, as the principal Press officer, in putting England's second city back on the world map. More to the point she has forgiven me for basing the heroine of the first opera I had performed largely on her. She still smokes and could appear yet once more, is a thought that occurred. For a reason which will become clear at the end of this column and which I offer as a handy tip to budding librettists, I was anxious to steer clear of the new opera's plot for as long as possible. So I asked Denis why he had given up smoking. He knew why I had: in a word, cancer. In his case it was the discovery after one uncertain performance on stage that nicotine was damaging his ability to hit that High C which contributes so much to the excitement of his art. The connection was irrefutable. Thus it won't be long – he will demonstrate the fact shortly at La Scala Milan, as well as Covent Garden – that he will move from being the Crown Prince to being the King of the High Cs.

We agreed we regretted the necessity, and wished we could smoke, *My Lady Nicotine* will not take any stern, puritan line, will not join the fanatic proselytisers. We touched on the role of smoking in national finances. They seem to balance as arguments, pro and con. People should be as free to do themselves harm as much as good, whatever good is. All pleasures, did we think, carry their penalty? On the other hand, I pointed out, it would be a bold stroke – speaking as the librettist-as-hustler – if we could win a grant for the production from the Department of Health.

All that was fine, but for how long could I escape giving the bad news? How much more Frascati would we need? It was already past midnight. Diversions were launched. I gave an account of how earlier in the evening when I met Monica Foot at the opera house, she explained that while she had not seen this Verdi work before she had been reading an account of it in her Kobbe opera book. She touched on various scenes she was looking forward to, having only known them on gramophone records. She seemed very taken by a scene in a hermit's cave. I was puzzled. From my memory of the *Masked Ball* there was no hermit's cave. Yet here was an intellectual woman who was usually right about everything from the history of feminism to obscure 18th century novelists. Look, kid, I said nervously, I thought the *Masked Ball* was about this good, liberal, tormented king, a bit theatrical like the rest of us, who falls in requited, but innocent love with the wife of his great friend and servant and is, tragically, shot by the husband. I think there is a soothsayer, but no hermits, no caves. No hermits, she replied. No caves? Tell you what, I said, I think you opened the page of Kobbe at Verdi's *Force of Destiny*. That's a different kettle of intrigue.

Did we mind, she asked, if she smoked? We did not at all, although we could see that, socially, this can be a difficult matter in restaurants, and wondered if we could somehow incorporate a scene in *My Lady Nicotine*, perhaps some dramatic punch-up between smokers and the anti-fag lobby. Perhaps not. I described, still playing for time, the moving aria, at least moving to me since it is rich in deeply-felt self-pity, in which the tenor hero – who has to give up drinking spirits as well as smoking – feels he has lost all his personality without these two props, and quite by chance used the phrase about "teaching grandmothers to suck eggs." When, I asked Monica and Denis, when did they think had been the Golden Age of egg-sucking? At which the great tenor, still innocent of his fate, revealed that in his youth in Pontarddulais he had been expert in sucking eggs. He used to paint them. That, it seems, is why eggs are sucked. He described how it is done and a revolting business it sounds, however, expert grandmothers in West Wales may still be at the pastime. It was difficult to prevent him sending for an egg to demonstrate, but we managed. We asked Monica to blow smoke in our faces so that we could remember the good times. That's a scene in the opera.

It was now long past one in the morning – the cafe owner was a fan of Denis – and so I said I had bad news. About the tenor in *Lady Nicotine*, I said. That keen "Bont" face turned. No, he said, you aren't serious? I nodded. It's always the same, said Denis. In *Traviata* Violetta dies and I'm crying; in *Boheme* it's Mimi goes and I'm crying: tonight in the Masked Ball, I'm shot dead. Why is it always the tenor? There you go, I said, a phrase I've just picked-up from the young. Tell me, he said. It's ironic really, I said, as if reporting on an event over which I had no control. The heroine fancies you, wants to save you by persuading you to give up smoking, succeeds in doing so, and then discovers that, as a non-smoker, she doesn't much care for you. But look on the bright side, I said, would you really care for a girl like that? A hard lot these Morriston librettists, said Denis. Monica concurred.

Western Mail, 11th November 1986.

The Amis Industry

A social comedy, now obscure, but gathering strength, is being played out in Wales on which I feel it my duty to report. I have two good reasons. First, I can see a manner in which I can turn it to my personal gain. Secondly, I recognise in it profit to my home town of Swansea. It concerns Kingsley Amis's novel *The Old Devils,* which won the Booker Prize and is selling like Welsh cakes. For all the author's explicit instructions the novel is being taken to be about Swansea and men and women who might have lived in the town. That is not his fault. He is not being sued by anyone. An important character in the novel is a broadcaster, Alun Weaver, who returns to Wales. He is of the sort we known as the "professional" Welshman. In the trade there is a rather specialised game of guessing which Mr Amis has in mind. Indeed, I was rather shocked that one Swansea soul wondered if I had any connection with the role. However, I am in the clear since, unlike Alun Weaver, I do not have white hair. Mr Amis makes the cruel joke that Weaver dyes his hair white. Surely none of our telly heroes do that. Moreover, he is a womaniser, which leaves out a loyal soul like myself. It must be an impure fiction.

More to the point is that this Weaver figure makes much of his connection with a famous Welsh poet "Brydan." Let us take it that Brydan is Dylan Thomas. Swansea is rich in the Dylan trade. So is Laugharne. There is, I'm told, a Dylan bar in Bangor. Statues, theatres, plaques, posters, illuminated verses, memoirs, junk of several sorts, turn a penny for the poet's fame. All this took place after he was dead. Why should Swansea not celebrate Kingsley Amis's connection and celebrate while he is still alive? Indeed, why just Swansea? We spent a weekend in Cardigan Town with the Amises in 1956, not all that far from the place Dylan Thomas was shot at not so long before. This, therefore, is a patent on the Amis industry. How many people know, for example, although they may be persuaded to care, that there was once a meeting between Dylan Thomas and Kingsley Amis? And that it took place in the early Fifties in a pub – the Uplands in Swansea – which may well be the boozer dismayingly described in *The Old Devils?*

And, from my memory of the occasion, that Mr Amis was a bit miffed, that Mr Thomas would not go back to his place for a drink, but went off instead with some Swansea boys? I claim that.

There will, of course, be a plaque or two at University College, Swansea, where Mr Amis taught. I was one of his students in 1949, but in a whole year only went to one of his lectures. My problem was that I was living at home at Morriston and his lectures were at nine in the morning, which was too early for me. A classmate who became my wife said that I ought to come and hear this chap, and so I made an effort and went once, and he said he was glad to see me since he had heard about me. We all became friends. There should be a plaque, too, in the Mumbles where the Booker prize-winner lived when he was beginning to write *Lucky Jim.* He was a dazzling, reckless host, if impoverished. I left there, one uneasy night when I had just been commissioned in the RAF, when all around were against the Korean war, thinking I was away to battle taking the Mumbles train. I had gone to my farewell party with a tin of rabbit stolen from my grandmother in Morriston – those were hard times – because we felt the Amises were short. That Kingsley Amis was to become famous, and the new twt about the place, Martin, equally, were prospects no one dreamed of. I claim that, too, if this industry is to come to anything.

After the success and fame of *Lucky Jim* there were to be such parties. Kingsley Amis now believes those years in Swansea were his happiest times. In the past 25 years he has mixed with a smaller circle there, but in that earlier times there was an exuberance in the company that lends itself to celebration which a diminishing group remember as a golden age. Being commercial about all this, though, and appreciating that the Swansea or West Glamorgan councils can't go putting up plaques everywhere, which of the two Uplands houses will prove most worthy? Here was the party where John Braine of *Room at the Top* behaved daftly. There was the darts match with Anthony Powell and his wife. On the other hand, there was the long night with Philip Larkin and all that jazz. And the game I was blamed for with oranges in which a professor was concussed. Which council, I wonder, will claim the fame for marking the spot when, playing our game of cricket on the beach, Kingsley said he had brought his lunch and was resting and produced a bottle of vodka, when we had our sandwiches. In the Fifties he was the only man with a motor-car among us, and needed his wife to drive.

In some ways I am not best qualified to launch this industry since, while we remain courteous we fell out over the Vietnam war in 1967,but believe it is better for the campaign to be launched by a Swansea boy rather than by some alien by and by. Worse, I think it is a vexed matter, this memorialising of artists, and certainly Mr Amis is, in fiction, a great artist. It may be a pity that so many writers – Yeats, Waugh, Eliot – have political views we may regret, but equally, there are so many on the Left who are bad artists, and even worse people. Is it proper, though, to praise so formally during a lifetime and let the profits roll? Having made my claim, I leave the matter there.

Western Mail, 25th November 1986.

Be lucky like me – CHECK

There comes a time and this is it, when even the cool, informed, compassionate, middle-aged Welsh columnist cracks with joy. Had I still the old talent of skipping in the street, I would have danced a few days ago along the Wye Valley from the St Lawrence Hospital in Chepstow. For the first time in a strange, year-long struggle my surgeon did not cross his fingers in a cautious benediction as I left. With just one small operation to go on my poor mouth, it really does look as if the cancer has gone away. That next surgery will keep me silent for a week, which will give a few a chance to win a word in edgeways. I write this partly because I cannot give my mind to anything else. Also because, yet again, the medical people think my experience could be useful in driving away fear. That message is clear. Cancer must not be feared.

The meanderings that follow may suggest that my case is peculiar. Who would expect otherwise? What is clear is that had I not been caught early, and had not behaved so, I would probably be dead. Therefore do not be afraid. If anything troubles you – check. If there is fright in your mind, even, check. Do not let fear of the word cancer inhibit you. Statistics, for what they are worth, propose that, like the Ancient Mariner, cancer stoppeth one in three. Most afflicted are cured. It is seldom a journalist can do anything practical – as opposed to other forms of good work – so that this is my contribution. I'm aware, every day, that few people can be as lucky as I have been. Like most, I have witnessed some people I've loved die of cancer. This is another reason why the affliction is so confusing. You realise that you did not understand. Therefore, when you are struck down yourself you need a heart of stone or the imagination of a gnat not to be shocked at your incomprehension then, nor to know a new truth in your experience. Quite apart from a concern about your own fate, memory makes for a troubled, if moving, revelatory time.

My experience I offer, therefore, in the hope it may be

277

useful. Not everyone's problems will be comparable. One of mine was that the tumours were in my mouth. The cancer lay there. On the swift discovery, half of my mouth was taken out. Other tumours remained.

How were we to know that they, too, were not to flower into the malign. The surgery was painful, but I'm sure that is common to all surgery. It hasn't been nice to have to learn to force my teeth apart and chew. Having to give up smoking and drinking spirits, those props of life, has been a struggle, except that I knew that fellow sufferers had said sod it and chosen the grave. My surgeon could have sent me, as he sent others, for chemotherapy, or radium needles stuck in the face, but we seem to have taken a gamble. Therefore, I've lived a year knowing the tumours were in my mouth and that they might, like the other, have needed another major operation. We sat it out. This week he looked, if the thought can be conceived, even more pleased than did myself. It's true I'm fond of a gamble myself. Not that I've known a poker game quite so long drawn out. In the meantime, and how long it seems, I'd been talking with a few medical people curious about the case. I learned about the importance of spirit, will and emotion in fighting cancer. One influence was a Roman Catholic woman who works with cancer cases and, like so many, is keen on the relationship between stress, emotional shock and grief as a source. She, therefore, believes in the power of the spirit, will, and, of course, religion, in its defeat.

Being a Church in Wales cum Annibynwyr boy, I've always been as dubious about Roman Catholics as about Marxists – I wonder what the latter say to cancer patients, Love Lenin, or Stalin? Dream of the death of capitalism? The considered view from this fashionable school which sees a connection between private grief or shock of one sort or another and cancer captured my mind. This was a year ago when I learned the bad news. As is happened I had fallen ill from what I thought a dirty trick played by someone I had seen as a friend. By chance at the very time I read an article about a book I'd written. The reviewer was the Aberystwyth historian Gareth Williams. He

278

wrote that I "had the instincts of a bar-room brawler." This surprised me since I had always taken myself to be a sweet, affable, if mischievous soul. The remark set me thinking, frightened as I was, waking up in cold sweat from night to night. One of cancer's oddities for me, having spent a life reporting on others around the globe, was that it made me think of myself for the first time. Cancer is the enemy within. Therefore I took Mr Williams's judgement aboard. I decided I would be a bar-room brawler. I would fight in my mind with a fury I never knew I possessed, the perpetrator of the dirty trick.

If the spiritual school were correct, if the power of the will was the answer, that would be the target of my rage. The exercise was made tolerable from the knowledge that the object of this bizarre form of homeopathy would neither know nor care. There are other reasons for fighting to stay alive, given the argument of spirit and will has force. Many argue that the affection of family and friends is enough. Certainly, I have been embarrassed to learn that a soul so diffident as myself has in such hard times had so many friends. Even so, I think a distinctive fight may have proved useful. But who is to tell? What works in one case may not work in another. I have to go back to the hospital for another five years to check that the cancer has not returned, and I'll know that a few who were operated on when I was, are dead, and others will come in and, if disfigured, survive, or not, and always know that I was lucky. Life, for me, is changed forever and it is quite a problem to know how to behave. That is a matter for writing elsewhere. The point of this is simple – be lucky like me. Check.

Western Mail, 9th December 1986.

1987

Happy End

How often we have asked and myself in my role, as chairman of the Welsh Union of Writers, as often as most: does Wales have the arts council it deserves? The other night at Abergavenny, in a fit of open-mindedness, a different question presented itself: does the arts council have the Wales it deserves?

The occasion was the performance by the St Donat's Music Theatre, sponsored by the Welsh Arts Council, the South-east Wales Arts Association, and Allied Steel and Wire Ltd, of the Bertolt Brecht-Kurt Weill *Happy End*. The question was raised by the fact that the hall was barely half-full for a brilliant performance of a dazzling work which contains in *Bilbao* and *Surabaya Johnny* two of the most wonderful songs of the century. It is in other ways, too, a funny, wry musical drama, touching on crime, sin, the sinister, and true love conquering all. Its closing line is relevant: 'Why rob a bank when you can own one?' The cast and band, in passing, were not at all intimidated either by a thin audience or poor acoustics, with Mr Wyn Davies, of the WNO, conducting in fine Weill style, and Rosamund Shelly singing the favourite songs as well as I've heard. But why were we so few? True, the night was cold, snow firm in the hedgerows, but the roads were clear. Perhaps the performance was not well advertised; and it was the case that the friends I dragged with me had not known it was on. The tickets were £3 and £4. But Abergavenny and district is well-heeled.

Could it be that *Happy End,* and its creators Brecht and Weill, are regarded as being avant-garde, far-out, foreign and modern? Was that the reason? Much as I had suspected to be the explanation when there were only a handful of us in the audience for the same work at the New Theatre, Cardiff, in

1975? This, if true, would be a remarkable comment on the state of theatre, even the politics of theatre, and especially of the idea of the avant-garde, that movement whose function, apart from generally shocking the bourgeoisie or staid, is to offer fresh insights into society. I find it peculiarly remarkable since *Happy End* is exactly the same age as myself, 57 and a quarter, which strikes me as having been around a long time. And it may be, too, that my judgement that night in Abergavenny was partly governed by *Happy End* having no less a peculiar private importance.

And that is another difficulty of age: each experience has a memory. This is made worse if you have a good memory. In work the gift of almost total recall is a boon since it saves so much industry. In life otherwise it can be a curse leading to an inability to throw dogeared remembrances with their texts of melancholy, guilt or fury on the fire along with defunct papers. The shame is that senility cannot be selective, or so they say. It becomes a bit much when even a simple pleasure like hearing *Surabaya Johnny* in a town hall in Gwent is intruded upon by a vivid past. In the early Sixties in Berlin I spent some time with a colleague of both Brecht's and Weill's, the revolutionary theatre and cinema director Erwin Piscator. His secretary was a friend of mine. I would sit agape since it was Piscator who had invented the theatrical style in the early Twenties, which has subsequently been thought of as Brechtian. He had established it with his production of the *Good Soldier Schweik* in which Brecht lent a hand. He had worked closely with Carola Neher for whom *Surabaya Johnny* was written. One chat was especially dramatic the night we were expecting the Russian tanks to roll in as the Cuban missile crisis was at its height in 1962. I was there, rather stupidly, for *Panorama* when I wouldn't have stood much chance had the Soviet troops come through. However, there was a new production of the *Marriage of Figaro,* all of us sitting there listening to transistor radios in the auditorium and agreeing that if we had to go, what finer music to go by? As it happened no tanks rolled, but we weren't to know.

Piscator was certainly the avant-garde in the Twenties and Thirties. He and his friends were Communists battling honestly with the Nazis. With hindsight we can see that, by their political attitudes in alliance with the Comintern, they contributed to the defeat of social democracy in the Weimar Republic, but that was not clear at the time. There are some people to whom it is not clear even now. What is even stranger is that there has been so little change in the idea of what is novel in the theatre. Piscator's famous techniques in his use of cinema within theatre, in his concept of 'alienation', that political use of Busoni's aesthetic, putting, with an irony that seems seldom appreciated, such a high art form to what was taken to be a Marxist concept are still treated as avant-garde so much later.

This, I think, is a failure of our time, and that it is serious is shown by the fashion in which radical chic writers and ideologues abused the tragic miners' strike in imitation of times past. Antique middle-class agitprop that for Piscator was grave and relevant became a kind of knee-jerk. Nothing seemed to make the point more clearly than a final new memory of *Happy End* in Abergavenny. In 1936 Piscator and his friend, Carola Neher, escaped from Hitler to Moscow to make a movie for Uncle Joe Stalin. *The Revolt of the Fisherman of Santa Barbara.* Stalin suddenly turned against the left-wing intelligentsia who had served him well in Berlin. Piscator happened that week to be in Switzerland. Carola Neher, for whom Brecht and Weill had written the great songs, was not so lucky. She died in a Soviet labour camp. After the performance in Abergavenny, the cast were at the Walnut Tree restaurant. Egon Ronay has just given it the prize as the best British place to eat.

Western Mail, Feburary 1987

Coincidences

At what point do coincidences become portents? One case is when you return from a trip aboard and find at home three important books about the history of the Labour Party and a recent number of the *Western Mail* in which an opinion poll reveals that the Conservative Party leads Labour in Wales. I tried reading it upside-down, holding the paper up to the light: it was no good. There is was. Tory 37, Labour 34, Alliance 24.

What would they make of it, all those Labour heroes of Dr Kenneth O. Morgan's new study? What melancholy eloquence would Aneurin Bevan, whom Dr John Campbell writes about, have offered? For James Callaghan whose memoirs now appear, the poll has an extra poignancy: it suggests that Labour will not win the Cardiff seat he has held since World War II. I daresay the late Jim Griffiths of whom Dr Morgan writes affectionately would offer a Biblical thought. After the 1955 election defeat, orating in an Aberavon chapel, his hand on the Big Book, that rich Ammanford voice fell to a sotto voce. He said, 'The harvest is past, the summer is ended, and we are not saved'. He was very pleased to be congratulated on that piece from Jeremiah, yet Jim went on to be the first Labour Welsh Secretary of State. We should be wary of prophecy. Even so, in these sheaves of current texts about the Labour Party, there are tea-leaves to be observed. Inevitably, most of the evidence lies in the ideas and career of Aneurin Bevan, for my money, as that of many, the greatest of Labour leaders in intelligence, passion and style.

Dr Campbell's biography has a built-in, self-confessed disability. It is a 'political' study. That is, it eschews a complete portrait. In the case of most politicians this might not matter much: in Aneurin Bevan's it does, since his background, personality and mode of life were peculiarly relevant to his ideas and force both in national and international affairs.

This limitation of Dr Campbell's has already had one happy effect in stimulating debate about Bevan. In the *New Statesman* the Welsh historian Professor Dai Smith has published a long attack on the book's failure to appreciate the importance of Nye Bevan's Welsh socialist background, which may be a sign that Dr Smith will hurry-along his own fuller work on Bevan.

There's a lot in Dr Smith's essay I don't agree with. He does though, touch on a matter of key importance, one as much of fact as interpretation about the great Welsh socialist's last days, one that has always puzzled me. Dr Campbell, like most writers about Bevan, makes much of the 1959 General Election which Labour lost under Hugh Gaitskell's leadership and with Bevan then his faithful deputy. The source for this is gloomy conversation with the celebrated journalist Geoffrey Goodman who accompanied Bevan during the campaign.

Dr Smith resists the idea that words then of despondency should be used as an epitaph for Bevan's ideas. I think he is right for this reason.

Not long after the election I had a long lunch with Aneurin Bevan. While I had met him briefly a few times before and had heard some of his great speeches both inside and outside the House of Commons and admired him since adolescence, this was different. Here he was with Pierre Mendes-France, the former French socialist prime minister, offering his considered view of the future.

It was a difficult time for the Labour Party with the row about Clause 4 at its height. It was a bit tricky for me, too, since one of my jobs at the *New Statesman* at the time was to try and make some sense of the Bevanite critique of the German SPD's abandoning Marxism at Bad Godesberg. All hands were welcome on deck.

However, memory of Bevan's analysis at that lunch tends to support Dr Smith's view. Bevan confessed to being disappointed at the manner in which workers and their families were being so occupied by Harold Macmillan's materialism. He had hoped society would be different. He went on to say, though, that this did not mean that dream of Socialism and, as he could properly and proudly claim to have shown, its practical expression was dead. Humanity had not suddenly lost the capacity to be noble. A means would be found.

I offered the view, partly because it still surprised me then that the Socialist intellectuals I worked with were invariably public school and Oxbridge people, that his Socialism sprang unlike theirs from the fact of heavy industry where the comradeship created was always necessary, in shared danger. When that industry passed, might not the dream fade? He didn't see why.

It doesn't follow, of course, that this memory of a great man in ebullient social form necessarily means that he was not profoundly dismayed. If he was though, he disguised it well. He cheerfully put up with, and generously debated, a notion I had at the time that a Marxist proletariat did not exist, but that voters were more like Leibniz's monads.

When lunch broke-up I asked him if it was true that when he had been Minister of Housing he had been presented with a plan whereby old people would live in houses together; and that he had opposed it on the grounds that it would be wrong for the old so to live where they would often see funerals pass by. That kind of insight was as much to do with his greatness as the affection, even awe in which he was held by such heroic Europeans as Milovan Djilas and K. S. Karol. Small wonder that some of the pygmies who opposed him found so large a character and patrician impossible to comprehend.

That was a long time ago and many have gone to different destinations. For myself, for what its worth, I left the Labour Party and was involved in the discussions which led to the involved founding of the SDP, believing it important that the Centre-left realigned and that the extreme or Marxist Left hived itself off into a new party thus, in the end, ensuring that the Tories would be in a permanent minority. It could happen sooner than we thought. The Labour Party forgot one of Bevan's famous aphorisms – I can still hear that light tenor voice with the slight hammer before "P": "Politics is about power and only about power."

Western Mail, 22nd April 1987.

Days of wine and roses

The days of wine and roses, as we've always known, are not long. The poet was right about that. The pressing question now is whether or not they are to grow shorter,because shaping-up to collide are the forces behind the Government's Bill to extend pub hours, and those in Heartbeat Wales who tell us that one in three male adults in Wales – not to mention those female topers in East Dyfed – are drinking dangerously.

I find these statistics or, at least, their interpretation, surprising. Wales has never struck me as a heavy-drinking nation. The French and Germans drink more than twice as much. Drinking on a scale that has shaken even a well-trained soul like myself, occurs in Dublin, at Martini-time in San Francisco in pre-cocaine days, or in the company of writers in Warsaw.

Indeed after a week with the last group in the early 'Seventies I was so shaken I asked, my doctor for a blood test. He gave it. I put the blood in the fridge overnight, took it to the hospital. My doctor rang me and said the hospital had sent him a report saying: This man is dead. I hadn't known my wife had turned off the fridge.

Let's suppose, though, that the Welsh statistics are grave. I doubt if much solace will be found or much good done by angry debate about extending pub hours. When drink is harmful it is the drink, or the state of mind, that does the damage not the pub. If it is the case that there are three kinds of drinkers – that is, those who drink because they are happy and sociable, those who drink because they are melancholy and nervous, and those who drink because they are still all these things at different times: then drink they will.

Tourists in Wales will mostly benefit from longer pub hours. The scornful will argue that there is the world of difference of an afternoon between contemplating the Towy rain in Nantgaredig over a pint of Felinfoel, and, say, sipping a Californian champagne in Santa Barbara considering the Pacific, or a Montrachet in the lavender fields of the Var, or even a Valpolicella across the Venetian waters from San Giorgio: it is merely a qualitative distinction. The principle, as any West Walian publican will tell you, is the same.

Arguments against drink need to be more subtle since the matter is complicated. In this the former Welsh chapel experience, now, to coin a phrase, dissipated, could be valuable. These great days of the Band of Hope and the Rechabites in which so many of us were nurtured may have gone; some of their lessons are not helpful; others may be.

Mainly, as I remember them, they were two-fold but yet connected. Hellfire was one prospect. Drink was evil and sinful. That this was so evident in life around us. There were we, religious, in families that were tidy and striving; while there were they, the Godless down the terrace, or row, drinking like rodneys, scrounging for clothes for the children and generally a bad lot. Only loose women drank.

Even as late as 1953 when I first met Richard Burton in the Copper House at Cwmafan his wife and mine had to take a walk up the Foel since they were not allowed into the pub, even had they wished to brave opinion by so doing. And that was when Port Talbot had already become the centre of the Welsh steel industry and it took a furnace melter four pints after a shift just to make up for sweat lost.

So that the first thing for those who wish to contend with the perils of drink in Wales to grasp – as perhaps they do – is that the task is hard, the prospect of success small. They are grappling with the human condition. Appeals to the cost for the Health Service will be of little use. The robust soak will respond that the Health Service exists to help him: that is what hospitals are for.

Those who have not seen the wretched condition in which people die from cirrhosis of the liver will not be persuaded. There is still an illusion that you go 'pop' like a champagne cork. To give an account of the wretched state of the alcoholic seldom helps. It astonished me when for a time I was acting the good samaritan to a friend, and trying to find him a berth in a London hospital, to discover how little an alcoholic might drink. Neurotic and chemical factors were usually at work. To visit those lower depths can, though, be chilling but even then not persuasive.

The intelligence of the drinker is irrelevant. Tell him or her that 'moderation' is the model, and the reply will be that they are drinking because, among other things, it is precisely moderation that they are trying to avoid. Excess is the appeal. This response will come as much from the bright as the thick. And, of course, it grows serious when no solace can be brought to families struck down by the brutalities and fecklessness of drink, to beguile the drinker into some impossible hope.

What I suspect will not help, though, is a preaching tone. The teetotal may not be useful, much as a eunuch is probably not effective in accounts of the perils of fornication. I am sure I'm not alone in having had cancer of the mouth and to be told that I must never drink spirits again for the rest of my life or I wouldn't have one, to have given them up. Neither, I guess, am I alone in not missing them at all. Yet, no sermon, nor statistics, would have convinced me.

Exaggerating the problem, too, will not help. This week I found a small group of Welshwomen, all in the prime of life, troubled that they had read some professor's view that a reasonable amount for a woman to drink was three glasses of wine a week. With the natural awe of their kind in the face of the written academic work, they had taken this nonsense seriously. Such propaganda is counter-productive.

But we all carry out backgrounds with us. I have a clear memory from the age of nine. In Brynhyfryd elementary school in Swansea, as in all such Welsh schools in the 'Thirties, we had an annual temperance lecture. A chart was hung on the wall, the visual aid of the time. Coloured columns illustrated the strength of various alcoholic drinks and the menace they held.

On the extreme left was a tall, virulently green column. This was the most wicked drink: green chartreuse. I recall now my eyes widening and that childish resolve. When I grew up – that was going to be my drink. And for a long time, it was.

Western Mail, 1987

Cold virtue offers little comfort to poor and sick

Uncommon experience can often carry a common message; an eccentric particular, as in this case, may illustrate a general, if gloomy point. The story has to do with money, capitalism, the Stock Exchange, a private crisis and bizarre resolution. Its elements are naivety, stupidity, cynicism, cunning and a fascinating if unwished-for experience. Like most Welshmen of my generation, I had never bothered with the Stock Exchange, had regarded it as an antisocial gambling den, an alien world. One company I had invested in reluctantly, since I'd argued for its creation and was persuaded I should put some money where my mouth was, and went to the money-lenders. I saw that as a pension when senility set-in. At this stage in the narrative, Naivety and Stupidity stumble into the limelight. Suddenly struck down with illness and unable to earn any money, I realised that I had neglected to take out any insurance. How, you ask, could anyone who had been self-employed all his working life, have been quite so arrogant?

There, seemed, of course, a fair chance that the matter wouldn't occupy me for too long, that the rest of my brooding would be done underground or, with luck, in the company of angels. But there are always other people to think about. Robert Louis Stevenson's classic definition of many of us – "Romantic Bohemians haunted by duty" – is never far away, and can always temper despair or self-pity. So, what was to be done? At which, entering stage right, Cynicism and Cunning appear, driving Naivety and Stupidity, however briefly, from the stage. Those lessons in mathematical logic learned at the feet of Karl Britton at University College, Swansea, in the late 'Forties now had an unexpected value. The questions suggested themselves automatically. First, if it was not possible to earn money by working, how was it possible to make money by not working? Gambling on horses, Welsh rugby or by-elections were not sure things. It was going to be quite enough of a gamble anyway to cash-in capital intended for old age, especially if there wasn't going to be one.

However, hadn't it always been the faith that the Stock Exchange was a gambling den? What about that? Did the same handicap work there as with the horses? Here the Welshman is at a disadvantage with the Scot. Scotland has a long history of indigenous banking, perhaps a more powerful factor in political nationalism than we appreciate. We are not so familiar with markets and their fixing. Nevertheless, it must be the case with the Stock Exchange as elsewhere that for every winner, there is a loser. How to be a winner?

Commonsense would suggest that, as with horse-racing, inside information must matter. Knowing which jockey is fixed, which gee-gee doped – without such detail to hand, profit is a matter of chance. The logic thus offered by Cynicism looked promising. What, now, could Cunning do to overcome the difficulty of guaranteeing success?

Behaving like a plain citizen riding the Tory tide would not be good enough. Consider, for example, the recent launching of Rolls-Royce. Quite apart from the absurdity of the Government's pretending that the programme of privatisation is a means of creating a "shareholding democracy" even the deal of transactions is a nonsense. The punter might borrow £10,000 to invest, receive £350 worth of shares, have paid interest on his loan and then have had to pay £25 to sell those few shares. Meanwhile, Rolls-Royce would have held that £10,000 for a few days. Multiply that a hundred times – and guess who was the sucker?

As it turned out, cunning played a small role. Having announced my cool strategy to all who visited, many of whom put it down to my more-than-usual demented state, there was one friend who revealed a secret. It really is remarkable how people you think you have known well for ten years can turn out to be something quite different. He had been doing well all tht time out of people he knew who were doing things in the City. "Was this legal?" I asked, "having this insight into the future behaviour of companies?" It seems it was merely gossip raised to the level of prophecy. Of such is the nature of capitalism. And so it went and the crisis is ending and I grew popular passing on the good word to other friends until it was possible to resume work, when I more or less put Satan behind me, fascinated by the insight into his talents. I never knew what any of the companies did, if indeed they did anything.

The full force of this parable, for such it is, only became clear to me in the early hours of last Friday. Here was Mrs Thatcher and the Tory Party winning the third election in a row, an achievement without precedent. Certainly it was due in part to an antiquated electoral system which was undemocratic. But it was a system the two principal parties refused to change. Even with that system though, the Tory victory in the United Kingdom was probably due to a separate factor: the Labour Party's defence policy. It was this policy of unilateral nuclear disarmament which mainly had contributed to the creation of the Social Democratic Party, to the departure of many from the Labour Party. The triumph of CND within the Labour Party – as indeed in Plaid Cymru – brought about a triumph for all they, and many others, detest.

The irony, or, rather, folly is tragic. Many, although not all, in CND are good, idealistic, troubled men and women. They are also people who, like most of us, deplore economic and social policies which produce unnecessary poverty and unemployment. Yet by their attitude to nuclear policy it seems they have allowed a victory for the very Tory policies they deplore. Will they think themselves one day naive and stupid? Wish that, if not cynical and cunning, they might not at least have been silent? When next they orate against the miseries of Thatcherism, will they have the grace to admit that the perfections of their conscience have encouraged those miseries?

Naturally they will say, the party workers, the propagandists and the orators as they return, mostly, to their comfortable homes and jobs, that it was all the fault of those of us who while social democrats, did not share their view of the nuclear question. To the pure all others are impure. Cleverly, no doubt, they will turn this argument on its head. I think that won't wash. They knew that their policy would probably lead to an election lost whatever the economic factors and yet they persisted. I doubt if such cold virtue will much comfort the poor and the sick.

Western Mail, 16th June 1987.

Smoking

Now seems as good a time as any, while the evening sun shines and before the nights draw in, to raise the question. Since it is a matter that should rate low on all moral, practical and spiritual scales – it's to do with smoking – inevitably therefore it raises more bad temper, distress and genuine puzzlement than grave issues to do with the soul immortal. Such are the times in which we live. The question is this: Does the host have an obligation to make a guest content? Or to put it the other way around: Does the guest have a duty to meet the wishes of the host? I mention the state of the weather since a practice has grown of hosts asking guests if they would mind going out into the garden or no doubt, if a garden is not available, the street, if they wish to smoke. What if the night is black and the wind howling, or the rain falling or snow or ice underfoot? Before reporting on a week's research – research, incidentally, which left every group in which I raised the subject squabbling nastily – I will declare my own position so that no one will suppose that this report is objective or, if it comes to that, other than confused.

Being now a statistic in the anti-smoking lobby's propaganda as someone who had half his mouth removed because of cancer caused as much as heavy smoking as – my preferred source of the cause – emotional shock, I do not mind at all if my guests smoke. This may be because my family still smoke, but I suspect it has more complicated a justification. Anyone brought up in South Wales in the 'Forties on the great Hollywood films is always a smoker in his heart. Eroticism as well as lingo was graced by the romance of the dream factory. Not even a long contest with the Grim Reaper can disturb so powerful a cultural hold, it seems. A cigarette is more than a smoke, so that even the spectacle of another smoking, while I must not, ludicrously evokes a melancholy as sweet almost as a Schubert song rather than a hospital terror. There is another Welsh factor, one which, perhaps wrongly, I assumed still carried weight. The guest was always the most important person in the house. There might be little to offer, but what there was, was given first to the visitor. Preachers and teachers might exploit this trait, if often struck me: but there it was. Smoking, of course, was never an issue since most men smoked. Even had it been, though, I cannot imagine anyone asking a guest to do other than he or she wishes. I still have the spirit.

Inevitably, there is a Welsh ambiguity. Why, for instance, should the Welsh word for "guest" – *gwadd* – be the same as for "mole"? We may find it charming to call the mole ruining the lawn, a guest; the semantic interest grows when we think of a guest burrowing into a household.

But, then, peoples who remember their peasant origin are hospitable. All who have travelled in the Middle or Far East have known the joys and miseries of the gifts offered.

One of my own instructive memories was of the generosity of a Sheikh in Kuwait. One day a television colleague, claiming that he was the most important member of our entourage, accepted the loan of a yacht. The next day when it was a grand banquet, it seemed I was the more important. Therefore, I had to eat the sheep's eye of honour. (What was instructive was that whereas I had learned to avoid working with upper-class men on the skids, I now gathered that middle-class Marxists on the make – for such was my colleague – were just as shifty and and selfish).

Muslims, anyway, need to be hospitable. For them "God is the Guest" and I haven't yet heard a compatriot, for all our tradition, say "Duw yw'r garahoddedig".

In this question, though, as much as in affairs like Glyndŵr, the Merthyr Rising or the General Strike, considering the Welsh past comes to be useless as well as sentimental. The very idea that a guest should smoke him or herself daft in a house of non-smokers has come to seem absurd to young Welsh friends who are in every other way the very models of old hospitality, generous to many a fault.

Research has thrown up some eccentricities. A Right-wing man who used to play rugby for Pontypool said that he allowed no one to smoke in his house. He then went on to say that he had been guest of honour at some big dinner in Pittsburgh and had there insisted no one smoked. He saw no inconsistency in this absurdity. If he has rights as host, then surely he abandons them as guest.

And then there was a the Leftist feminist who had cunningly circumvented the fanaticism of some of her kind by arguing that she should be allowed to smoke since the sisterhood had to recognise the overwhelming need for cigarettes, so distressed was she at the triumph of male chauvinism in general. She found this very amusing, so did I.

Another smoker, a man, reported that he had anticipated winter, having been asked to move outside in summer to indulge himself. He now asks, when invited anywhere to lunch or dinner, if smoking is forbidden. If it is, he refuses to accept. I see him now, as the snow falls, speaking in an increasingly frantic tone, to the faces of absent friends he detects in the shapes of the smoke he blows at his family.

The most common of the disputes that broke out as this researcher departed was between those who maintained that to be in the presence of cigarette smoke was bad for the health; and those who said – "Well, in that case, Jack, or Jill, Sion or Sian, what about the fumes in the street from lorries and motor cars, you dope, or clown, or idiot, or sledge parod?" I forsee a winter of social discontent.

Western Mail, 11th August 1987.

Eugene Onegin

Only the conviction that compatriot Welsh opera-lovers are quite unacquainted with envy or jealousy enables me to write what follows. About hatred, affection, despair, frivolity or cowardice I would not be so certain. But if there are two emotions which the briefest knowledge of the fate of heroes and heroines of grand opera should steer us clear of, as if from a plague, then it is those of the green-eyed monster. What happened was this. Like all opera fanatics I had been reading the reviews of the Covent Garden performances by the Kirov of Leningrad. This was their first visit to Britain since the war. Each fulsome notice of *Boris Goudonov,* the *Queen of Spades* and *Eugene Onegin* darkened my gloom, stirred self-pity. Why had I been so slow? Why could I not afford a ticket? They were to be at the Birmingham Hippodrome. Yet every performance there had been sold out for months, Cinders was missing the Ball. Morose was the word.

At which, as the tears began to fall – this writer is not a librettist for nothing – the telepone rang. It was an old pal, Monica Foot. Did I want a ticket for the Kirov *Eugene Onegin?* That authentic Oxford accent had never sounded so warm to the ear. (She is a Big Wheel in Birmingham). Did I realise that it would conicide with the 21st anniversary of our first meeting? Of course. She would remember since one of her children had been born the next day. How suitable, therefore, I said, that it should be *Onegin.* And what is that supposed to mean, she asked, more sharply?

Outside the Hippodrome the Birmingham Women's Campaign for Soviet Jewry were demonstrating. Of Gorbachev they demanded, "Deeds not words". Most of us accepted their leaflets quietly. Communists who did not, offered the pickets some penetrating thoughts, like, What about the Lebanon? What about the PLO? Even, puzzlingly, What about Nicaragua? One curiosity of the scene was that, just as it is held that old married couples come to look alike, so did all these white-haired Marxists. No doubt it's due to having embraced a creed for a lifetime.

In nearly 40 years of opera-going – and this is why I caution against envy – I have never seen a finer performance than this *Onegin*. In musical quality it compares with both the Domingo-Margaret Price *Otello* at Covent Garden six years ago and the Geraint Evans-Della Casa-Wechter-Jurinac *Figaro* in Vienna in 1961; and in that quality and drama with the Callas-Gobbi *Tosca* which I thought, until now, I would recall as unique.

So stunning was this portrayal that for the first time in my life I regretted that I knew the plot and the libretto. I was so consumed by the drama that I wished it would all come as a surprise. How pale, for all their merits, recent productions of *Onegin* in Cardiff and at Covent Garden came to seem.

But was our delight, we wondered, a delight shared by an ecstatic audience, due to so many separate years of disappointment in opera houses in the West? Beforehand we had been swapping yarns of miserable evenings spent raging at the way – at the Welsh National as much as elsewhere – in which East European Marxists had traduced masterpieces. Mrs Foot quoted an example new to me. In Sicily at the Palermo Opera House she had seen Mozart's *Magic Flute* directed by the East German Goetz Friedrich, a notorious case. This genius had set Mozart's sublime work in Cuba. Sorastro's temple had been manned by whiskered guerrillas. That, I conceded, had upstaged the Welsh National. Their genius had a clutch of serfs. Was this, I asked wittily, because Friedrich realised Sorastro rhymed with Castro? Not that Mrs Foot has anything against the Left, having been always a prominent feminist, not to mention an officer of the Labour Party, even if her heart is still with the Black Hand anarchists. I tried to cheer her up by saying that I'd seen a production in Moscow at the Bolshoi that did not have Cubans storming about in Figaro. In the bar, yes, but not on stage.

This Leningrad *Onegin* equally was free of producers' or directors' megalomania. So what was it about the production that will be radiant forever in the memory? And are there any lessons to be learned? *Onegin,* which Tschaikovsky derived from Pushkin's great poem, was presented as a passionate romantic work. A tale in which each main character makes the wrong decision in his or her emotional life can seem, in Western or any inadequate productions sentimental or mannered. Here Lensky's death in the duel is tragic; Tatyana's wistful nobility is unbearably touching; Onegin is clearly a self-pitying melancholic who deserves his fate. Why should this be? It wasn't only because all concerned were Russian: the tale is universal. Rather it was because the conductor, who was also the producer, Yuri Tenirkanov, has the talent, the time and the desire to present the work as the composer wrote it. Nothing has come between him and Tschaikovsky's purpose. Naturally it is a help when you have singers who not only sing like angels, but look like Hollywood film stars of the 'Thirties. Also that your designer has clearly such a budget that every set rouses applause; and can create with such a luxury as Britain has probably never known.

And when you have an orchestra so in cahoots with the general purpose that they can take such an astonishing gamble as to let fly with a brilliance and uproar of brass and percussion to hit the end of Tatyana's *Letter* aria quite confident that the soprano will be perfectly in accord then there's no more to say. Naturally a lot more was said since the hotel I was in, the Albany, kept the party going. One day we may have an opera house in the Cardiff Dockland – and the gossip in Tory circles is that the plan is still alive. Had we one, the Kirov could have come. What we will never have is a Conservatoire like Leningrad's that can produce the Kirov. The WNO might, though, imitate their humility in the face of a composer's genius. In the meantime we can just brood on the oddity that if you want to see high art maintained in great wealth and with no trace of Marxist nonsense, you need to see a Leningrad production.

Western Mail, 25th August 1987.

'Thatcherism'

Trying always to be first with the news, I thought you would like to know that the intellectual fashion designed in Paris, one that should take us up comfortably to the new millenium in 14 years time, is none other than a concern with death. This information will soon reach the universities and so percolate through teachers to students. Wales should be, to coin a phrase, a fruitful graveyard for this novel trend.

Parisians have a particular problem. A batch of their thinkers, Althusser, Lacan, Barthes, Braudel whose work has produced cosmically some hilarious consequences – at least in my view – died recently at much the same time. God, we knew, had been dead for just over a century; now Marxism has also died: therefore what can be left? Even the British Labour Party is abandoning socialism.

This interest in mortality, if it catches on, will, of course, delight the Pope. It will not specially dismay those Christians who, like myself, have always intended to conduct their lives, or excuse them, by believing that our time here is merely a rehearsal for more of the same conducted more successfully hereafter. Gloom is all that can be forecast for the rest, those who have made a profession of defunct idealogies – at least, those whose minds are still alive enough to recognise what's happening.

All of which high-flown stuff, you may say, is all very well for some, but what about the rest of us? The question can be answered in an unusually practical manner in Wales. Or, if it cannot be answered, at least Wales lends itself to the question being asked.

The heart of the problem facing the French, as the British, is dealing with what is loosely, if universally, known as "Thatcherism". Call it self-interest raised to the level of faith, if you like. British opposition parties are in disarray. The SDP, for which some of us had high hopes, seems needlessly to commit suicide by joining with Liberals when, if there is one enduring fact of British political life it is that the Liberals will not win power. Plaid Cymru is not flourishing.

However, Wales, like Scotland and unlike England voted powerfully against "Thatcherism". This may merely be because these two countries are not profiting from it. There is nothing cynical about this, since elections are always won on self-interest graced, with luck, by eloquence. Or it may be because Wales and Scotland are waking up to a sense of national identity. Whichever it is, let's take what's happening in quite conventional terms before considering the future in the light of Parisian thinking. (In the olden days we prophets used to take to the mountains: now we take to aeroplanes, Rhoose becomes Sinai). There are clear signs that a new Welsh approach is being adopted in the matter of devolution, one very different from the disastrous campaign of 1979. Then it was organised from the top. What was especially ludicrous was that the "top" Labour government was not supported by its own party in Wales in any proper manner. The present Labour leader Neil Kinnock was hostile. Entrenched Labour councils were equally so. I recall interviewing for television a group of Welsh-speaking West Walians who would vote against because they feared they would suffer financially.

Several powerful Labour local politicians in Wales now regret their attitude in the 'Seventies. How, they ask, were they to know then that a Tory Government would assume a steady power and so centralise government that local authorities would become the meaningless creatures Mrs Thatcher has made them? Creatures that will soon become even more emasculated? The approach of the new campaigners is to move more quietly among the people, to work, in the idiom, from the grassroots upwards. It will, I gather, be a year or so before important public moves are made. Not, I'm sure, that this careful approach will lack its public outbreaks. Only the other day we heard that a Cardiff district was in favour in a small poll, news that 30 years ago would have stunned us. Now it tends to raise a smile since that part of Cardiff is stiff with workers in the Welsh-language industry and bourgeois members of Plaid Cymru. I'd be more persuaded by a poll in Swansea, now that we are being realistic and not repeating 1979.

Hopeful as all this may be, I wonder if the Parisian experience doesn't offer a more dashing argument. If "Thatcherism" has seen off the Marxist intelligentsia why not turn Thatcherism against itself? Without Wales and Scotland the Tories would have a permanent majority in England. If self-interest is the Tory creed, why not be truly self-interested and give the Celtic (or Iberian) lot self-government? If privatisation is such a good thing, why not privatise Wales? Mrs Thatcher could then be in Downing Street till the millenium. I can see that the argument might dismay some. Would a parliament in Cardiff be quite as happy to subsidise the Welsh language as is Westminster? (I would hope it would). Would Neil Kinnock be happy not to have any chance of being Prime Minister, his colleagues to abandon hope of Cabinet places? Still, we have all made sacrifice for the country, in one way or another. Surely they could.

At which his friend, knowledgeable about constitutional matters, as I am not, tells me that I neglect to grasp that the Tories are both ideological and sentimental about the United Kingdom and will never yield Wales and Scotland. At which, equally, I point out that perhaps no one has ever shown them before how they could make a profit out of the plan.

Western Mail, 23rd September 1987.

So, long live our differences

There are few merits in belonging to small nations. Large neighbouring peoples are anxious to overwhelm you either by force or by serious cultural invasions. Unless lucky, you tend to be poorer; the dangers of a self-defeating paranoia are seldom avoided. The vigorous are always tempted to pack their bags and leave and thus increase the difficulties of those left behind. We Welsh, like the Irish, the Poles, the Czechs, have keened this sad song to a fine pitch. In Wales there has been one strong counterattack to this condition, one that is becoming increasingly fashionable in political analysis. What we have is "community". That warm, sentimental essence of the national soul is always argued for: its preservation is vital for survival. I wonder. A recent, curious event leads me to think that perhaps the merit of a small nation, that the real strength of Wales or at least Welsh people,is precisely that they are not a "community" but rather a collection of remarkable histories which incorrigibly refuse to fit the politician's or ideologue's categories. What follows may be read simply as an odd Armistice Day tale, or as something more revealing of the kind of people we are.

Through the post I received from kind historical researchers in Treboeth, Swansea, where I spent my childhood, press cuttings of the death of my grandfather Elias Morgan. He died just before I was born in 1929. Among the cuttings was a picture of him taken just before his death at the grave of his second son Philip in Salonika in Greece. Philip had served with his brother Charles my father, throughout the Great War and died just before the Armistice. That my uncle's grave was in Salonika I had known. The shadow of that war had hung over my Treboeth upbringing and again, in the episode when I had been permitted in 1961 to be the first British television correspondent into Communist Bulgaria.

There I had been approached by M16 to ask if I was interested – most of my colleagues had been invited at dinners at their Oxbridge college. Some feelers, as I now take them, had also been put-out by the KGB. Therefore as I travelled down through Thrace to the border, wondering if I could nip-over to see my father's brother's grave, inevitably I was struck by how cosmopolitan the Welsh experience was turning-out to be. It was all a long way from Treboeth, I thought.

As it happened, I never visited the grave since there was a difficulty with the authorities and I saw instead, if briefly, the inside of the Sofia gaol. But I compensated by falsely informing the MI6 man that I had seen what might have been nuclear troop movements on the Thrace border being, no doubt wrongly, under the impression that he hadn't helped me much. As for the KGB, I left their chap with a copy of Djilas' banned portrait of Stalin as the dwarf gangster, a gesture that amused him.

But what the Treboeth historian also sent me, along with that picture of my grandfather at the Salonika grave, was a press cutting of his will. Here was some document. Naturally, it is of more interest to me than it possibly could be to anyone else, except that it has, I think, raised that matter of a strength of a people being their peculiarities rather than a nationhood held in common. In a phrase, the fewer the people, the more they should treasure the attention concentrated on the individual. If, in the Biblical sense, there is a special providence in the fall of a sparrow, then similarly there should be in the celebration.

There are two ways of taking family history. Being more intrigued by the future than the past, I've tended to ignore it. I'd been told about battles as Rebecca Rioters and how the soldiers had been so frightened of a forbear in Velindre that they took his son to Swansea gaol instead. Told of my great grandfather walking daily over the mountain from Llandybie to Llangyfelach. That my grandfather Elias had built five schools in Swansea, scores of houses; the Mond nickel works in Clydach. Naturally, I knew that in the Thirties we were the most well-off family in Treboeth; that my mother had been a servant in my father's house: that when we were subsequently impoverished it was my mother's family of colliers and tinplate workers who helped us out in the cottages without light or hot water.

We just crossed the street in Treboeth from one world to another. It didn't trouble me, except for sadness for my parents, since I had always been the spoiled boy of all my many brothers in my mother's family. Anyway, there was singing, football, girls. What has astonished me about this Press-cutting of a will is that my grandfather left his children, my father among them, what would be half a million pounds apiece in present values. I have heard tales of how my father's other brother John, after whom I was named, spent the money. His parties for the Swansea rugby and soccer teams are still spoken of by survivors. He died when I was young when his sports car went out of control into a cliff at Caswell.

In the days when I was playing rugby in Swansea and wearing cardboard inside my shoes as usual to keep the rain out, an old All White told me he had once followed my father up Treboeth hill after seeing him offer the tram conductor a pound note, not knowing the fare was a penny, so taken was he with this glamorous figure. My father could not remember. Where did the money go? This case may strike some as eccentric. I suspect its importance, if any, is that it is not, but rather that each case is eccentric, and that it is the recognition that our strength is not in our community but in our differences that should see us through.

Western Mail, 10th November 1987.